Colloquial

Arabic of Egypt

Colloquial Arabic of Egypt provides a step-by-step course in spoken Egyptian Arabic – the most widely understood dialect in the Arab world. Combining a user-friendly approach with a thorough treatment of the language, it equips learners with the essential skills needed to communicate confidently and effectively in Egyptian Arabic in a broad range of situations. No prior knowledge of the language is required.

Key features include:

- Arabic in romanization form throughout, with optional Arabic script supplement
- emphasis on modern conversational language with clear pronunciation guidance
- progressive introduction to the Arabic alphabet to aid familiarity with simple labels and signs
- grammar section and bilingual glossaries for easy reference
- stimulating exercises with lively illustrations
- new e-resources at www.routledge.com/cw/colloquials offering supplementary materials for teachers and learners, including extra activities (and answers), vocabulary lists and cultural information, ideas for group activities linked to each unit in the course, listing of the complete Arabic alphabet, notes comparing Egyptian and Standard Arabic and downloadable additional audio tracks.

Balanced, comprehensive and rewarding, this new and revised edition of *Colloquial Arabic of Egypt* offers an indispensable resource both for independent learners and for students taking courses in Egyptian Arabic.

Audio material to accompany the course is available to dowload free in MP3 format from www.routledge.com/cw/colloquials. Recorded by native speakers, the audio material features the dialogues and texts from the book and will help develop your listening and pronunciation skills.

By the end of this course, you will be at Level B1 of the Common European Framework for Languages and at the Intermediate–Mid level on the ACTFL proficiency scales.

THE COLLOQUIAL SERIES

Series adviser: Gary King

The following languages are available in the Colloquial series:

Afrikaans
Albanian
Amharic
Arabic (Levantine)
Arabic of Egypt
Arabic of the Gulf and
  Saudi Arabia
Basque
Bengali
Breton
Bulgarian
Burmese
Cambodian
Cantonese
Chinese (Mandarin)
Croatian
Czech
Danish
Dutch
English
Estonian
Filipino
Finnish
French

German
Greek
Gujarati
Hebrew
Hindi
Hungarian
Icelandic
Indonesian
Irish (forthcoming)
Italian
Japanese
Kazakh
Korean
Latvian
Lithuanian
Malay
Mongolian
Norwegian
Panjabi
Persian
Polish
Portuguese
Portuguese of Brazil
Romanian

Russian
Scottish Gaelic
Serbian
Slovak
Slovene
Somali
Spanish
Spanish of Latin
  America
Swahili
Swedish
Tamil
Thai
Tibetan
  (forthcoming)
Turkish
Ukrainian
Urdu
Vietnamese
Welsh
Yiddish
Yoruba
  (forthcoming)
Zulu (forthcoming)

COLLOQUIAL 2s series: *The Next Step in Language Learning*

Chinese
Dutch
French

German (forthcoming)
Italian
Russian

Spanish
Spanish of Latin
  America

Colloquials are now supported by FREE AUDIO available online. All audio tracks referenced within the text are free to stream or download from www.routledge.com/cw/colloquials. If you experience any difficulties accessing the audio on the companion website, or still wish to purchase a CD, please contact our customer services team through www.routledge.com/info/contact.

Colloquial
Arabic of Egypt

The Complete Course for Beginners

Jane Wightwick and Mahmoud Gaafar

Routledge
Taylor & Francis Group

LONDON AND NEW YORK

Third edition published 2014
by Routledge
2 Park Square, Milton Park, Abingdon, Oxon OX14 4RN

and by Routledge
711 Third Avenue, New York, NY 10017

Routledge is an imprint of the Taylor & Francis Group, an informa business

First edition by Russell McGuirk published by Routledge 1986
Second edition by Jane Wightwick and Mahmoud Gaafar published by Routledge 2004

British Library Cataloguing in Publication Data
A catalogue record for this book is available from the British Library

Library of Congress Cataloging in Publication Data
Wightwick, Jane.
Colloquial Arabic of Egypt : The Complete Course for Beginners / Jane Wightwick and Mahmoud Gaafar. -- Third edition.
pages cm. -- (The Colloquial Series)
Text is in English and Arabic.
1. Arabic language–Textbooks for foreign speakers–English. 2. Arabic language–Dialects–Egypt. I. Gaafar, Mahmoud. II. Title.
PJ6307.W52 2014
492.7'82421–dc23
2013036779

ISBN: 978-1-138-95803-6 (pbk)

Publisher's Note
This book has been prepared from camera-ready copy provided by the authorsl.

Contents

Hello and welcome!

> **In this unit you will learn about:**
> - greetings and simple courtesies
> - saying your name
> - saying where you come from
> - singular pronouns ('I', 'you', 'he', 'she')
> - making simple sentences
> - how the Arabic script works
> - how to recognize these Arabic letters: ث ت ب ا

My family

> **In this unit you will learn about:**
> - members of the family
> - plural pronouns
> - describing possession
> - masculine and feminine words
> - asking simple questions
> - how to recognize these letters: ي ن
> - reading some simple words in Arabic script

Acknowledgements

We would like to acknowledge the various reviewers who via the publisher gave us detailed and invaluable feedback on the first edition of *Colloquial Arabic of Egypt*. Their input has helped enormously when preparing this third edition. We appreciate also the support we received from the Routledge team, particularly Samantha Vale Noya, Andrea Hartill, Isabelle Cheng and Sarah May.

Thanks also go to our families in England and Egypt for helping us with the photographs – and acting as models in some of them – and to Charles and Maha for the pictures of their elegant villa in Ein Sukhna.

For the new edition recordings, we would like to thank Najla Shawqi for adding her voice to the existing models, and our good friend Eric for the audio recording.

The publishers would like to thank the following for the permission to reproduce photographs: p77: Henk Vrieselaar/Shutterstock; p178: Zurijeta/Shutterstock; p179: Patryk Kosmider/Fotolia; p206: photka/Shutterstock; p222: TanArt/Fotolia

Introduction

The Arabic language

Arabic is often thought of as having separate 'spoken' and 'written' forms. The 'spoken' being the various dialects of the 20 or so Arabic-speaking countries, and the 'written' being the Standard Arabic taught in all schools and understood by educated Arabs. It is true that most conversations take place in the colloquial language and most written material is in Standard Arabic. But the factor determining which is used has more to do with the formality of the situation rather than how the communication is delivered. A high-level televised political debate would probably be conducted in Standard Arabic but a soap opera would be in colloquial. Communication between different Arab nationalities tends to include at least elements of Standard Arabic where dialects might contain unfamiliar words.

Egyptian colloquial is perhaps the most vibrant and universally understood of the many spoken dialects of Arabic. Egypt is the centre of popular Arab culture, exporting its films, soap operas, popular programmes, songs and advertisements to fill the mushrooming airtime of the Arabic TV channels.

The differences between the colloquial and the Standard are less apparent the more elevated the subject matter becomes. Even at the basic level, it tends to be vocabulary that is most affected. The structure of the language remains largely recognizable. So, whichever way you approach the language – from an initial study of the colloquial or of Standard Arabic, you will be able to expand your knowledge to other areas.

How to use the course

Colloquial Arabic of Egypt will introduce you to the spoken Arabic of Egypt, using the capital city Cairo as its model. Egypt is a big country and accents vary from region to region, but the Cairene dialect is the most widely understood and therefore the most useful.

We strongly recommend that you study *Colloquial Arabic of Egypt* with the accompanying audio. It is very difficult to master the sounds of Arabic without hearing them spoken by native speakers. The audio not only includes all the dialogues recorded by authentic Egyptian actors, but also additional listening and speaking exercises which will help improve your fluency.

 Sections of the course that appear on the audio are marked with the headphones symbol.

Above all, it is important to enjoy your learning and to have a go at communicating right from the start. Nobody will mind if you make a mistake and foreigners speaking Arabic are still rare enough for you to make a real impression.

Structure of the course

Colloquial Arabic of Egypt is comprised of 15 units, two of which are review units (Unit 8 and Unit 15). The other teaching units are based around two or three natural dialogues.

Here are the main features of each unit:

 Summary of aims

An initial summary of the main teaching points of the unit to prepare you for what you will learn, or for later reference.

 Dialogues

The dialogues have all been carefully scripted not only to present the language, but also to convey the Egyptian patterns of speech and sense of humour.

 Vocabulary

Each dialogue is followed by a vocabulary panel showing new and significant items of vocabulary.

Language points

These sections expand on the language of the dialogue, explaining important language structures and expressions.

Cultural points

Some concepts require more explanation, for example an indication of their cultural significance, or in which situation they are used. Information of this kind is given in these sections.

Exercises

The numerous exercises and activities encourage your active participation and consolidate what you have learnt. All four skills of listening, speaking, reading and writing are included.

Downloadable eResources

A new feature of this edition is the free downloadable eResources (www.routledge.com/9780415811316). You will find a host of useful material that will help you with your study: additional practice activities, extra topic vocabulary, cultural information, reference material and downloadable audio. All of this material is linked to particular sections of the course and marked with the eResources symbol.

The Arabic script

Each teaching unit ends with a section introducing you to the Arabic alphabet, giving you the opportunity to read some of the vocabulary of the unit in Arabic script. When you feel more confident, you can use the script supplement and the glossaries to enhance your reading skills.

Abbreviations used in the course

sing.	singular
pl.	plural
fem.	feminine
masc.	masculine
lit.	literally
adj.	adjective

The sounds of Arabic

Colloquial Arabic of Egypt uses romanized Arabic in the main course, although there is an optional section at the end of each unit for those who are interested in gaining familiarity with the Arabic script.

You may already be familiar with the Arabic script, through previous knowledge of Standard Arabic or other Arabic-script languages such as Persian and Urdu. In this case you will still find the romanized text useful as it shows the vowel sounds and word stress in a way that the Arabic script cannot. However, we have included the Arabic script in the glossaries at the back of the book and a special *Arabic script supplement* gives the dialogues and other key listening texts in Arabic script.

The difficulty of rendering the sounds of Egyptian Arabic accurately on paper has been brought home to us by the amount of debate this aspect has engendered amongst reviewers of the original edition. We have adopted a particular method of romanization, but it will never be an exact science. There are no rules which tell you whether a particular sound should be written as 'e' or 'i', 'ey' or 'ay', 'ee' or 'ii'. Individual speakers will vary slightly as they do in any language and some sounds do not have an exact transliterated equivalent. In the end there is no substitute for listening and mimicking what you hear.

The audio that accompanies the course will enable you gradually to assimilate and practise pronunciation in the context of meaningful words and phrases – more useful than practising isolated unconnected sounds. But for reference, we are including an outline of the main features of Egyptian Arabic pronunciation.

Arabic sounds (Audio 1; 2–6)

Consonants

Consonants are non-vowels. The Arabic language in general relies mainly on consonants to convey meaning. The vowels sounds are more flexible and vary from country to country and from region to region.

Many consonants are pronounced in a similar way to their English equivalents, but some need special attention:

Sound	Pronunciation notes
kh	pronounced as if clearing your throat and saying 'h' at the same time, like the 'ch' in the Scottish 'loch' or the German pronunciation of 'Bach'
r	pronounced more trilled than the English 'r'
gh	pronounced like a French 'r' (as in 'rue') in the back of the throat
'	glottal stop, as in the Cockney pronunciation of 'bottle' as bo'ul
q	'q' pronounced in the back of the throat; uncommon in Egyptian Arabic as usually becomes a glottal stop (')
H	pronounced as a breathy 'h' as if breathing on glasses to clean them; written with a capital letter in the romanization to distinguish it from a regular 'h'
S	pronounced as a hard, emphatic 's' with the tongue on the roof of the mouth rather than behind the teeth; written with a capital letter in the romanization to distinguish it from a regular 's'
D	pronounced as a hard, emphatic 'd' with the tongue further back on the roof of the mouth than a regular 'd'; written with a capital letter in the romanization to distinguish it from a regular 's'

T	pronounced as a hard, emphatic 't' with the tongue on the roof of the mouth rather than behind the teeth; written with a capital letter in the romanization to distinguish it from a regular 't'
Z	pronounced as a hard, emphatic 'z' with the tongue on the roof of the mouth rather than behind the teeth; written with a capital letter in the romanization to distinguish it from a regular 'z'; uncommon in Egyptian Arabic as is often pronounced as **D**
9	the famous Arabic guttural consonant, the letter **9ayn** (ﻉ) has no equivalent in European languages. For this reason, we have followed convention and used a **9** to show this letter in the romanization. The sound comes from the stomach and is a little like saying 'ah!' while constricting your throat. It takes time to master this sound and you need to hear it to try and reproduce it. But don't worry too much at first as the context will help you to be understood.

Vowels and diphthongs

Vowels and diphthongs (vowel combinations) vary from Standard Arabic to colloquial, from dialect to dialect, speaker to speaker, word to word. For example, the verb 'to write' is pronounced **yáktub** in Standard Arabic but **yíktib** in Egyptian colloquial; one Egyptian might say **mush 9áawiz** ('I don't want') and the next **mish 9áayiz**. Some Egyptian colloquial vowel sounds hover between different sounds, and you could write the word for 'you' as **énta**, **ínta** or **ánta**.

Below is the system of transliterations we have settled on for this course. Your best policy is to use the romanization for reference but also to listen to the individual words and phrases and mimic the pronunciation you hear.

Sound	Pronunciation notes
i	as the 'i' in 'sit', but sometimes closer to the 'e' in 'set'
ii	as the 'ee' in 'feed'
a	as the 'a' in 'sat'
aa	as the 'ar' in 'far'
u	as the 'u' in 'pull'
uu	as the 'oo' in 'boot'
oh	as the 'oa' in 'boat'
ay	as the 'ay' in 'lay'
aw	as the 'ow' in 'now'

Doubled consonants

Take care to pronounce double consonants twice the length of single consonants. It sometimes helps to imagine that there is a hyphen in between the doubled letters, e.g. **mudár-ris** (teacher), **húw-wa** (he).

Word stress

Word stress (emphasis) is marked on the romanization by an accent above the stressed vowel, e.g. **yíktib** (to write), **húwwa** (he). The stress can move if endings are added, e.g. **mudárris** (male teacher), **mudarrísa** (female teacher), **mudarrisíin** (teachers). Moving stress is a particular feature of Egyptian Arabic; examples and explanations are given throughout the units.

The Arabic alphabet

Here are the Arabic letters in alphabetical order with their Egyptian pronunciation, together with the Modern Standard Arabic pronunciation for comparison.

	Letter name	Standard Arabic	Egyptian Arabic
ا	alif	*	*
ب	baa	b	b
ت	taa	t	t
ث	thaa	th (as in 'thin')	t or s
ج	giim	j	g
ح	Haa	H	H
خ	khaa	kh	kh
د	daal	d	d
ذ	thaal	th (as in 'this')	d or z
ر	raay	r	r
ز	zaay	z	z
س	siin	s	s
ش	shiin	sh	sh
ص	Saad	S	S
ض	Daad	D	D
ط	Taa	T	T
ظ	Zaa	Z	Z or D
ع	9ayn	9	9
غ	ghayn	gh	gh
ف	faa	f	f
ق	qaaf	q	' or q

ك	kaaf	k	k
ل	laam	l	l
م	miim	m	m
ن	nuun	n	n
ه	haa	h	h
و	waaw	w	w
ي	yaa	y	y

*alif can be pronounced as a short vowel (e.g. **a, u** or **i**) or as a long **aa** sound.

For more details on how the letters join and other features of the script, see the script sections at the end of each unit.

Download additional notes contrasting Modern Standard Arabic and Egyptian for those who already have some familiarity with Arabic.

Unit One

áhlan wa sáhlan!

Hello and welcome!

In this unit you will learn about:

- greetings and simple courtesies
- saying your name
- saying where you come from
- singular pronouns ('I', 'you', 'he', 'she')
- making simple sentences
- how the Arabic script works
- how to recognize these Arabic letters: ث ت ب ا

Cultural point

The exchange of greetings and courtesies is an important part of communication in Egypt, as it is generally in the Arab world. Initial exchanges can take several minutes and can be accompanied by kissing of cheeks, embraces and handshakes. It is possible to find an Arabic greeting for almost any occasion, such as getting your hair cut, swallowing your medicine, returning from a journey – and each has its own specific reply.

In this unit you will learn some of the more common everyday greetings. Later, you will meet some more expressions and their replies which you can add to your repertoire.

Basic greetings (Audio 1; 7)

Practise the Arabic sounds you'll need for some basic greetings before you move on to the first dialogue.

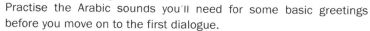
Dialogue 1

SabáaH il-khayr (Audio 1; 8)

Hassan is visiting his friend Gaber. Gaber's mother opens the front door.

See if you can hear the Arabic for 'Hello' and 'Good morning' in the dialogue.

Hásan:	SabáaH il-khayr yaa Tant.
umm(i) gáabir:	áhlan yaa Hásan. izzáyyak yábni?
Hásan:	il-Hámdu lilláah. gáabir SáaHi?
umm(i) gáabir:	áywa, min bádri.

Hassan:	*Good morning 'auntie'.*
Gaber's mother:	*Hello Hassan. How are you, dear?*
Hassan:	*Fine thanks. Is Gaber awake?*
Gaber's mother:	*Yes, since early on.*

Vocabulary

SabáaH il-khayr	good morning (*lit.* 'morning of prosperity')
yaa	commonly used when addressing people directly, e.g. **yaa Hásan, yaa Tant**
Tant	'auntie': derived from the French 'tante' and used widely to address older female relatives and friends
áhlan	hello; a fuller version is **áhlan wa sáhlan** (hello and welcome)
izzáyyak	how are you? (to a male)
yábni	'my son': a contraction of **yaa + ibni** ('my son')
il-Hámdu lilláah	'thanks be to God': a common reply to **izzáyyak** ('how are you?') meaning 'fine thanks'
SáaHi	awake
áywa	yes; no = **la'**
min bádri	since early on (*lit.* 'from early')

Language points

Male, female and groups

In English, when we talk *indirectly* about a single male, a single female or a group of people we use 'he', 'she' or 'they' accordingly. But when we talk *directly* to one or more people, we use the word 'you' regardless of whether they are male or female or how many there are. In contrast, Egyptian Arabic also has three different words for 'you' (and by extension for 'your'), reflecting the gender and number of people being addressed. This means that many greetings and basic questions sound slightly different depending on who is addressed. For example, the phrase 'how are you?' in the dialogue changes as follows (the part meaning 'you' is underlined):

izzáy<u>yak</u>	how are you? *(to a male)*
izzáy<u>yik</u>	how are you? *(to a female)*
izzay<u>yúku</u>	how are you? *(to a group)*

We'll introduce more about groups, or plurals, later in this course. Concentrate for the moment on the differences in the basic greetings between talking to a male and a female.

 ## Replies to greetings (Audio 1; 9)

Many common greetings have standard replies. These replies are useful to know, but you do not always have to respond according to the standard formula. Look carefully at these greetings and replies and then practise using them with the recording.

Greeting	*Reply*
good morning ('morning of prosperity') **SabáaH il-khayr**	good morning to you ('morning of the light') **SabáaH in-nuur**
good afternoon/evening ('evening of prosperity') **masáa' il-khayr**	good afternoon/evening to you ('evening of the light') **masáa' in-nuur**
hello **áhlan**	hello to you **áhlan biik** *(fem. **áhlan bíiki**)*

goodbye ('[go] with safety') **má9a s-saláama**	goodbye to you ('may God keep you safe') **alláah yisallímak** (*fem.* **alláah yisallímik**)
how are you? **izzáyyak?** (*fem.* **izzáyyik?**)	fine, thanks ('thanks be to God') **il-Hámdu lilláah**

Exercise 1

Fill in the missing words in these short exchanges.

1 – **SabáaH il-khayr.**
   – _____ **in-nuur.**

2 – **áhlan.**
   – _____ **bíiki.**

3 – **masáa'** _____ .
   – _____ **in-nuur.**

4 – **izzáyyak?**
   – _____ **lilláah.**

5 – _____ **s-saláama.**
   – _____ **yisallímik.**

Exercise 2

How would you say these in Arabic?

1 Hello Hassan.

2 Hello to you. (*talking to a male*)

3 Good evening 'auntie'.

4 Good evening to you.

5 How are you? (*asking a male*)

6 How are you? (*asking a female*)

7 Thanks be to God.

8 Good morning Gaber.

9 Goodbye 'my son'.

10 Goodbye to you. (*talking to a male*)

Dialogue 2

 ísmak eh? **(Audio 1; 10)**

At the start of a radio quiz show, we are invited to meet the contestants who are students from different cities in Egypt.

---

1   Is the first student called Mona or Sara?
2   Where is Kamal from?
3   Who is from Port Said?

IL-MUZÍÍ9:	Dayf ráqam wáahid ... ísmik eh?
MÓNA:	ána ísmi móna. ána min iskindiríyya.
IL-MUZÍÍ9 :	áhlan móna. Dayf itnáyn ... ísmak eh?
KAMÁAL:	ána ísmi kamáal. ána min aswáan.
IL-MUZÍÍ9 :	Dayf taláata?
SAMÍIRA:	w-ána samîira. ána min buur sa9îid.

BROADCASTER:	*Guest number one ... what's your name?*
MONA:	*My name's Mona. I'm from Alexandria.*
BROADCASTER:	*Hello Mona. Guest two ... what's your name?*
KAMAL:	*My name's Kamal. I'm from Aswan.*
BROADCASTER:	*Guest three?*
SAMIRA:	*And I'm Samira. I'm from Port Said.*

 Vocabulary

Dayf	guest
ráqam	number
ísmak eh? *(fem.* **ísmik eh?***)*	What's your name?
ána ísmi ...	My name's ...
ána min ...	I'm from ...
wi/w-	and; contracted to **w-** when the next word begins with a vowel

Note: Be careful to pronounce the Arabic **s** in ísmi as a true 's' sound (as in 'sit'). English speakers tend to pronounce 's' in the middle of a word as a 'z' sound, with 'isn't' becoming 'izzunt'. Avoid this in Arabic – an **s** is an **s** and a **z** is a **z**, wherever they appear in a word.

Cultural point

The Arabic for 'Egypt' is **maSr**. In everyday speech **maSr** is often also used to refer to Cairo, although its official name is **al-qáahira**. Cairo is divided into several main districts, such as **ig-gíiza** (Giza), **maSr ig-gidíida** (Heliopolis) and **iz-zamáalek** (Zamalek).

Egypt's second largest city is **iskindiríyya** (Alexandria) on the Mediterranean coast. Other major northern cities are **buur sa9íid** (Port Said) and **is-sways** (Suez), while **lú'Sur** (Luxor), **aswáan** (Aswan) and **asyúuT** (Asyut) are important towns in the south.

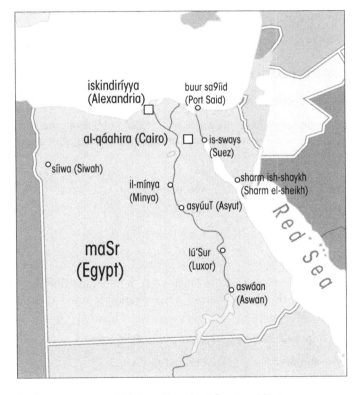

Download some more useful information about Egypt and its towns.

 Language points

Numbers 1–5

Numbers are vital for communication in any language. Begin by making sure you can remember the first five.

wáaHid	one
itnáyn	two
taláata	three
arbá9a	four
khámsa	five

Personal pronouns: singular

■ Subject pronouns

Subject pronouns are words such as 'I', 'you', 'he', 'she', etc. Arabic distinguishes between a male 'you' (**ínta**) and a female 'you' (**ínti**):

ána	I
ínta	you *(masc.)*
ínti	you *(fem.)*
húwwa	he
híyya	she

There is no equivalent of the English 'is', 'am' or 'are' (the verb 'to be') in Arabic. So you can make simple sentences and questions without any verb:

ána min buur sa9íid.	I [am] from Port Said.
híyya samíira.	She [is] Samira.
ínta kamáal?	[Are] you *(masc.)* Kamal?
húwwa min aswáan.	He [is] from Aswan.
ínti min maSr?	[Are] you *(fem.)* from Egypt?

■ Attached pronouns

As their name implies, attached pronouns are added to the *end* of words. They can be used as the equivalent of the English possessive pronouns ('my', 'your', 'his', 'her').

Here are the singular attached pronouns added to the word **ism** ('name'):

ísmi	my name
ísmak	your name *(masc.)*
ísmik	your name *(fem.)*
ísmuh	his name
ismáhaa	her name

When talking about names, it is common (but not required) to use both a subject *and* an attached pronoun:

(ána) ísmi kamáal.	My name's Kamal.
(húwwa) ísmuh gáabir.	His name's Gaber.
(híyya) ismáhaa móna.	Her name's Mona.

As you heard in Dialogue 1, attached pronouns can also be added directly to the word **izzáyy** to ask how someone is:

izzáyyak?	How are you? *(masc.)*
izzáyyik?	How are you? *(fem.)*
izzáyyuh?	How is he?
izzayyáhaa?	How is she?

Note: The emphasis, or word stress, can change in Egyptian Arabic if endings are added. In the examples above, the attached pronoun meaning 'her' causes the stress to shift to the next syllable. Compare **ísmuh** ('his name') and **ismáhaa** ('her name'); **izzáyyuh** ('how is he?') and **izzayyáhaa** ('how is she?').

Exercise 3

Match the shirts with the correct Arabic numbers.

taláata

itnáyn

khámsa

arbá9a

wáaHid

Exercise 4

Match the questions with the correct replies.

1 ínti móna?

2 ínta min buur sa9íid?

3 húwwa min iskindiríyya?

4 híyya min aswáan?

5 ísmuh eh?

6 ínta Hásan?

a áywa, húwwa min iskindiríyya.

b la', ána gáabir.

c la', híyya min lú'Sur.

d áywa, ána móna.

e áywa, ána (masc.) min buur sa9íid.

f húwwa ísmuh kamáal.

Exercise 5

Give the questions for these answers.

1 ána ísmi móna.

2 híyya ismáhaa samíira.

3 ána ísmi maHámmad.

4 áywa, ána *(fem.)* min lú'Sur.

5 áywa, ána gáabir.

6 áywa, húwwa min iskindiríyya.

Exercise 6 (Audio 1; 11)

You are meeting Gaber for the first time. Below is your initial conversation. Read the conversation and try to memorize your part, adding your own name and home town. Then join in the conversation on the recording, playing your part.

GABER: SabáaH il-khayr.

You: SabáaH in-nuur. ísmak eh?

GABER: ána ísmi gáabir. w-ínta (w-ínti)?

You: ána ísmi ... *(add your name)*

GABER: ána min iskindiríyya. w-ínta (w-ínti)?

You: ána min ... *(add your home town)*

GABER: áhlan wa sáhlan biik (bíiki) fi maSr.

You: áhlan biik yaa gáabir.

Dialogue 3

ána ingilizíyya (Audio 1; 12)

Rita Stanley arrives at a restaurant where she has earlier reserved a table. She is greeted by the *maître d'*.

---

1 **Where is Rita from?**

2 **Which table is she directed to?**

IL-METR:	áhlan wa sáhlan yaa madáam. ism HaDrítik?
RITA STANLEY:	Stanley.
IL-METR:	Stanley? HaDrítik min iskindiríyya?!
RITA STANLEY:	la', la'. ána min Liverpool. ána ingilizíyya!
IL-METR:	itfaDDáli. tarabáyza khámsa.

MAÎTRE D':	*Hello and welcome, Madam. Your name?*
RITA STANLEY:	*Stanley.*
MAÎTRE D':	*Stanley? Are you from Alexandria?!*
RITA STANLEY:	*No, no. I'm from Liverpool. I'm English!*
MAÎTRE D':	*Please come (this way). Table five.*

Vocabulary

áhlan wa sáhlan	hello and welcome (a fuller version of **áhlan**)
madáam	madam: the male equivalent is **ustáaz** ('sir' or 'Mr')
ism	name
HaDrítik	a polite formal way of saying 'you/your' to a woman
ingilizíyya	English (*fem.*)
itfáDDal	come this way; here you are/please (take this, etc.)
(*fem.* **itfaDDáli**)	
tarabáyza	table

Cultural point

The *maître d'* is joking when he asks Rita Stanley if she is from Alexandria. Stanley Bay, St Stephano Beach, Gleemonopolo Beach, Camp de Cesar and Miami Beach are all names of areas in Alexandria from a bygone era when the city was a magnet for Mediterranean people.

Language point

Polite 'you'

We've met the words **ínta** and **ínti**, meaning 'you'. However, these are not normally used to address a stranger or an older adult for the first time, particularly in a service situation. Instead, Egyptians use an expression which literally means 'your presence':

Hadrítak	you (*polite, masc.*)
Hadrítik	you (*polite, fem.*)

Notice that the ending meaning 'your' changes from **-ak** for a man to **-ik** for a woman (see Attached pronouns on page 17):

HaDrítak min ig-giiza?   Are you (*polite, masc.*) from Giza?

HaDrítik min iskindiríyya?   Are you (*polite, fem.*) from Alexandria?

If you want to ask politely about someone's name, you add the word **ism** (name) directly in front of **Hadrítak/Hadrítik**:

ism HaDrítak eh?   What's your (*polite, masc.*) name?

ism HaDrítik móna?   Is your (*polite, fem.*) name Mona?

Exercise 7 (Audio 1; 13)

Listen to the recording of a travel agent from Nile Tourism (**in-niil lis-siyáaHa**) meeting a visitor off the train from Alexandria and decide if the following are true or false.

1   The conversation takes place in the evening.

2   The travel agent is called Widaad.

3   The visitor is called Mohammed Amin.

4   The visitor is from Alexandria.

5   The travel agent is also from Alexandria.

Language point

Nationalities (Audio 1; 14)

Nationalities usually end in **-i** for the masculine and **-íyya** for the feminine. Listen and repeat the nationalities.

Masculine	Feminine	Nationality
ingilíizi	ingilizíyya	English
máSri	maSríyya	Egyptian
amriikáani	amriikaaníyya	American
iskutlándi	iskutlandíyya	Scottish
ostoráali	ostoralíyya	Australian

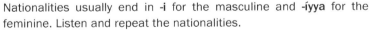

ána ingilizíyya.	I'm English. *(fem.)*
húwwa máSri.	He's Egyptian.
ínta amriikáani?	Are you American? *(informal, masc.)*
HaDrítik iskutlandíyya?	Are you Scottish? *(polite, fem.)*
híyya ostoralíyya.	She's Australian.

Note: The stress, or word emphasis, usually falls on the *syllable before last* in Egyptian Arabic. Notice how the stress (shown by the accent above the vowel) moves in the feminine nationalities because an additional syllable has been added: **máSri/maSríyya**.

 Download a vocabulary list of additional nationalities.

 Exercise 8 (Audio 1; 15)

Complete these Arabic questions and statements to match the English in brackets.

1 ínta _____ (Egyptian)?

2 ínti _____ (Egyptian)?

3 ána *(masc.)* _____ (English).

4 ána *(fem.)* _____ (English).

5 húwwa _____ (American).

6 híyya _____ (American).

7 HaDrítak _____ (American)?

8 la', ána *(masc.)* _____ (Scottish).

9 HaDrítik _____ (American)?

10 la', ána *(fem.)* _____ (Scottish).

Now say the completed expressions out loud, paying particular attention to the moving word stress. Check your pronunciation with the recording.

Exercise 9

Make these sentences and questions feminine, as in the example.

ínta ingilíizi. → ínti ingilizíyya.

1	ínta máSri?	4	HaDrítak ingilíizi?
2	húwwa iskutlándi.	5	ána ostoráali.
3	ána amriikáani.	6	húwwa ostoráali?

Exercise 10 (Audio 1; 16)

Listen to Rita Stanley describing herself:

áhlan. ána ísmi Rita Stanley. ána ingilizíyya. ána min Liverpool.

Now describe yourself in a similar way. Try to speak out loud as this will give you confidence. Record yourself and listen to the recording to improve your delivery and accent.

Learning with a friend or in a class?
Download ideas for practising personal information.

The Arabic script

ﺍﺏ
ﺕ

Familiarity with the Arabic script is not essential to using this course or to communicating in Egyptian colloquial. However, some knowledge of the script will enrich your learning if you have not mastered it through previous studies. Once you can recognize all the letters and understand the principles of how they join, you will be able to read Arabic street signs, product labels and other simple written material.

The Arabic script is not as difficult to decipher as it might at first appear. There are 28 letters of the alphabet – only two more than English; there are no capital letters; and words are normally spelt as they sound.

In each unit of *Colloquial Arabic of Egypt*, you will be presented with a group of letters until you are familiar with the complete Arabic alphabet.

Arabic letters

Some Arabic letters share the same shape but have varying numbers of dots above and below to distinguish them. For example:

ب   the letter **baa**, pronounced 'b' as in '<u>b</u>at'

ت   the letter **taa**, pronounced 't' as in '<u>t</u>in'

ث   the letter **thaa**, formally 'th' as in '<u>th</u>in', but usually pronounced 't' or 's' in spoken Egyptian Arabic

Other letters have their own unique shape. For example:

ا   the letter **álif** can represent several vowel sounds. It can be pronounced as a short vowel, e.g. **a, u** or **i**, or as a long **aa**

Joining letters

Arabic is written from *right to left*. Most letters will join to other letters before and after in a word. When another letter is joined, the original generally loses its left-hand 'tail' (or flourish). Look how these letters join:

(read from right to left)

$$ ب + ا = با $$
$$ ت + ب = تب $$
$$ ب + ث = بث $$
$$ ب + ث + ت = بثت $$

Six Arabic letters, one of which is **álif**, only join to the letter before but never to the following letter:

(read from right to left)

$$ ا + ب = اب $$
$$ ت + ا + ب = تاب $$
$$ ا + ب + ث = ابث $$
$$ ب + ت + ا = بتا $$

Unit Two

9ílti

My family

In this unit you will learn about:

- members of the family
- plural pronouns
- describing possession
- masculine and feminine words
- asking simple questions
- how to recognize these letters: ن ي
- reading some simple words in Arabic script

Dialogue 1

 ta9áala! (Audio 1; 17)

Samira is from Port Said but today she is in Cairo taking part in a surprise student radio quiz. Her family is back home.

___

What relation is Hassan to Samira?

UMM(I) SAMÍIRA:	yaa Hásan! ta9áala! úkhtak fir-rádyo!
HÁSAN:	úkhti?
UMM(I) SAMÍIRA:	bi-súr9a. 'uul l-abúk ta9áala!
HÁSAN:	bába! bába! ta9áala ísma9 bíntak fir-rádyo!
ÁBU SAMÍIRA:	bínti? haat ir-rádyo hína yaa Hásan yábni.
UMM(I) SAMÍIRA:	la'. íHna hína! ta9áala ínta lir-rádyo!

SAMIRA'S MOTHER:	*Hassan! Come here! Your sister's on the radio!*
HASSAN:	*My sister?*
SAMIRA'S MOTHER:	*Quickly. Tell your father to come here!*
HASSAN:	*Dad! Dad! Come and listen to your daughter on the radio!*
SAMIRA'S FATHER:	*My daughter? Bring the radio here, Hassan, my son.*
SAMIRA'S MOTHER:	*No. We're here! You come to the radio!*

Vocabulary

ta9áala! (*fem.* **ta9áali**)	come here!
rádyo	radio; **fir-rádyo** = on the radio (*lit.* 'in the radio')
bi-súr9a	quickly
'uul (*fem.* **'úuli**) **li ...**	tell ... (*lit.* 'say to ...'). **'uul l-abúk** = tell your father
ísma9! (*fem.* **ismá9i**)	listen!
haat! (*fem.* **háati**)	bring!
íHna	we
hína	here

Members of the family

umm	mother
ab	father
ukht	sister
akh	brother
bint	daughter
ibn	son
wiláad	children
gohz	husband
miráat	wife

To talk about your own or someone else's family ('Layla's husband', 'my wife', etc.), use the word for the member of the family directly followed by a name or an attached pronoun. There's is no need for the equivalent of the English 'of' or possessive 's.

gohz láyla	'husband [of] Layla', i.e. Layla's husband
wiláad áHmad	'children [of] Ahmed' i.e. Ahmed's children
úkhtak	your *(masc.)* sister
miráati	my wife

The two words **ab** (father) and **akh** (brother) become **ábu** and **ákhu** when followed by a name or an attached pronoun.

ábu gáabir	Gaber's father
ákhu samíira	Samira's brother
akhúhaa	her brother

Note: Arabic does not like clusters of three consonants such as the 'kst' sound in the English word 'next' (which would be pronounced 'nekist' if it were an Arabic word). If a combination of words results in a consonant cluster, a 'helping' vowel is inserted. So **umm + samíira** is pronounced as **umm(i) samíira** (Samira's mother). Significant helping vowels are shown in brackets in the first few units.

Exercise 1

Complete the relations on Ahmed's family tree. Pay attention to whether the relation is male (♂) or female (♀).

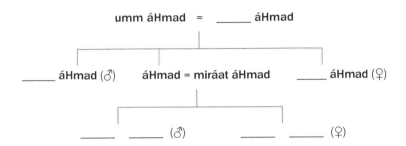

umm áHmad = _____ áHmad

_____ áHmad (♂)   áHmad = miráat áHmad   _____ áHmad (♀)

_____ _____ (♂)   _____ _____ (♀)

 Download a list of additional family members.

 Language points

Personal pronouns (plural)

In Unit 1 you met the singular pronouns. Now here are the plurals:

íHna	we
íntu	you *(pl.)*
húmma	they

Remember that there are three words for 'you'. The pronoun varies depending on whether you are addressing a male (**ínta**), a female (**ínti**), or a group (**íntu**).

Exercise 2

Rephrase these sentences using one of the plural pronouns above, as in the examples.

> **ána wi-samíira hína!** → **íHna hína!**

1 **húwwa wi-miráatuh hína?**

2 **ínta w-ínti fir-rádyo!**

3 **ána wi-góhzi min iskindiríyya.**

4 **ínti wi-wiláadik min buur saa9íid?**

5 **wiláad áHmad fi aswáan.**

6 **ána w-íbni fi maSr.**

Possession

The Arabic equivalent of the English possessive pronouns ('my', 'your', 'our', etc.) are attached pronouns joined to the end of a word. For example, **wiláad** means 'children', but **wiláadi** means 'my children'. Here is a reminder of the singular attached pronouns:

wiláadi	<u>my</u> children
wiláadak	<u>your *(masc.)*</u> children
wiláadik	<u>your *(fem.)*</u> children
wiláaduh	<u>his</u> children
wiláadhaa	<u>her</u> children

Now here are the plural attached pronouns:

wiláadna	<u>our</u> children
wiláadku	<u>your *(pl.)*</u> children
wiláadhum	<u>their</u> children

The attached pronouns can change slightly depending on whether the word they are attached to originally ends in a consonant (non-vowel) or a vowel, as shown in the following table:

	After consonant	Example (**wiláad**)	After vowel	Example (**ábu**)
my	-i	wiláadi	-ya	abúya
your (*masc.*)	-ak	wiláadak	-k	abúk
your (*fem.*)	-ik	wiláadik	-ki	abúki
his	-uh	wiláaduh	-h	abúh
her	-haa	wiláadhaa	-haa	abúhaa
our	-na	wiláadna	-na	abúna
your (*pl.*)	-ku	wiláadku	-ku	abúku
their	-hum	wiláadhum	-hum	abúhum

Note: Remember that if an attached pronoun starts with a consonant *and* the word before already ends in two consonants, then a 'helping' vowel is put between the word and the ending to prevent a cluster of three consonants, e.g. **bínti** (my daughter), but **bint(í)na** (our daughter); **ísmak** (your name), but **ism(á)haa** (her name). Notice how the stress shifts onto the helping vowel since an extra syllable has been added to the word.

 ## Exercise 3

Write these combinations with attached pronouns and then decide what they mean, as in the example.

ab + ána ➜ abúya (my father)

1 **ab + ínti**

2 **ibn + íHna**

3 **ukht + ána**

4 **ism + ínta**

5 **umm + íntu**

6 **akh + húmma**

7 **bint + ínti**

8 **wiláad + húwwa**

9 **gohz + híyya**

10 **akh + ána**

11 **miráat + ínta**

12 **ism + húwwa**

13 **ab + íHna**

14 **wiláad + húmma**

Exercise 4

Re-write these sentences, changing the subject, as in the examples.

ána ísmi samíira. [she] → híyya ism(á)haa samíira.

íbnak fir-rádyo? [your *(pl.)* son] → ibn(ú)ku fir-rádyo?

1 ána ísmi kamáal. [he]

2 bínti hína? [your *(fem.)* daughter]

3 abúya min aswáan. [our father]

4 góhzi ísmuh 9osmáan. [her husband]

5 úkhtuh fir-rádyo. [their sister]

6 úmmuh ism(á)haa láyla. [your *(masc.)* mother]

Exercise 5

Fill in the missing words in these short exchanges about names.

1 – ísmak _____ ?
– ána _____ Hásan.

2 – _____ eh?
– ána _____ samíira.

3 – bíntik _____ eh?
– _____ _____ móna.

4 – abúku _____ eh?
– _____ _____ kamáal.

5 – miráatuh _____ _____ ?
– _____ _____ láyla.

6 – ibn(ú)ku _____ _____ ?
– _____ _____ áHmad.

Exercise 6 (Audio 1; 18)

Look at Samira's family tree and listen to the description.

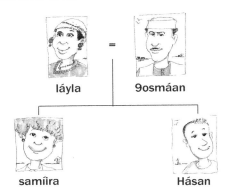

ána ísmi samîira w-ána min buur sa9îid.
akhúya ísmuh Hásan w-úmmi ism(á)haa láyla.
bába ... abúya ... ísmuh 9osmáan.

Now make up a similar description for Widaad's family from Giza.
Start with **ána ísmi widáad ...**

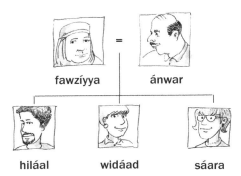

Exercise 7

Make up a few sentences about your own family and their names.
Try to say the description out loud to practise speaking.

Cultural point

The Red Sea

The Egyptian Red Sea coast is a popular holiday destination for both Egyptians and international tourists – famous for its marine life, long sandy beaches and year-round sunshine. Since the early 1980s, there has been a huge explosion in the number and size of resorts on the Red Sea. Amongst the most well-known are **sharm ish-shaykh** (Sharm el-sheikh) and **dáhab** (Dahab) on the Sinai peninsula; **ghardá'a** (Hurghada) and **il-9ayn is-súkhna** (Ein Sukhna) on the west coast.

Download more information about the Egyptian Red Sea resorts.

Dialogue 2

miin di? (Audio 1; 19)

Gaber is showing his friend Hassan a photo from his family album.

1	Who is the girl in the photo?
2	Who is the older man?
3	Where was this photo taken?

HÁSAN:	miin di yaa gáabir?
GÁABIR:	di khaTíbti widáad.
HÁSAN:	w-ímta l-fáraH in sháa' alláah?
GÁABIR:	il-fáraH fiS-Sayf.
HÁSAN:	wi-da miin?
GÁABIR:	da kháali amíin bitáa9 ostorálya.
HÁSAN:	wiS-Súura di fayn yaa gáabir?
GÁABIR:	sharm ish-shaykh.

HASSAN:	*Who's that, Gaber?*
GABER:	*That's my fiancée Widaad.*
HASSAN:	*And when is the wedding, God willing?*
GABER:	*The wedding is in the summer.*
HASSAN:	*And who's that?*
GABER:	*That's my uncle, Amin, the one in Australia.*
HASSAN:	*And where's this picture [taken], Gaber?*
GABER:	*Sharm el-sheikh.*

Vocabulary

miin?	who?
da (*fem.* **di**)	this/that
khaTíbti (*fem.*)	my fiancée; the masculine equivalent is **khaTíibi**
ímta?	when?
fáraH	wedding
in sháa' alláah	If Gods wills/God willing. Phrase universally used when talking about future events.
iS-Sayf	the summer. **fiS-Sayf** = in the summer
kháal	maternal uncle (mother's brother). Paternal uncle is **9ámm**. Aunt equivalents are **kháala** and **9ámma**.
bitáa9	connected with, belonging to
ostorálya	Australia
fayn?	where?
Súura	photo/picture

Language points

Gender of nouns

All Arabic nouns (words which name an object, a person or an idea) are either *masculine* or *feminine*. It is easy to tell them apart as almost all feminine nouns end with -a (and almost all masculine nouns do not):

fáraH *(masculine)*	wedding
rádyo *(masculine)*	radio
Súura *(feminine)*	photo/picture
kháala *(feminine)*	aunt (maternal)

The main exceptions are some feminine nouns that *don't* end in -a, but which refer to females or countries/cities, e.g. **umm** (mother), **bint** (daughter/girl), **maSr** (Egypt), etc.

il (the)

The word for 'the' is **il**. There is no separate word for 'a/an/some':

bint	(a) girl/(a) daughter
il-bint	the girl/the daughter
fáraH	(a) wedding
il-fáraH	the wedding
wiláad	(some) children
il-wiláad	the children

■ Sun letters

Certain initial letters cause the **l** sound of **il** to 'assimilate', in other words to change to the sound of the following letter, which is pronounced doubled. For example:

Súura	(a) picture
iS-Súura	the picture
rádyo	(a) radio
ir-rádyo	the radio

This assimilation happens with letters which represent sounds produced towards the front of the mouth, in the same region as the **l** sound of **il**. With the exception of **k** and **g**, these sounds are usually made with the tongue against the back of the teeth. The letters that assimilate are known as *Sun letters* since the Arabic word for 'sun' (**shams**) itself begins with the assimilating sound **sh**. The full list of Sun letters is as follows:

> **t, d, z, n, r, s, sh, k, S, T, D, Z, l**, and sometimes **g**

Do not worry too much about this aspect at the beginning. You will be easily understood if you pronounce **il** before a Sun letter; but gradually you will develop the habit of assimilating the sounds.

■ After a vowel

If **il** follows a word ending in a vowel, the **i** is dropped, and the **l** sound elided with the preceding vowel:

ímta l-fáraH?	When's the wedding?
fiS-Sayf (= **fi** + **iS-Sayf**)	in the summer
wil-wiláad (= **wi** + **il-wiláad**)	and the children

Exercise 8 (Audio 1; 20)

Practise pronouncing the Sun letters correctly. Follow the instructions on the recording.

Exercise 9

Decide if these words are masculine or feminine and then write them with the appropriate form of **il**, as in the example.

> **Súura** → *feminine* **iS-Súura** (the picture)

1	**ibn**		6	**tarabáyza**
2	**ráqam**		7	**kháal**
3	**umm**		8	**masáa'**
4	**Sayf**		9	**kháala**
5	**SabáaH**		10	**Dayf**

Language point

Demonstratives: da/di/duul

Egyptian Arabic makes no distinction between 'this' and 'that', or 'these' and 'those' (*demonstratives*). However, the demonstratives do change depending on the gender and number of what they refer to: **da** for a masculine word, **di** for a feminine word and **duul** for plurals.

Simple statements and questions can be formed using these demonstratives:

di Súura.	This/That [is a] picture.
da kháali.	This/That [is] my uncle.
di umm(i) gáabir.	This/That [is] Gaber's mother.
di khaTíbti widáad.	This/That [is] my fiancée Widaad.
miin di?	Who [is] this/that *(fem.)*?
miin duul?	Who [are] these/those?

If you want to say the equivalent of 'this/that wedding' (rather than 'this/that <u>is a</u> wedding'), you need to make the noun definite by adding **il** and then add **da/di/duul** *after* the combination:

il-fáraH da	that wedding (*lit.* 'the wedding that')
iS-Súura di	this picture ('the picture this')
il-wiláad duul	those children ('the children those')

Exercise 10

How would you say these in Arabic?

1 Who's this? *(pointing at a man)*

2 That's my maternal uncle, Hassan.

3 Who's this? *(pointing at a woman)*

4 That's Hassan's daughter.

5 And who are these?

6 Those are her children.

7 And this picture?

8 That's my brother in Sharm el-sheikh.

 Download extra activities to practise **di**, **da** and **duul**.

 Language points

Attached pronouns on feminine nouns

When an attached pronoun is added to a feminine noun, the feminine ending -a usually changes to -t if the attached pronoun begins with a vowel, or to -it if the attached pronoun begins with a consonant:

Súura picture   → **Súrtak** your *(masc.)* picture
    → **Suurítna** our picture

kháala (maternal) aunt   → **khálti** my aunt
    → **khaalíthum** their aunt

Notice how the stress can move and how the long vowel in **Súura** and **kháala** shortens when an attached ending beginning with a vowel is added. Another example from Dialogue 2 of this vowel shortening is the long **ii** in **khaTíiba** (fiancée) which shortens to **i** when the attached pronoun meaning 'my' is added, producing **khaTíbti** (my fiancée).

Pay special attention to feminine nouns that have a doubled letter before the ending -a, for example **9ámma** (paternal aunt). In this case, the ending changes to -it before all attached pronouns to avoid a cluster of three consonants:

9ámma (paternal) aunt   → **9ammíti** my aunt
    → **9ammíthum** their aunt

Exercise 11 (Audio 1; 21)

 Practise using attached pronouns with these feminine nouns:

Súura kháala khaTíiba 9ámma

Follow the prompts on your recording.

Using bitáa9

bitáa9 is a useful word, roughly meaning 'belonging to' or 'connected with'. The feminine is **bitáa9it**.

kháali bitáa9 ostorálya	my uncle connected with Australia
iS-Súura bitáa9it láyla	the picture belonging to Leila

bitáa9/bitáa9it can also be used with the attached pronouns:

ir-rádyo bitáa9i	the radio belonging to me; i.e. my radio
iS-Súura bitaa9íthaa	the picture belonging to her; i.e. her picture

And for short answers:

ir-rádyo da bitáa9 miin?	Whose radio is that?
bitáa9i.	It's mine.
iS-Súura di bitáa9it miin?	Whose picture is that?
bitaa9íthaa.	It's hers.

Download extra activities to practise attached pronouns.

Forming questions

There is no special question form in Arabic. You can turn a sentence into a question by simply raising your voice at the end:

húwwa min buur sa9íid.	He's from Port Said.
húwwa min buur sa9íid?	Is he from Port Said?

The position of question words, such as **miin?** (who?), **fayn?** (where?) or **ímta?** (when?), is flexible and they are often put at the end of the question:

miin da?/da miin?	Who's that?
fayn iS-Súura di?/ iS-Súura di fayn?	Where's this picture [taken]?

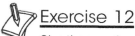

Exercise 12

Give the questions for these answers, as in the example.

da íbni áHmad. → miin da?

1 **duul wiláad ukhti.**

2 **di bínti sáara.**

3 **iS-Súura di fi maSr.**

4 **il-rádyo bitáa9 úmmi.**

5 **il-fáraH fiS-Sayf.**

6 **khaTíbti fi dáhab.**

Exercise 13 (Audio 1; 22)

Imagine you are showing your photo album to an Egyptian friend. Listen to the recording and answer her questions as prompted. You will hear a model answer after the pauses.

Learning with a friend or in a class?
Go to the website for ideas for practising introductions.

تاب The Arabic script

Here are two more letters of the Arabic alphabet:

ن   the letter **nuun**, pronounced 'n' as in 'net'

ي   the letter **yaa**, pronounced 'y' as in 'yet', or 'ii' like the 'ee' in 'bee'

Joining letters

When at the beginning or in the middle of a word, **nuun** and **yaa** have the same basic shape as **baa**, **taa** and **thaa** in Unit 1.

(read from right to left)

ن + ب = نـب

ي + ث = يث

ب + ن + ت = بنـت

ا + ن + ا = انـا

They only retain their differences when written at the end of a word:

(read from right to left)

ب + ن = بـن

ا + ي = اي

ث + ا + ن = ثان

ب + ن + ت + ي = بنـتي

Vowels

Modern written Arabic does not normally show short vowels (a, e, i, o, u) as part of the script. These can be included as symbols above and below the main script, but they are usually only added for children's books or religious texts. For example, the word **bint** is written without the short **i**:

bint (girl/daughter) = بنـت (b/n/t)

However, if a word starts with a short vowel, this will be shown by an **alif**, sometimes with a small symbol called a *hamza* above or below:

ab (father) = أب (alif/b)

ibn (son) = ابـن (alif/b/n)

The attached pronoun **-i** ('my') is written with ي yaa joined to the end of the noun:

(read from right to left)

ابـن (son) + ي (my) = ابـنـي (my son) íbni

Exercise 14

See if you can match these words you have met to the Arabic script.

1	ínta (you)	بنتي	a
2	yaa ('hey')	اثنين	b
3	bínti (my daughter)	أنا	c
4	íbni (my son)	ابني	d
5	ána (I)	أنت	e
6	itnáyn (two)	يا	f

Unit Three

tíshrab shay?

Would you like some tea?

In this unit you will learn about:

- offering food and drink
- accepting and refusing politely
- some Egyptian dishes and drinks
- jobs and occupations
- making words plural
- how to make simple sentences negative
- recognizing these Arabic letters: ح ح خ

Cultural point

Food and drink are a very important part of Arab hospitality. You will nearly always be offered a hot or cold drink if you go to someone's house – some **shay** (sweet black tea often in a glass) or **áhwa** (coffee), or perhaps **Háaga sá9a** (a cold drink) or **kárkaday** (hibiscus tea).

You may be offered cakes, perhaps the traditional syrupy **ba'láawa** (baklava – filo pastry and nuts), **lú'mit il-'áaDi** (fried dough balls), **basbúusa** (semolina cake) or the ubiquitous mock-cream gateau. If it is near eating time, you will probably be invited to join the meal.

Download more information about Egyptian hospitality.

Dialogue 1

tíshrab shay? (Audio 1; 23)

Gaber's mother offers Hassan some morning refreshments while he waits for his friend to get ready.

---

1   Is Hassan offered tea or coffee?
2   Does he accept the offer of sweet porridge?

UMM(I) GÁABIR:	tíshrab shay yábni?
HÁSAN:	la' shukrán yaa Tant. líssa sháarib.
UMM(I) GÁABIR:	tákul Tába' bilíila?
HÁSAN:	bilíila? ána amúut fil-bilíila!
UMM(I) GÁABIR:	Táyyib, u'9úd yábni!

GABER'S MOTHER:	*Would you like some tea, dear?*
HASSAN:	*No, thank you, auntie. I've just had a drink.*
GABER'S MOTHER:	*Would you like to eat a bowl of sweet porridge?*
HASSAN:	*Porridge? I adore porridge!*
GABER'S MOTHER:	*Then sit down, dear!*

Vocabulary

shay	tea
shukrán	thank you
Tába'	plate/bowl/dish
bilíila	sweet porridge, a morning dish made with milk and grain
ána amúut fil ...	I adore ... (*lit.* 'I die in the...')
Táyyib	OK, well; a common expression sometimes shortened to just **Tab**
u'9úd!	sit down!

Language point

Offering food and drink

In Dialogue 1, you heard two simple phrases for offering drink or food. In both cases you need to add the ending **-i** if offering to a female:

tíshrab ...?	Would you like (to drink) ...?
(fem. **tishrábi ...?)**	
tákul ...?	Would you like (to eat) ...?
(fem. **tákli ...?)**	

Notice how the addition of the feminine verb ending -i affects the pronunciation. Adding -i to **tíshrab** causes the stress to move to the second syllable: **tishrábi**; adding -i to **tákul** causes the u to drop out altogether: **tákli.** This kind of change is typical of spoken Arabic in general and of Egyptian Arabic in particular, so listen out for it on the recordings.

You could also use a third, more general phrase which is not restricted to offering food or drink. Again add the feminine verb ending -i if offering to a female:

tiHíbb ...?	Would you like ...?
(fem. **tiHíbbi ...?)**	

Exercise 1

Practise offering guests food and drink. Offer these items as in the example. (You will find the Arabic for the items in Dialogue 1 or in the Cultural point before the dialogue).

> tea *(to a female guest)* ➔ **tishrábi shay?**

1 coffee *(to a male guest)*

2 baklava *(to a male guest)*

3 baklava *(to a female guest)*

4 hibiscus tea *(to a female guest)*

5 a cold drink *(to a male guest)*

6 semolina cake *(to a male guest)*

7 semolina cake *(to a female guest)*

8 coffee *(to a female guest)*

Responding to offers

The simplest responses to any offer are:

áywa, min fáDlak   Yes, please.
(to a female min fáDlik)

la', shukrán.   No, thank you.

If refusing an offer, it is courteous to add an explanation so that you don't hurt your host's feelings. A common explanation is that you have just eaten or drunk something before arriving. In Dialogue 1, Hassan says:

la', shukrán. líssa sháarib.   No, thank you. I've just had a drink.

The word **líssa** in this context means 'just', and **sháarib** means 'drinking', so the phrase literally means 'just drinking'. You will learn more about Arabic '-ing' words (*active participles*) in Unit 4, but for the moment we'll stick to the two useful ones in the context of food and drink: **sháarib** (drinking) and **wáakil** (eating).

líssa sháarib.   I've just had a drink.

líssa wáakil.   I've just had something to eat.

If you are female, you will need to use the feminine version of the two words: **shárba** (drinking) and **wákla** (eating).

líssa shárba.   I've just had a drink. *(fem.)*

líssa wákla.   I've just had something to eat. *(fem.)*

 Exercise 2 (Audio 1; 8)

 Practise accepting and refusing offers politely. Follow the instructions on the recording.

 Exercise 3

Unscramble these sentences and questions, as in the example:

áhwa gáabir yaa tíshrab?   ➜   tíshrab áhwa yaa gáabir?

1 yaa basbúusa tákul gáabir?

2 shúkran wáakil líssa la'

3 fáDlik min áywa

4 widáad shay tishrábi yaa?

5 Tant la' shárba líssa yaa shúkran

6 Hásan bilíila tákul Tába' yaa?

7 fil amúut bilíila ána

8 yábni Táyyib u'9úd

Exercise 4

Match the questions with their correct replies, for example **1e**. (Take special note of the gender of the speaker as shown in the picture, and whether the questions are directed at a man or at a woman. This will give you a clue to the answer.)

1   tíshrab shay?   áywa, ána amúut fil-bilíila.   a

2   tishrábi áhwa?   la' shúkran. líssa wákla.   b

3   tákli Tába' bilíila?   áhwa? la' shúkran. líssa shárba.   c

4   tishrábi shay?   la' shúkran yaa Tant. líssa sháarib.   d

5   tíshrab áhwa yábni?   shay? áywa, min fáDlak.   e

6   tákul Tába' bilíila?   shay? áywa, min fáDlak.   f

Learning with a friend or in a class?
Download ideas to practise offering and responding.

Dialogue 2

 Tába' il-yohm eh? **(Audio 1; 25)**

Rita Stanley is now seated at her table in the restaurant. A waiter approaches.

What does Rita choose to eat?

IG-GARSÓN:	tishrábi eh HaDrítik? 9aSíir? kóhla? kárkaday?
RITA STANLEY:	máyya min fáDlak. Tába' il-yohm eh?
IG-GARSÓN:	Tába' il-yohm kabáab wi-kófta, wi-9andína wára' 9ínab, sabáanikh, omlíit. HaDrítik tiHíbbi máSri?
RITA STANLEY:	áywa. háatli k-kabáab wi-sálaTa.
IG-GARSÓN:	wáaHid kabáab wi-sálaTa!

WAITER:	*What would you like to drink? Juice? Cola? Hibiscus tea?*
RITA STANLEY:	*Water, please. What's the dish of the day?*
WAITER:	*The dish of the day is kebab and kofta, and we have stuffed vine leaves, spinach, omelette. Would you like Egyptian (food)?*
RITA STANLEY:	*Yes. Bring me a kebab and salad.*
WAITER:	*One kebab and salad!*

Vocabulary

tishráb eh? (fem. **tishrábi eh?**)	What would you like to drink?
Tába' il-yohm	dish of the day
9andína	we have
háatli ... (fem. **haatíli**)	bring me ...

(For drinks and dishes, see the list that follows.)

Food and drink

Here are the drinks and snacks you have met so far in this unit, together with a few more popular items.

máyya	water
9aSíir	juice
kóhla	cola
bíira	beer
nibíit	wine
kárkaday	hibiscus tea
shay	tea
áhwa	coffee; **áhwa** is also used to mean a traditional coffee shop
lában	milk
kabáab	kebab, lamb cubes
wára' 9ínab	(stuffed) vine leaves
kófta	minced meat (served as part of kebab or as meat balls/fingers)
fuul	fava beans (baked slowly overnight)
Ta9míyya	fried discs of bean paste; also known as **faláafil**
omlíit	omelette
sabáanikh	spinach
bámya	okra, ladies' fingers
sálaTa	salad
sandawítsh	sandwich
ruzz	rice
9aysh	bread

Exercise 5 (Audio 1; 26)

 Practise offering the drinks and snacks in the list on page 49. Follow the instructions on the recording.

 Download a list of additional drinks and snacks.

Language points

To have

The equivalent of the English verb 'to have' ('I have', 'you have', 'he has', etc.) is expressed by using the word **9and** (roughly meaning 'at' or 'chez') and the appropriate attached pronoun (see Unit 2):

9ándi	I have (*lit.* 'at me')
9ándak	you (*masc.*) have
9ándik	you (*fem.*) have
9ánduh	he has
9andáhaa	she has
9andína	we have
9andúku	you (*pl.*) have
9andúhum	they have

Notice that when the attached pronoun needs a helping vowel, the stress moves along the word, so that it always falls on the penultimate syllable (the one before last).

These expressions can be used by themselves:

9andína wára' 9ínab.	We have stuffed vine leaves.
9ándi akh ísmuh tom.	I have a brother called ('his name is') Tom.

They can also be combined with nouns or pronouns:

ána 9ándi ukht ismáhaa móna.	I have a sister called Mona.

gáabir 9ánduh kháala   Gaabir has an aunt called Sara.
ismáhaa sáara.

Exercise 6

Change these Arabic sentences and questions to match the new subject in brackets, as in the example.

9andína wára' 9ínab. (they) ➔ **9andúhum wára' 9ínab.**

1 **9ándi akh ísmuh tom.** (she)

2 **9ánduh bint ismáhaa náadya.** (we)

3 **ínta 9ándak wiláad?** (you, *fem.*)

4 **9andúhum kárkaday?** (you, *pl.*)

5 **híyya 9andáhaa ibn.** (I)

6 **Hásan 9ánduh akh ísmuh gamáal.** (Widaad)

7 **sáara 9andáhaa khaal fi buur sa9íid.** (Gaber)

8 **ána wi-miráati 9andína Dayf.** (Ahmed and his wife)

Construct phrases (iDáafa)

Construct phrases relate two nouns together. Sometimes in English the two words are linked using words such as 'of', e.g. 'bowl of balila', 'father of Widaad'; or the possessive 's, e.g. 'Widaad's father', 'Kamal's salad', 'my daughter's picture'.

In Arabic a construct phrase is made by putting the two nouns directly together. There is a special term for these constructs: **iDáafa**, literally meaning 'addition'. Note carefully the order of the words. You can remember the Arabic order by mentally adding 'of' between the words:

ábu widáad	father of Widaad/Widaad's father
sandawítsh Ta9míyya	(a) falafel sandwich ('sandwich [of] falafel')
Tába' bilíila	(a) bowl of sweet porridge
9aSíir laymúun	(a) lemon juice ('juice [of] lemon')

The feminine ending **-a** changes to **-it** when the noun is first in a construct phrase (see also Attached pronouns, Unit 2):

sálaTit sabáanikh	spinach salad
Súurit bínti	my daughter's picture

If the construct phrase is definite (i.e. *the* bowl of porridge), then the article **il-** is added *only* to the second word:

Tába' il-bilîila	the bowl of porridge
Tába' il-yohm	the dish of the day
sálaTit is-sabáanikh	the spinach salad

Download extra activities to practise **iDáafa** construct phrases.

Cultural point

Throughout Egypt, there are traditional juice stalls selling delicious freshly-squeezed juices made from local fruit and vegetables. You usually drink a glass on the spot, but it is sometimes possible to take away bottles. Prices are very reasonable.

Exercise 7

Choose an appropriate word from the list below to complete the phrases, as in the example. Some of the phrases may have more than one correct answer.

Tába'   plate/dish/bowl

sandawítsh   sandwich

izáaza   bottle

kubbáaya   glass

_____ **máyya** ➜ **izáazit máyya/kubbáayit máyya**
(a bottle of water/a glass of water)

1 _____ **bilíila**

2 _____ **ruzz**

3 _____ **kóhla**

4 _____ **shay**

5 _____ **Ta9míyya**

6 _____ **bámya**

7 _____ **fuul**

8 _____ **9aSíir laymúun**

Exercise 8 (Audio 1; 27)

Listen to Widaad and Gaber ordering lunch in a restaurant. Put a tick in the table below beside the items of food and drink that they choose, as in the example.

	Water	Lemon juice	Cola	Spinach	Okra	Kebab	Rice	Salad
Widaad	✔							
Gaber								

Exercise 9 (Audio 1; 28)

You are ordering an Egyptian breakfast. You want to order coffee, a falafel sandwich and a plate of beans. Prepare what you're going to say and then answer the waitress's questions on the recording.

Dialogue 3

HaDrítik bi-tishtághali eh? (Audio 1; 29)

A journalist is conducting interviews in the street for a radio programme about jobs and careers. He speaks to three passers-by.

---

1   What are the names of the three interviewees?
2   What is the job of the second interviewee?

IL-MUZíi9:	ism HaDrítik eh, yaa madáam?
SAYYÍDA 1:	ísmi záynab sarHáan.
IL-MUZíi9:	wi-HaDrítik bi-tishtághali eh?
SAYYÍDA 1:	ána mudarrísa – mudarrísit kímya.
IL-MUZíi9:	w-ism HaDrítak eh, yaa ustáaz?
RÁAGIL 1:	ána id-duktúur áHmad muníir.
IL-MUZíi9:	wi-HaDrítak bi-tishtághal hína fi maSr?
RÁAGIL 1:	la', mish hína. ána duktúur fi faránsa.
IL-MUZíi9:	wi-HaDrítik, yaa áanisa?
SAYYÍDA 2:	ána ísmi sámya nuur w-ána muDíifa fi maSr liT-Tayaráan.

BROADCASTER:	*What's your name, Madam?*
WOMAN 1:	*My name's Zeinab Sarhan.*
BROADCASTER:	*And what do you do?*
WOMAN 1:	*I'm a teacher – a chemistry teacher.*
BROADCASTER:	*And what's your name, Sir?*
MAN 1:	*I'm Doctor Ahmed Munir.*
BROADCASTER:	*And do you work here in Egypt?*
MAN 1:	*No, not here. I'm a doctor in France.*
BROADCASTER:	*And you, Miss?*
WOMAN 2:	*My name's Samya Nur and I'm a flight attendant with Egypt Air.*

Vocabulary

bi-tishtághal eh? (*fem.* **bi-tishtághali eh?**)	What do you do? (*lit.* 'you work what?')
kímya	chemistry
mish hína	not here
faránsa	France
áanisa	'Miss': a common way of addressing younger, unmarried women
maSr liT-Tayaráan	Egypt Air

(For occupations, see the list below.)

Occupations (Audio 1; 30)

Here are some occupations. The feminine of most occupations is formed by adding **-a**. Listen and repeat them, taking note of how the stress can move in the feminine.

Masculine	Feminine	Translation
mudárris	**mudarrísa**	teacher
duktúur	**duktúura**	doctor
muDíif	**muDíifa**	flight attendant
muHáasib	**muHásba**	accountant
muhándis	**muhandísa**	engineer
mumássil	**mumassíla**	actor
muHáami	**muHaamíya**	lawyer
Táalib	**Taalíba**	student

Note: **mudarrísit kímya** (chemistry teacher, *lit.* 'teacher [of] chemistry') is another example of a construct phrase (**iDáafa**). **mudarrísa** ('teacher') ends with the feminine **-a**, and so this changes to **-it** when it is the first noun in a construct phrase.

Download a list of additional occupations.

Exercise 10

Make these sentences and questions feminine, as in the example.

> ána duktúur fi aswáan. ➜ ána duktúura fi aswáan.

1 ána muhándis fi amríika.

2 húwwa muDíif fi maSr liT-Tayaráan.

3 húwwa mudárris kímya.

4 ínta mumássil yaa ustáaz?

5 ána Táalib fi-iskindiríyya.

6 ínta Táalib hína?

Exercise 11

How do you say these in Arabic?

1 I'm an actor (*masc.*).

2 I'm an actor (*fem.*).

3 Are you (*fem.*) a doctor?

4 Are you (*masc.*) a student?

5 He's an accountant in Alexandria.

6 She's a lawyer in America.

7 I'm a flight attendant (*fem.*) with ('in') Egypt Air.

8 Are you (*fem.*) a chemistry teacher?

Language points

Negative phrases with mish

mish (also pronounced **mush**) means 'not' and can be used to make
many simple phrases and sentences negative:

> hína   here
> **mish** hína   not here

SáaHi	awake
mish SáaHi	not awake
ána duktúur.	I'm a doctor.
ána mish duktúur.	I'm not a doctor.
húwwa máSri.	He's Egyptian.
húwwa mish máSri.	He's not Egyptian.
di úmmi.	That's my mother.
di mish úmmi.	That's not my mother.

Exercise 12

You are the subject of mistaken identity! Someone is asking you questions and all the information is wrong. Correct them as in the example, using the feminine if you are a woman.

Say the sentences out loud to help practise speaking.

> ínta ingilíizi (ínti ingilizíyya)? ➔ la', ána mish ingilíizi (ingilizíyya)!

1 ínta iskutlándi (ínti iskutlandíyya)?

2 ínta (ínti) min Glasgow?

3 di bíntak (bíntik)?

4 da íbnak (íbnik)?

5 ísmak (ísmik) Stanley?

6 ínta mumássil (ínti mumassíla)?

Plurals

Plurals in English are usually formed by adding 's' or 'es' to the end of the singular (radio/radios; box/boxes, etc.). Some Arabic plurals are simple external endings like these, but others require changes to the internal vowels – similar to the English 'man/men' or 'mouse/mice'. Like these two English examples, the Arabic internal plurals have to be learnt individually, although there are common patterns.

In this unit we will concentrate on the external pluals. Internal plural patterns will be introduced in later units. The structure summary at the back of the book also gives common patterns and the glossaries show plurals for individual nouns.

■ External plurals

There are two external plural endings:

1 -íin: only used with nouns referring to people. Many (but not all) professions and nationalities can be made plural using the -íin ending:

   mudárris (teacher, *masc.*) ➔ mudarrisíin (teachers)

   mumássil (actor, *masc.*) ➔ mumassilíin (actors)

2 -áat: used with some feminine or masculine nouns, especially long nouns or those of foreign origin. Note that the feminine -a ending is removed before adding the plural -áat.

   tilifóhn (telephone, *masc.*) ➔ tilifohnáat (telephones)

   tarabáyza (table, *fem.*) ➔ tarabayzáat (tables)

In spoken Egyptian, the -íin plural is generally used for males *and* females (although Standard Arabic uses -áat for groups of females).

If the final vowel in the singular is a long vowel, this will shorten when the plural endings -áat or -íin are added:

   maTáar (airport) ➔ maTaráat (airports)

   sawwáa' (driver) ➔ sawwa'íin (drivers)

If a word ends with a vowel, an extra yy or y is added to ease pronunciation:

   máSri (Egyptian, *masc.*) ➔ maSriyyíin (Egyptians)

   mustáshfa (hospital) ➔ mustashfayáat (hospitals)

Exercise 13

Make these sentences and questions plural by changing the pronouns and using -íin, as in the example.

húwwa muhándis. ➔ **húmma muhandisíin.**

1 **húwwa mudárris.**	5 **húwwa máSri.**
2 **híyya muhandísa.**	6 **híyya ostoralíyya.**
3 **ána mumassíla.**	7 **ána muHáasib.**
4 **ínta mumássil?**	8 **ínti muhandísa?**

Exercise 14 (Audio 1; 31)

Now you are going to be interviewed.

a   Prepare information about your name, nationality, where you come from and your job. (If your job is not included in this unit or in the additional list of occupations on the website, try to find out what the word for it is or choose one of the jobs listed as an alternative.)

b   Practise answering the interviewer's questions on the recording. Keep repeating the interview until you are replying fluently in the pauses allowed.

The Arabic script   ﺍﺏ ﺕ

The three Arabic letters below share a distinctive shape. The individual letters are only distinguished by whether they have a dot below or above:

ﺡ   the letter **Haa,** pronounced as a breathy 'h'; imagine you are breathing on a pair of glasses to clean them

ﺝ   the letter **giim,** pronounced 'g' as in 'get' in Egyptian Arabic (but more formally pronounced as a soft 'j' as in the French 'je')

ﺥ   the letter **khaa,** pronounced in the back of the throat like the 'ch' in the Scottish 'loch'

The tail of these letters is only retained at the end of a word:

$$ح + ب = حب$$
$$ت + ح + ب = تحب$$
$$ت + ا + ج = تاج$$
$$ن + ي + ح = نيح$$
$$ب + خ + ت = بخت$$

Exercise 15

How many of these members of the family can you recognize in Arabic script? Look back at Unit 2, Dialogue 1 if you need help.

1 أب
2 بنت
3 أخ
4 أخت
5 ابن

Pronunciation (Audio 1; 32)

Listen to the recording and repeat these words you have met which include **Haa** or **khaa**. Pay special attention to the sounds underlined.

<u>H</u>ásan	Hassan
í<u>H</u>na	we
fára<u>H</u>	wedding
<u>kh</u>aal	uncle
<u>kh</u>ámsa	five
sabáani<u>kh</u>	spinach

Unit Four
fíihaa takíif?
Does it have air conditioning?

In this unit you will learn about:

- describing places and objects
- talking about where something is
- using adjectives for description
- rooms of the house and household items
- pronouncing 'emphatic' letters
- recognizing these Arabic letters: ل ش س

Dialogue 1

fíihaa kaam shibbáak? **(Audio 1; 33)**

A customer is calling 'Nile Tourism' (**in-niil lis-siyáaHa**) to ask about cruises between Luxor and Aswan in Upper Egypt. Widaad answers the phone.

1	How many windows does the cabin have?
2	Does it have a television?

IZ-ZIBÚUN	aló? in-niil lis-siyáaHa? maHámmad mawgúud?
WIDÁAD	la', mish mawgúud, yaa fándim. má9aak widáad.
IZ-ZIBÚUN	áhlan widáad. fiih kabíina bayn lú'sur w-aswáan?
WIDÁAD	áywa, fiih kabíina 'lux' ... kibíira.
IZ-ZIBÚUN	fíihaa kaam siríir?
WIDÁAD	siriiráyn foh' ba9D wi-tilifizyóhn ganb il-baab.
IZ-ZIBÚUN	wi-fíihaa kaam shibbáak?
WIDÁAD	shibbáak wáahid. bayn is-siríir wit-tarabáyza.

CUSTOMER	*Hello? Nile Tourism? Is Mohammed available?*
WIDAAD	*No, he's not available, sir. Widaad speaking.*
CUSTOMER	*Hello Widaad. Is there a cabin between Luxor and Aswan?*
WIDAAD	*Yes, there's a luxury cabin ... a large one.*
CUSTOMER	*How many beds does it have?*
WIDAAD	*Two bunk beds and a television next to the door.*
CUSTOMER	*And how many windows does it have?*
WIDAAD	*One window, between the bed and the table.*

Vocabulary

aló?	hello? (only used over the telephone)
mawgúud	present/available
mish mawgúud	not present/not available
yaa fándim	Sir/Madam
má9aak widáad	Widaad speaking (*lit.* 'with you Widaad')
kabíina	cabin
bayn	between
'lux'	luxury/first class

siríir	bed
siriiráyn foh' ba9D	bunk beds ('two beds above each other')
tilifizyóhn	television
ganb	next to
baab	door
shibbáak	window

Exercise 1 (Audio 1; 34)

Practise speaking on the phone. Follow the instructions on your recording.

Exercise 2

A customer phones the National Bank (**bank il-wáTan**). Put the opening conversation in the right order.
(Note: **uul li** = tell me)

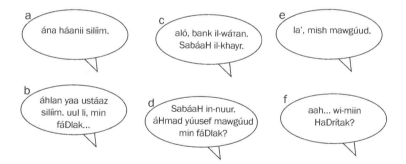

a ána háanii silíim.

c aló, bank il-wáTan. SabáaH il-khayr.

e la', mish mawgúud.

b áhlan yaa ustáaz silíim. uul li, min fáDlak...

d SabáaH in-nuur. áHmad yúusef mawgúud min fáDlak?

f aah... wi-miin HaDrítak?

Language points

fiih/fíihaa

fiih and **fíihaa** – both literally meaning 'in it' – are very useful phrases used to mean 'it has (got)' or 'there is/there are'.

    fiih is the masculine version which can also be used as a universal phrase without reference to a specific place:

fiih kabíina?	Is there a cabin (available)?
fiih mushkíla.	There's a problem (in general).
fiih bank 'uráyyib min hína?	Is there a bank near here?

fíihaa is the feminine version, which refers to features of a specific feminine place.

ik-kabíina fíihaa kaam siríir?	How many beds does the cabin have?
fíihaa tilifizyóhn?	Is there a television [in the cabin]?
il-9arabíyya fíihaa takíif.	The car has air conditioning.

Exercise 3

Use **fiih** or **fíihaa** to say these in Arabic.

1 Is there a problem?

2 The cabin has a table.

3 Is there air conditioning (in general)?

4 Is there a car (available)?

5 How many doors does the car have?

6 There's a bank next to the coffee shop.

Describing position (Audio 1; 35)

Dialogue 1 contains several words describing position. They are listed below together with some other common additions. Listen and repeat the words and phrases on the recording.

bayn	between	**taHt**	under
foh'	above/over	**'uddáam**	in front of
fi	in	**wára**	behind
ganb	next to	**9ála**	on

it-tilifizyóhn ganb il-baab. The television is next to the door.

fíih bortráy foh' is-siríir. There's a portrait above the bed.

ána wára l-baab. I'm behind the door.

Download a list of additional words and phrases to describe position.

Exercise 4 (Audio 1; 36)

Where am I? **ána fayn?** Gaber keeps moving around the room. Listen to him telling you where he is on the recording and track his progress by putting a cross on the picture below for each position he mentions.

Exercise 5

Use the positional words to make sentences, as in the example.

    fi (bint/kabíina) ➔ **il-bint fi k-kabíina**

1 **fi (wálad/kabíina)**

2 **ganb (siríir/baab)**

3 **'uddáam (ána/shibbáak)**

4   9ála (tilifizyóhn/tarabáyza)

5   bayn (siríir/tarabáyza + baab)

6   wára (rádyo/tilifizyóhn)

Positional words + attached pronouns

The positional words can be followed by the same attached pronouns that are used for possession (see Unit 2):

il-baab gánb<u>ak</u>.	The door is next to <u>you</u> *(masc.)*.
ish-shibbáak 'uddáam<u>na</u>.	The window is in front of <u>us</u>.
il-bank waráku<u></u>.	The bank is behind <u>you</u> *(pl.)*.
ána gánb<u>uh</u>.	I'm next to <u>him/it</u> *(masc.)*.

Watch out for the helping vowel that may be necessary when you add an attached pronoun to **ganb**, a word ending in two consonants (see Unit 2 for more details):

ána ganb(á)haa.	I'm next to her/it *(fem.)*.
híyya ganb(í)na.	She's next to us.
húwwa ganb(ú)ku.	He's next to you *(pl.)*.

Exercise 6 (audio online; WEB01)

Re-write these sentences using the correct attached pronoun, as in the example. As well answers in the Key, this exercise has a downloadable audio file for you to check your pronunciation.

it-tilifizyóhn ganb il-baab.   **→**   it-tilifizyóhn gánbuh.

1   il-bint ganb il-9arabíyya.

2   ána wára wiláadi.

3   híyya 'uddáam it-tarabáyza.

4   is-siríir taHt ish-shibbáak.

5   núura ganbak ínta w-áhmad.

6 fik-kabíina kaam siríir?

7 widáad mawgúuda fil-máktab?

8 il-'ahwa 'uddáam il-bank.

Download extra activities to practise positional words.

Dialogue 2

il-9arabíyya gidíida? **(Audio 1; 37)**

Hassan is admiring his friend Gaber's new car.

1	**Does the car have air conditioning?**
2	**Does it have a CD player or radio?**
3	**Does it have leather seats?**

HÁSAN	il-9arabíyya gidíida? mabrúuk 9aláyk!
GÁABIR	alláah yibáarak fiik.
HÁSAN	fíihaa takíif?
GÁABIR	la', ma fiiháash. bass fíihaa 'CD'.
HÁSAN	'CD'? fayn?
GÁABIR	ahó, taHt ir-rádyo.
HÁSAN	ik-kúrsi muríiH. da gild, yaa gáabir?
GÁABIR	la', ma fiish fil-modáyl da gild.
HÁSAN	ummáal?
GÁABIR	ik-kibíira, il-alfáyn 'cc' fíihaa gild wi-takíif.
HÁSAN	Táyyib, yálla bíina!

HASSAN	*Is the car new? Congratulations!*
GABER	*Thank you.*
HASSAN	*Does it have air conditioning?*
GABER	*No, it doesn't. But it has a CD.*
HASSAN	*A CD? Where?*
GABER	*There, underneath the radio.*
HASSAN	*The seat's comfortable. Is it leather, Gaber?*
GABER	*No, there isn't any leather in this model.*
HASSAN	*What then?*
GABER	*The big one, the 2000cc has leather and has air conditioning.*
HASSAN	*OK, let's go!*

Vocabulary

9arabíyya	car
mabrúuk 9aláyk	congratulations (*lit.* 'blessing on you')
alláah yibáarak fiik(i)	reply when offered congratulations (*lit.* 'may God bless you')
takíif	air conditioning
bass	but
kúrsi	seat/chair
gild	leather
modáyl	model (of car)
ummáal?	what then?
il-alfáyn 'cc'	the 2000cc
yálla bíina!	let's go!

 Language points

Adjectives

Adjectives are descriptive words. Here are those from Dialogues 1 and 2, together with some other useful adjectives:

gidíid new	**'adíim** old
kibíir big/large	**Sugháyyar** little/small
'uráyyib (min) near (to)	**bi9íid (9an)** far (from)
muríiH comfortable	
mawgúud present/available	
mabsúuT happy	

Adjectives come *after* the noun and change according to the gender and number of what they are describing. If the noun described is feminine, you will need to add the feminine ending **-a** to the adjective:

bayt kibíir	a large house *(masc.)*
kabíina kibíira	a large cabin *(fem.)*
is-siríir gidíid.	The bed is new *(masc.)*.

il-9arabíyya gidíida.	The car is new *(fem.)*.
il-bank bi9íid?	Is the bank far *(masc.)*?
il-'ahwa 'urayyíba min hína?	Is the coffee shop near here *(fem.)*?

Adjectives referring to people can often (but not always) be made plural by adding the external plural -íin:

maHámmad mawgúud?	Is Mohammed present/available?
widáad mawgúuda?	Is Widaad present/available?
il-wiláad mabsuuTíin?	Are the children happy?

To say, 'the new bed', rather than 'the bed is new', you need to add il- to the adjective as well as to the noun:

is-siríir gidíid.	The bed is new.
is-siríir ig-gidíid	the new bed
ik-kúrsi muríiH.	The chair is comfortable.
ik-kúrsi il-muríiH	the comfortable chair
il-9arabíyya 'adíima.	The car is old.
il-9arabíyya il-'adíima	the old car

Exercise 7 (Audio 1; 38)

Practise feminine adjectives. Follow the prompts on the recording.

Exercise 8

Find the correct ending to complete the sentence or question, for example **1d**.

1 gáabir ...	a ... muríiH.
2 il-wiláad ...	b ... iS-Sughayyára.
3 íHna wára ...	c ... tarabáyza?
4 ínti ...	d ... mabsúuT.
5 fíihaa ...	e ... ik-kibíir.
6 ik-kúrsi ...	f ... mabsúuTa?
7 húwwa fil-bank ...	g ... il-baab ik-kibíir.
8 ána 'uddáam il-'ahwa ...	h ... mawguudíin?

 Download extra activities to practise adjectives.

Active participles ('ing' words)

Active participles are words such as 'eat<u>ing</u>' or 'sleep<u>ing</u>'. In Arabic, they can be used to describe what is happening at the moment (as you have met in Unit 1).

gáabir SáaHi?	Is Gaber awake ('waking')?
la', húwwa náyim.	No, he's asleep ('sleeping').

They can also sometimes be used to describe the recent past (as you have met in Unit 3).

ána líssa sháarib.	I've just had a drink ('just drinking').
húwwa líssa wáakil fuul.	He's just eaten ('just eating') beans.

Active participles behave like adjectives. They can be made feminine by adding -**a**, and plural by adding -**íin**.

widáad SáHya?	Is Widaad awake?
la', híyya náyma.	No, she's sleeping.
il-wiláad SaHyíin?	Are the children awake?
la', húmma naymíin.	No, they're sleeping.
híyya líssa shárba.	She's just had a drink.
íHna líssa waklíin fuul.	We've just eaten beans.

Note: the short **i** of the active participle drops out when the feminine or plural ending is added. In addition, any initial long vowel will shorten with the stress moving to the final syllable in the plural. For example: **sháarib, shárba, sharbíin.**

Active participles are a common feature of Egyptian Arabic and will be covered in further detail in Unit 6.

Exercise 9

Choose an appropriate active participle from the list below to complete the phrases. Don't forget to make the participle feminine or plural if required.

SáaHi	awake ('waking')
náyim	sleeping
wáakil	eating
sháarib	drinking

1 **gáabir SáaHi? la', húwwa** _____ .

2 **tishrábi shay yaa bínti? la' shukrán, líssa** _____ .

3 **widáad náyma? la', híyya** _____ .

4 **tákul Ta9míyya yaa áHmad? la' shukrán, líssa** _____ .

5 **tákli fuul yaa móna? la' shukrán, líssa** _____ .

6 **tishrábu kóhla yaa wiláad? la' shukrán, líssa** _____ .

7 **shhhhh! il-wiláad** _____ **fik-kabíina.**

8 **samíira fayn? híyya** _____ **fis-siríir.**

Language point

Is not/Are not

■ **mish** (not)

An adjective (or active participle) can be made negative by adding **mish** ('not'):

is-siríir mish muríiH.	The bed isn't comfortable.
il-9arabíyya mish kibíira.	The car isn't large.
úmmi mish mabsúuTa.	My mother isn't happy.
húmma mish naymíin.	They aren't sleeping.

■ ma fiish/ma fiiháash (there isn't/there aren't)

The phrases **fiih** and **fíihaa** can be made negative by adding **ma** before and **-sh** after:

ma fiish mushkíla.	There isn't a problem.
ma fiiháash takíif?	Doesn't it have air conditioning?
ma fiish fil-modáyl da gild.	There isn't any leather in this model.
ma fiish mudarissíin hína.	There aren't any teachers here.

Exercise 10

Make these sentences and questions negative as in the example:

fiih siríir taHt ish-shibbáak. → ma fiish siríir taHt ish-shibbáak.

1 fiih Súura foh' is-siríir.

2 fíihaa takíif?

3 il-9arabíyya 'adíima.

4 fiih kúrsi ganb il-baab.

5 ik-kúrsi muríiH.

6 fiih CD taHt ir-rádyo.

7 il-wiláad mawguudíin.

8 fíihaa shibbáak?

9 il-bayt kibíir.

10 fiih bank 'uráyyib min hína?

Exercise 11

Choose the correct words from the box to complete the sentences describing the picture. Don't forget to add **il-** where necessary.

tilifizyóhn	tarabáyza	siríir	shibbáak	kúrsi	rádyo	baab

1 fiih siríir taHt _____ .

2 fiih _____ 'uddáam it-tarabáyza.

3 fiih _____ 9ála t-tarabáyza, bass(i) ma fiish _____ .
4 is-siríir bayn _____ w-_____ .
5 ish-shibbáak foh' _____ .

Rooms of the house

bayt, buyúut	house, houses
óhDa, ówaD	room, rooms
ohDt in-nóhm	bedroom
ohDt is-súfra	dining room
ohDt il-o9áad	living room/sitting room
iS-Salóhn	(guest) sitting room
il-máTbakh	kitchen
il-Hammáam	bathroom
is-Sáala	hall
il-balakóhna	balcony

Download a list of additional household vocabulary.

Cultural point

Accommodation in Egypt

In the past individual houses were common in Egypt, with the grander villas surrounded by lush gardens. Nowadays, with the pressure to accommodate a growing population, most city-dwellers live in apartment blocks, often closely packed. In the search for affordable accommodation, many families are moving further and further from the city centres. Greater Cairo has grown dramatically and satellite towns have sprung up in the middle of the desert around Cairo.

Many apartment blocks have a doorman, **bawwáab** (from the Arabic for door, **baab**) or **Háaris il-a9qáar** ('property guard'). The doorman often lives in the block, sometimes with his family, and undertakes cleaning and maintenance duties, as well as general fetching and carrying.

The culture of hospitality dictates that traditionally every house would have a separate guest sitting room, **iS-Salóhn**, while the family would use the living room, **ohDt il-o9áad**. Modern pressures on living space mean that there are often not enough rooms to allow for a separate guest room, but the traditional welcome remains.

Exercise 12 (Audio 1; 39)

Listen to Widaad describing her bedroom and decide if the sentences below are true or false.

1 ohDt in-nóhm Sughayyára.

2 fíihaa shibbáak kibíir.

3 ma fiiháash balakóhna.

4 fiih bortráy foh' is-siríir.

5 ik-kúrsi mish muríiH.

6 fiih takíif fi ohDt in-nóhm.

Exercise 13

Now try to say a few things describing where you live. Use the examples in this unit as models and adapt them according to the features of your house or apartment.

Learning with a friend or in a class?
Download ideas to practise describing your home.

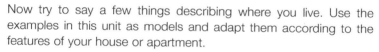

The Arabic script

The following pair of Arabic letters have a distinctive shape:

 س the letter **siin**, pronounced 's' as in 'sit'.

ش the letter **shiin**, pronounced 'sh' as in 'sheet'.

As usual, the tail is only retained at the end of a word:

ش + ب = شب

ش + ا + ب = شاب

ن + ا + س = ناس

خ + س = خس

ح + س + ن = حسن

Another useful letter is:

ل   the letter **laam**, pronounced 'l' as in 'lit'.

This letter is sometimes confused by beginners with **alif** (ا), with which
it combines to produce the Arabic article **il-** (ال 'the'). The two letters
look similar when the **laam** loses its tail, but remember that **alif** is a
non-joining letter and so will always be followed by a space, whereas
laam joins to the following letter:

$$ا + ل + خ = الخ$$

$$ا + ل + ب + ن = البن$$

$$ش + ا + ل = شال$$

 Exercise 14

Match these Arabic words you have met with the transcription.
Can you remember what they all mean?

a	itnáyn	جنب	1
b	bayn	شاي	2
c	ganb	بس	3
d	akh	بين	4
e	lában	تحت	5
f	bass	خال	6
g	shay	اثنين	7
h	bayt	أخت	8
i	ukht	أخ	9
j	taHt	لبن	10
k	khaal	بيت	11

Unit Five

eh kamáan?

Anything else?

In this unit you will learn about:

- saying what you want and need
- talking about quantity and price
- Egyptian souvenirs
- picnic food
- colours
- more about plurals
- numbers 1–100
- recognizing these Arabic letters: ظ ط ض ص

Dialogue 1

9awzíin galabíyya **(Audio 1; 40)**

Gaber needs to go to Khan El Khalili bazaar in old Cairo.

1	How is Gaber going to the bazaar?
2	What does he want to buy for his fiancée, Widaad?
3	What does he want to buy for his mother?

GÁABIR:	ta9áala ma9áaya khan il-khalíili.
HÁSAN:	bil-9arabíyya g-gidíida?
GÁABIR:	Táb9an! 9awzíin galabíyya li-widáad wi-kánaka naHáas li-úmmi.
HÁSAN:	w-ána kamáan miHtáag 'amíiS ábyaD lish-shughl.
GÁABIR:	fíkra. w-ána bárDu 9áawiz 'umSáan gidíida.
GABER:	*Come with me to Khan El Khalili.*
HASSAN:	*In the new car?*
GABER:	*Of course! We want a galabeyya for Widaad and a copper coffee pot for my mother.*
HASSAN:	*And I also need a white shirt for work.*
GABER:	*(Good) idea. I want new shirts too.*

Vocabulary

ma9áaya	with me: **ma9áa** (with) + **ya** (me)
Táb9an	of course
galabíyya (*pl.* **galaalíib**)	galabeyya: the famous long Egyptian robe
li-...	for. **li-widáad** = for Widaad; **li-úmmi** = for my mother
kánaka	small pot with wooden handle for brewing coffee
naHáas	copper
kamáan	also
'amíiS (*pl.* **'umSáan**)	shirt
ábyaD	white
shughl	work: **lish-shughl** = for [the] work
fíkra	(good) idea
bárDu	too/also

Cultural point

At some point when visiting Egypt, you're sure to want to buy some souvenirs to take home – perhaps a **galabíyya**, the traditional long flowing robe, a **shíisha** water pipe for smoking the local **tunbáak** (tobacco mixed with molasses), some pottery, jewellery or copper plates and utensils such as the jug-shaped **kánaka** used for brewing Arabic coffee. If you are in Cairo, you could visit Khan El Khalili bazaar – a large market in old Cairo famous for all kinds of products and crafts. There are specific districts for different artisans and traders: a spice market, a gold street, a district for copperware, etc.

A visit to an Egyptian tailor (**tárzi**) is also an eye-opener. Take along the latest Italian fashions and they will run you up duplicates made-to-measure in a couple of days and for a fraction of the price.

Read the download for more insight into Egyptian souvenir sellers.

Language point

Need and want

The equivalent of the English 'want' is **9áawiz**, also pronounced **9áayiz**. This is an active participle (see Unit 4) rather than a verb and literally means 'wanting'. Like other active participles it behaves like an adjective, changing to **9áwza/9áyza** in the feminine and **9awzíin/9ayzíin** in the plural. It is not necessary to add the personal pronoun ('I', 'you', etc.) when the context is clear:

(ána) **9áawiz**	I *(masc.)* want
(ána) **9áwza**	I *(fem.)* want
(íHna) **9awzíin**	we want
(húwwa) **9áawiz**	he wants, etc.

miHtáag ('need') is also an active participle and works in a similar way to **9áawiz**:

(ána) **miHtáag**	I *(masc.)* need
(ána) **miHtáaga**	I *(fem.)* need
(íHna) **miHtaagíin**	we need
(húwwa) **miHtáag**	he needs, etc.

Exercise 1

Use the appropriate form of **9áawiz** to fill in the gaps in the sentences below, as in the example:

(ána, *masc.*) _____ **'amíiS.** ➜ (ána) **9áawiz 'amíiS.**

1 (ána, *fem.*) _____ **sálaTa.**

2 (íntu) _____ **galaalíib?**

3 (ínti) _____ **áhwa?**

4 (húwwa) _____ **shay.**

5 (íHna) _____ **9arabíyya gidíida.**

6 (híyya) _____ **kánaka naHáas?**

7 (húmma) _____ **kabíina lux.**

8 (ínta) _____ **'umSáan?**

Exercise 2

Everyone's going to the market together. Make sentences about what they need using the pictures and the correct form of **miHtáag**:

Then try to make two or three more sentences about what *you* need from the market. (Remember to use the feminine form if you are female or the plural if you speaking on behalf of a group.)

1 widáad

4 gáabir wi-Hásan

2 gáabir

5 ábu Hásan

3 umm(i) gáabir

6 umm(i) w-ábu gáabir

Language point

Numbers 1–12 (Audio 1; 41)

number	short form	translation
wáaHid		one
itnáyn		two
taláata	tálat	three
arbá9a	árba9	four
khámsa	khámas	five
sítta	sitt	six
sáb9a	sába9	seven
tamánya	táman	eight
tís9a	tísa9	nine
9áshara	9áshar	ten
Hidáashar		eleven
itnáashar		twelve

The short form is generally used when the numbers 3–10 are put in front of a noun (rather than by themselves):

ínta 9áawiz tálat galaalíib? Do you want three galabeyyas?

ána miHtáag árba9a.   I need four.

feeh táman mudarrisíin? Are there eight teachers?

la', khámsa.   No, five.

Exercise 3 (audio online; WEB02)

 How would you say the following in Arabic? (As well answers in the Key, this exercise has a downloadable audio file for you to check your pronunciation.)

1 three shirts

2 five galabeyyas

3 ten teachers

4 four engineers

5 Do you *(fem.)* want four galabeyyas?

6 No. I *(fem.)* want three.

7 Do you *(pl.)* need seven shirts?

8 No, we need five.

 Dialogue 2

 HáaDir (Audio 1; 42)

Listen to a woman buying what her family needs for a picnic lunch by the river.

1	**How many loaves of bread does she want?**
2	**How much are the apples today?**

IS-SAYYÍDA:	iddíini 9ílbit gíbna rúumi wi-rub9 kíilu zaytúun.
IL-BAYYÁA9:	HáaDir yaa madáam. wi-HaDrítik miHtáaga 9aysh?
IS-SAYYÍDA:	háatli itnáashar raghíif báladi, min fáDlak.
IL-BAYYÁA9:	eh kamáan?
IS-SAYYÍDA:	9awzíin Tubáa' wára' wi-shúwak biláastik.
IL-BAYYÁA9:	máashi.
IS-SAYYÍDA:	bikáam it-tufíáaH?
IL-BAYYÁA9:	it-tufíáaH bi-9áshara gináyh.
IS-SAYYÍDA:	9áshara? leh? da bi-tamánya fi kull(i) Hítta.

WOMAN:	*Give me a packet of hard cheese and a quarter of a kilo of olives.*
SHOPKEEPER:	*At your service, madam. And do you need bread?*
WOMAN:	*Bring me twelve baladi (countryside) loaves, please.*
SHOPKEEPER:	*What else?*
WOMAN:	*We want paper plates and plastic forks.*
SHOPKEEPER:	*OK.*
WOMAN:	*How much are the apples?*
SHOPKEEPER:	*The apples are ten (Egyptian) pounds.*
WOMAN:	*Ten? Why? They're eight everywhere.*

Vocabulary

iddíini	give me
9ílba (*pl.* **9'ílab**)	packet/box/tin: **9ílbit gíbna** = packet of cheese. The feminine **-a** ending changes to **-it** in this construct phrase (see Unit 3).
rub9 kíilu	quarter of a kilo; **nuSS(i) kíilu** = half a kilo
zaytúun	olives
HáaDir	at your service, a phrase frequently used by shopkeepers and other service providers
háatli (*fem.* **hatíili**)	bring me
raghíif (*pl.* **raghífa**)	loaf
eh kamáan?	anything else? what else?
Tába' (*pl.* **Tubáa'**)	plate
wára'	paper
shóhka (*pl.* **shúwak**)	fork
biláastik	plastic
máashi	OK/fine, a common and very useful word
bikáam?	how much?; literally 'for how much'; an expression used to ask about cost/price only.
tufféaH	apples
gináyh	[Egyptian] pound; often abbreviated to LE (from the French *livre égyptienne*)
leh?	why?
fi kull(i) Hítta	everywhere (*lit.* 'in all places')

Cultural point

Most corner shops in Egypt sell the basic ingredients for a tasty picnic. From a baker or street stall you can buy traditional flat pitta-type bread which comes in two main varieties: **9aysh báladi** (wholemeal 'countryside' bread) and **9aysh sháami** (white 'Syrian' bread), as well as many western varieties. Local cheeses include **gíbna rúumi**, a hard cheese similar in flavour to Parmesan, and **gíbna báyDa**, a soft feta-type cheese. Egyptian/Armenian cured beef, **basTúrma**, is excellent and you will also find accompaniments such as **zaytúun** (olives) and **tórshi**, strongly-flavoured vegetable pickles.

Language points

Materials

To express what something is made from, simply add the material directly after the item:

kánaka naHáas	copper coffee pot
shúwak biláastik	plastic forks
Tubáa' wára'	paper plates

Internal plurals

In Unit 3 you learnt that Arabic plurals can be *external* (-**îin** or -**áat**) or *internal* (similar to the English 'mouse/mice').

In this unit there are several examples of internal plurals. Although there is no hard-and-fast rule about which type of plural to use, internal plurals are generally used with shorter, more basic words.

It is best to learn each internal plural individually with its singular. However, it helps to realize that internal plurals follow the principle of changing the internal vowels, but retaining the consonants (non-vowels):

wálad (boy/child) ➜ **wiláad** (children)

bank (bank) ➜ **bunúuk** (banks)

9ílba (packet/tin) ➜ **9ílab** (packets/tins)

'amíiS (shirt) ➜ **'umSáan** (shirts)

Slowly you will begin to hear patterns and to connect similar internal plurals, in much the same way that you would connect 'mouse/mice' with 'louse/lice'.

Exercise 4

Write down and say out loud the plurals for the following familiar words, as in the example. Look back at the vocabulary lists if you need to remind yourself of the plural for an individual word.

wálad (boy/child) ➔ wiláad (children)

1 9ílba (box, packet, tin)

2 bank (bank)

3 Tába' (plate, dish)

4 'amíiS (shirt)

5 galabíyya (galabeyya)

6 raghíif (loaf)

7 tarabáyza (table)

8 muhándis (engineer)

9 shóhka (fork)

10 tilifóhn (telephone)

Numbers and plurals

An unusual feature of Arabic is that only the numbers 3–10 are followed by a plural noun. From 11 upwards the number is followed by a *singular* noun:

khámas 'umSáan	five shirts
sába9 wiláad	seven children
Hidáashar 'amíiS	eleven shirts (*lit.* 'shirt')
itnáashar raghíif	twelve loaves (*lit.* 'loaf')

Exercise 5

Ask for the following in the quantities shown, following the example:

'amíiS (4) ➔ iddíini arbá9 'umSáan, min fáDlak.
(Give me four shirts, please.)

1 'amíiS (11)

2 galabíyya (3)

3 shóhka biláastik (12)

4 Tába' (6)

5 **9ílba** (4)

6 **raghíif** (10)

7 **Tába' wára'** (11)

8 **'amíiS** (8)

Exercise 6 (Audio 1; 43)

Listen to a man buying some groceries in a local shop. Decide if the sentences are true or false:

1 The conversation takes place in the morning.

2 The man wants half a kilo of cheese.

3 He wants eight loaves of bread.

4 He only wants a bottle of cola to drink.

5 The olives are 20 LE for a quarter of a kilo.

6 The man is not happy with this price.

Exercise 7 (Audio 1; 44)

You have written yourself the following list for a picnic on the beach. Prepare what you will need to ask for in the shop and then join in the dialogue with the shopkeeper on the recording.

(Note: 150g = **míyya wi-khamsíin graam**)

> bread (10 loaves, baladi)
>
> 1/2 kg hard cheese
>
> 8 plastic plates
>
> 4 cartons juice
>
> olives (ask about price)

Language points

Collective nouns

Some grammatically singular nouns – particularly fruit, vegetables and other items found usually in groups – have a plural meaning. These are called *collective nouns*, for example.

zaytúun	olives
tuffáaH	apples
laymúun	lemons
bayD	eggs

If you want to refer to a single item in the group, i.e. 'an olive', you need to add the feminine -a ending:

zaytúuna	an olive
tuffáaHa	an apple
laymúuna	a lemon
báyDa	an egg

Dual (two items)

Two items are usually expressed by using a special dual ending: -áyn. You have met an example of this in Unit 4 in the phrase for bunk beds, **siriiráyn foh' ba9d** (*lit:* 'two beds above each other').

siríir	a bed
siriiráyn	two beds
raghîif	a loaf
raghiifáyn	two loaves

Note: the stress moves to the dual ending: **siríir, siriiráyn**.

If the singular word ends with the feminine -a this changes to -t when the dual ending is added (or -it after two consonants):

tuffáaHa	an apple
tuffaaHtáyn	two apples
9îlba	a packet/tin
9ilbitáyn	two packets/tins

Exercise 8

Add the dual ending to make these singular nouns refer to two items.

1 **wálad** (a boy/child)

2 **bayt** (a house)

3 **bint** (a girl)

4 **shibbáak** (a window)

5 **Tába'** (a plate/dish)

6 **shóhka** (a fork)

7 **laymúuna** (a lemon)

8 **mushkíla** (a problem)

9 **Táalib** (a student)

10 **báyDa** (an egg)

Download additional examples of duals and plurals.

Dialogue 3

bi-káam di? (Audio 1; 45)

Gaber is selecting a new galabeyya in the shop. The shopkeeper is offering three colours: lemon yellow (**áSfar laymúuni**); light blue (**ázra' fáatiH**) and purple (**banafsígi**).

1	Which colour galabeyya does Gaber like best?
2	What does Gaber ask the shopkeeper about this galabeyya?

GÁABIR:	masáa' il-khayr. 9áawiz galabíyya Haríimi Sáyfi.
IL-BAYYÁA9A:	ma'áas eh?
GÁABIR:	wásaT. záyyik ínti kída.
IL-BAYYÁA9A:	il-alwáan 9andína áSfar laymúuni w-ázra' fáatiH wi-banafsígi.
GÁABIR:	Hílwa il-banafsígi. bi-káam di law samáHti?
IL-BAYYÁA9A:	di bi-míyya wi-9áshara, wiz-zár'a wiS-Sáfra bi-khámsa wi-tis9íin.

GABER:	*Good afternoon. I want a lady's summer galabeyya.*
SHOPKEEPER:	*What size?*
GABER:	*Medium. Like you.*
SHOPKEEPER:	*The colours we have are lemon yellow, light blue and purple.*
GABER:	*The purple's nice. How much is that, please?*
SHOPKEEPER:	*That one is 110 [pounds], and the blue one and the yellow one are 95.*

Vocabulary

Haríimi	for ladies/women; the men's equivalent is **rigáali**.
Sáyfi	summer: adjective from **iS-Sayf** ('the summer'); equivalent adjective from **ish-shíta** ('the winter') is **shítwi**
ma'áas	size
wásaT	medium
záyyik	like you: from **záyy** ('like') + **-ik** ('you', *fem.* ending)
kída	a common filler word, here used in its literal meaning of 'like this/that', but also to mean anything from 'that's the way it goes' to 'because I said so'.
lohn (*pl.* **alwáan**)	colour
áSfar laymúuni	'lemon-yellow': adjective from **laymúun**; this is a bright, vibrant yellow unlike the English 'lemon-yellow' which is usually a pale yellow.
ázra' fáatiH	light blue; opposite = **ázra' gháami'** ('dark blue')
banafsígi	purple
Hílw	nice/sweet: similar in meaning and popularity of use to its English translation
law samáHt (*fem.* **samáHti**)	(if you) please; an alternative to **min fáDlak/fáDlik**

Language point

Numbers 13–100 (Audio 1; 46)

Numbers 13–19 end in **-táashar**, the Arabic equivalent of '-teen'.
Numbers 20–90 end in the plural **-íin**, the equivalent of '-ty'.

number	translation
talatáashar	thirteen
arba9táashar	fourteen
khamastáashar	fifteen
sittáashar	sixteen
saba9táashar	seventeen
tamantáashar	eighteen
tisa9táashar	nineteen
9ishríin	twenty
talatíin	thirty
arba9íin	forty
khamsíin	fifty
sittíin	sixty
sab9íin	seventy
tamaníin	eighty
tis9íin	ninety
míyya	hundred

wi/w- ('and') is used to join units and tens, with the units coming first:

wáaHid wi-9ishríin	twenty-one
	(*lit.* 'one and twenty')
arbá9a wi-talatíin	thirty-four
tís9a wi-sab9íin	seventy-nine
sáb9a wi-tamaníin	eighty-seven
míyya wi-9áshara	one hundred and ten
míyya khámsa w-arba9íin	one hundred and forty-five

Don't forget that all numbers above ten are followed by a singular noun:

sittáashar lohn	sixteen colours
khámsa w-arba9íin bint	forty-five girls

Exercise 9

Say the Arabic for these figures:

5	8
11	16
22	46
75	90
62	31
106	158

 ## Exercise 10 (Audio 1; 47)

Now try some mental arithmatic! You'll hear some sums on the recording. Listen and work out the answers.

 Download extra activities to practise Arabic numbers.

 # Language points

Expressing price

Price is expressed using **bi-** ('with'):

bikáam di?	How much is that?
di bi-míyya wi-9áshara (gináyh).	That's 110 (pounds).
bikáam kíilo il-laymúun?	How much is a kilo of lemons?
bi-khámsa wi-talatíin (gináyh).	Thirty-five (pounds).

Exercise 11

Make up short exchanges about the price of these items, as in the example:

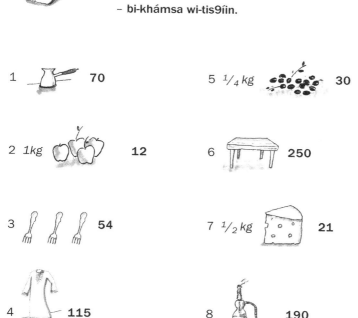

95   – bikáam il-'amíiS?

     – bi-khámsa wi-tis9íin.

1   70

5 ¹/₄ kg   30

2 1kg   12

6   250

3   54

7 ¹/₂ kg   21

4   115

8   190

More about adjectives

■ Colours **(Audio 1; 48)**

Most adjectives can be made feminine by adding the ending -a (see Unit 4). However, the basic colours have a different feminine form which should be used when describing a feminine noun. Practise your pronunciation by repeating the models on the recording:

masculine	feminine	translation
áSfar	Sáfra	yellow
ázra'	zár'a	blue
áHmar	Hámra	red
ákhDar	kháDra	green
ábyaD	báyDa	white
íswid	sóhda	black

Notice that the first time the shopkeeper mentions colours, she uses the masculine form as she is describing the masculine word colour (**lohn**) rather than the item itself:

il-alwáan 9andína áSfar laymúuni wi-ázra' fáatiH wi-banafsígi.	The colours we have are lemon yellow [colour], light blue [colour] and purple [colour].

However, the second time she is referring to the galabeyya (**galabíyya**), which is a feminine noun, and so she uses the feminine form of the colours:

... iz-zár'a wiS-Sáfra bi-khámsa wi-tis9íin.	... the blue one and the yellow one are 95.

■ Adjectives that don't change

Spoken Egyptian is somewhat flexible and, by convention, some adjectives don't usually change at all for the feminine (although they would in more formal Standard Arabic). Examples of adjectives that don't usually alter when describing a feminine noun are:

Sáyfi	for summer
shítwi	for winter
Haríimi	for ladies
rigáali	for men
búnni	brown
banafsígi	purple
laymúuni	lemon(y)

Exercise 12

Complete the dialogue with an adjective to match the English in brackets.

- 9áawiz 'amíiS _____ (*summer*).

- HáaDir. 9andína _____ (*blue*) gháami' wi- _____ (*red*).

- il-azra' _____ (*nice*).

- w-eh kamáan?

- miHtáag kamáan galabíyya _____ (*large*). 9andúku
  galaalíib _____ (*yellow*)?

- la', bass 9andína galaalíib _____ (*white*) wi-galaalíib
  _____ (*purple*).

- bikáam il-_____ (*white*) law samáHti?

Exercise 13 (audio online; WEB03)

Now put this dialogue in the correct order. (This exercise has a downloadable audio file for you to check your pronunciation.)

- kibíir. il-alwáan 9andúku eh?

- Hílw il-ákhDar. bi-káam da law samáHti?

- SabáaH il-khayr. 9áawiz 'amíiS shítwi.

- da bi-míyya khámsa wi-tamaníin gináyh.

- 9andína ábyaD w-ákhDar gháami' wi-búnni.

- ma'áas eh?

Learning with a friend or in a class?
Download ideas to practise colours.

Pronunciation: emphatic letters

There is a group of 'emphatic' letters in Arabic (see script section below for the Arabic names). These are the sounds 's', 'd', 't' and 'z' pronounced towards the back of the mouth with the tongue touching the top of the palate rather than against the teeth. This produces a duller, less sharp sound.

   In this course we have used a capital letter to distinguish these letters from their non-emphatic equivalents, for example **S**ayf ('summer'), ábya**D** ('white') and wása**T** ('medium').

 ## Exercise 14 (Audio 1; 49)

 Listen and repeat these pairs of words. The first word of each pair starts with a non-emphatic letter and the second with its emphatic equivalent.

1 **tiin** (figs)   **Tiin** (mud)

2 **sayf** (sword)   **Sayf** (summer)

3 **daar** (home)   **Daar** (harmful)

4 **siin** (letter **s**)   **Siin** (China)

5 **siláaH** (weapon)   **SaláaH** (goodness)

إِبْ تِ The Arabic script

This group of letters are formed in a similar way to each other, except that ص and ض have a small 'dink' and a tail after the initial shape, whereas ط and ظ have a downwards stroke.

ص   the letter **Saad**, emphatic 's'

ض   the letter **Daad**, emphatic 'd'

ط   the letter **Taa**, emphatic 't'

ظ   the letter **Zaa**, formally an emphatic 'z', but often
           pronounced as an emphatic 'd' in Egyptian Arabic

In common with other Arabic letters, ص and ض lose their tails (but retain the 'dink') when not at the end of a word. ط and ظ look very similar wherever they appear in a word:

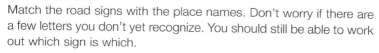

ن + ص = نص

ظ + ل = ظل

ح + ص + ب = حصب

ي + ط + ي + ح = يطيح

Exercise 15

Match the road signs with the place names. Don't worry if there are a few letters you don't yet recognize. You should still be able to work out which sign is which.

Note: the ـة or ة ending is the special feminine ending, pronounced -a.

a **TánTa** (Tanta)

b **aswáan** (Aswan)

c **asyúuT** (Asyut)

d **síiwa** (Siwa)

e **lú'Sur** (Luxor)

f **ig-gíiza** (Giza)

Unit Six
shákluh eh?
What does he look like?

In this unit you will learn about:

- describing appearance and age
- parts of the body
- items of clothing
- talking about what people are doing now or in the near future
- recognizing these Arabic letters: ذ د

Dialogue 1

yaa ibrahíim **(Audio 1; 50)**

Widaad is briefing Ibrahim, her assistant, about his important trip to Port Said dock tomorrow.

___
What is the name of the client Ibrahim is supposed to be picking up?
___

WIDÁAD: yaa ibrahíim, ínta Táali9 il-míina fi buur sa9íid búkra 9asháan 'Mister Laurence' biTáa9 'Sunshine Cruise'.

IBRAHÍIM: shákluh eh 'Mister Laurence' da?

WIDÁAD: Tawíil wi-shá9ruh áHmar. 9aynáyh milawwína wi-láabis naDDáara. istánna 9and(i) síllim il-márkib.

IBRAHÍIM: máashi yaa madáam widáad.

WIDAAD: *Ibrahim, you're going to the dock in Port Said tomorrow for Mr Laurence of Sunshine Cruise.*

IBRAHIM: *What does this Mr Laurence look like?*

WIDAAD: *Tall and his hair is red. His eyes are coloured and he wears glasses. Wait at the steps of the boat.*

IBRAHIM: *OK, Madam Widaad.*

Vocabulary

Táali9	heading up to/going to
míina	dock/port; airport = maTáar
búkra	tomorrow; today = innahárda; yesterday = imbáariH
9asháan	for/because of
miláwwina	coloured; when describing eye-colour this means 'not brown' (in contrast to most Egyptian eyes)
láabis	wearing/wears
naDDáara (*pl.* naDDaráat)	(pair of) glasses; when the plural ending áat is added the preceding long áa vowel is pronounced short and the word stress shifts to the end
istánna! (*fem.* istánni!)	wait!
síllim	steps/stairs
márkib (*pl.* maráakib)	boat

Language point

Describing appearance

■ Asking about appearance

The most common question used for asking about appearance is:

shákluh eh?	What does he look like? (literally 'his shape what?')
shákluh eh 'Mister Laurence' da?	What does this Mr Laurence look like? (literally 'his shape what this Mr Laurence?')

To ask the question about someone else, change the attached pronoun on the end of the word **shakl** appropriately:

shakláhaa eh?	What does she look like? (literally 'her shape what?')
sháklak eh?	What do you (*masc.*) look like? (literally 'your shape what?')

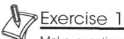

Exercise 1

Make questions about people's appearance using the appropriate attached pronoun as in the example. (Look back at Unit 2 if you need to remind yourself of the attached pronouns.)

húwwa ➔ shákluh eh? (What does he look like?)

1 ínti

2 íbnak

3 húmma

4 Hásan

5 umm(i) gáabir

6 bíntik

7 íntu

8 il-wiláad

■ Adjectives and expressions to describe appearance

Here are some useful adjectives and expressions to describe someone's appearance:

Tawíil/Tawíila	tall/long *(masc./fem.)*
'uSáyyar/'uSayyára	short *(masc./fem.)*
tikhíin/tikhíina	fat *(masc./fem.)*
rufáyya9/rufayyá9a	thin *(masc./fem.)*
9agúuz/9agúuza	old *(masc./fem.)*
shaabb/sháabba	young man/young woman
áSla9	bald
bi-shánab	with a moustache
bi-da'n	with a beard

Notice that the word stress shifts for the feminine of *short* and *thin*.

Exercise 2

How do say these in Arabic?

1   He's tall.

2   She's thin.

3   My mother is old.

4   Ibrahim is short and fat.

5   Hasan is tall with a beard.

6   My daughter is tall and thin.

7   My father is bald with a moustache.

8   Is he a young man with a beard?

Parts of the body (Audio 1; 51)

You heard the Arabic for 'hair' and 'eyes' in the Dialogue 1.
Now listen to the recording and repeat this list of parts of the body:

shá9r	hair
manakhíir	nose
bo'	mouth
9ayn (*pl.* **9aynáyn**)	eye
iid (*pl.* **iidáyn**)	hand
rigl (*pl.* **rigláyn**)	leg/foot
widn (*pl.* **widáan**)	ear
Sobáa9 (*pl.* **Sawáabi9**)	finger

■ Dual with parts of the body

As many parts of the body come in pairs, Arabic often uses the dual
-áyn ending (see Unit 5) to indicate the plural. In Egyptian Arabic this
can apply even when there are more than two of the parts in total (e.g.
'their hands'). When an attached pronoun is added to the dual, the final
n drops, leaving only **-áy-**:

rigláyn	legs
rigláyhaa	her legs
9aynáyn	eyes
9aynáyh	his eyes
iidáyn	hands
iidáyku	your *(pl.)* hands

To express 'my eyes', 'my legs', etc. you need to add the attached pronoun **ya** to the dual ending, producing **-áyya**:

| 9aynáyya | my eyes |
| iidáyya | my hands |

Exercise 3

Add the appropriate attached pronoun to the parts of the body below, as in the example:

shá9r (híyya) ➔ sha9ráhaa

1 shá9r (húwwa)

2 manakhíir (ána)

3 bo' (ínta)

4 9aynáyn (ínti)

5 Sawáabi9 (híyya)

6 iidáyn (íHna)

7 widáan (ínti)

8 shánab (húwwa)

9 rigláyn (ána)

10 9aynáyn (húmma)

Exercise 4 ((Audio 1; 52)

Listen to the four descriptions on the recording and match each one to the people below. Don't worry if you don't get every word. Just try and pick out the features. (Note: **ráagil** = man; **sitt** = woman)

a   b   c   d

Exercise 5 (Audio 1; 53)

A woman is arranging for a taxi to collect her, her father and her son from the airport (**il-maTáar**). The taxi driver wants to have some idea of what they all look like so he can identify them in the crowd. Look at the notes below and think about how you might describe their appearances.

woman:	not tall / black hair
father:	old / grey ['white'] hair / with a moustache
son:	tall / short red hair

You're going to play the part of the woman and talk to the taxi driver on the phone. Follow the prompts on the recording.

Dialogue 2

yaa ibrahíim (Audio 1; 54)

Ibrahim is at the port waiting for Mr Laurence. He rings Widaad back
at the office on his mobile phone.

1	Is Mr Laurence alone?
2	How old does Ibrahim guess Mr Laurence is?

IBRAHÍIM:	yaa madáam widáad, ána 9and síllim il-márkib. fiih khawáaga náazil láabis naDDáarit shams wi-bádla zár'a kóHli, wi-ma9áah wáHda sitt lábsa fustáan ákhDar.
WIDÁAD:	áywa yaa ibrahíim, yá9ni húwwa 'Mister Laurence' wálla mish húwwa?
IBRAHÍIM:	ána mish 9áarif yaa madáam. shá9ruh il-áHmar mish báayin 9áshaan il-itnáyn labsíin baraníiT.
WIDÁAD:	Táyyib, 9ánduh kaam sána yaa ibrahíim?
IBRAHÍIM:	Hawáali zayy arba9íin khamsíin kída.
WIDÁAD:	Táyyib yaa ibrahíim … is'áluh 'Are you Mr Laurence?'

IBRAHIM:	*Madam Widaad, I'm at the steps of the boat. There's a foreigner getting off wearing sunglasses and a dark blue suit, and with him is a woman wearing a green dress.*
WIDAAD:	*Yes Ibrahim, I mean, is he Mr Laurence or isn't he?*
IBRAHIM:	*I don't know, Madam. His red hair isn't showing because the two of them are wearing hats.*
WIDAAD:	*Well how old is he, Ibrahim?*
IBRAHIM:	*Something like about forty, fifty.*
WIDAAD:	*OK, Ibrahim … ask him 'Are you Mr Laurence?'*

Vocabulary

khawáaga	foreigner; a term commonly used to refer to Westerners
náazil	coming down/getting off
láabis	wearing

naDDáarit shams	sunglasses (*lit.* 'glasses [of] sun')
zár'a kóHli	dark blue; **kóHli** means 'the colour of kohl', the traditional dark blue eye makeup.
yá9ni	I mean/so/well; perhaps one of the most common words in spoken Egyptian. Used universally as a filler in much the same way as the English equivalents given.
ána mish 9áarif	I don't know
báayin	visible/obvious; **mish báayin** = not visible
9ánduh kam sána?	How old is he?
Hawáali	approximately/about
is'áluh	ask him

Cultural point

Egyptians wear a mix of traditional and Western dress. Many of the traditional items are designed to be cool and loose-fitting. Throughout Egypt you will see the **galabíyya**, the long flowing robe worn by both men and women. Other traditional items include a cotton skull cap, **Taa'íyya**, still popular in rural areas, and **shíbshib** (flip-flops).

The Islamic headscarf, or **Higáab**, is popular in Egypt, the full-face veil, or **niqáab**, less so. A sophisticated fashion industry has built up around the design and wearing of the **Higáab**. A women who chooses to wear the headscarf is called **muHaggába**, and one who wears the full-face veil is known as **munaqqába**.

Items of clothing

Look at the words used in Egypt for Western items of clothing and the example sentences. Notice that many of the words are derived from European languages, for example **banTalóhn** (trousers) from the French 'pantalon' or **báltoh** (coat) from the Italian 'paltò'.

bádla (*pl.* **bídal**)	suit
fustáan (*pl.* **fasatíin**)	dress
burnáyTa (*pl.* **baraníiT**)	hat
banTalóhn (*pl.* **banTalohnáat**)	trousers
bilúuza (*pl.* **biluzáat**)	blouse
'amíiS (*pl.* **'umSáan**)	shirt
gunílla (*pl.* **gunilláat**)	skirt
shuráab (*pl.* **shurabáat**)	(pair of) socks
gázma (*pl.* **gízam**)	(pair of) shoes
buut (*pl.* **buutáat**)	(pair of) boots
bálToh (*pl.* **baláaTi**)	coat
naDDáara (*pl.* **naDDaráat**)	(pair of) glasses

húwwa láabis bádla.	He's wearing a suit.
híyya lábsa fustáan.	She's wearing a dress.
íHna labsíin gízam.	We're wearing shoes.
íntu labsíin baláaTi?	Are you wearing coats?

Exercise 6 (Audio 1; 55)

Say what people are wearing. Listen to the items of clothing and then create sentences about what people are wearing, following the prompts on the recording.

Exercise 7

Make sentences describing what people are wearing following the pattern given.

(húwwa) → húwwa láabis 'amíiS.

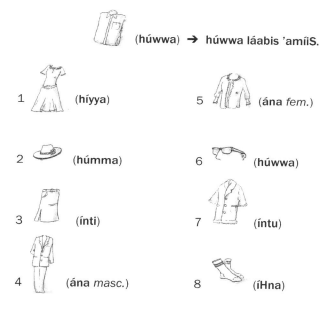

1 (híyya)

5 (ána *fem.*)

2 (húmma)

6 (húwwa)

3 (ínti)

7 (íntu)

4 (ána *masc.*)

8 (íHna)

Download extra activities to practise describing appearance.

Language point

More about active participles

As we have seen in previous units, active participles ('ing' words) are a common feature of Egyptian Arabic and can be used to describe what is happening at the moment (or in the near future).

In the masculine singular they are usually vowelled with a long **aa** followed by **i**. Remember that, although derived from verbs, active participles behave like adjectives in that the feminine adds **-a** and the plural adds **-íin**. These endings affect the word stress and the pronunciation of the preceding vowels.

■ Examples and uses **(audio online; WEBO4)**

Look at these common active participles. (You can download audio of the table to help you with the shifting stress patterns.)

Masculine	Feminine	Plural	Translation
náazil	názla	nazlíin	coming down/getting off
Táali9	Tál9a	Tal9íin	going up/heading to
láabis	lábsa	labsíin	wearing
9áarif	9árfa	9arfíin	knowing
náyim	náyma	naymíin	sleeping/asleep
SáaHi	SáHya	SaHyíin	awake
wáakil	wákla	waklíin	eating
sháarib	shárba	sharbíin	drinking

Active participles are a simple way of talking about what is happening without having to use the more complicated verb system. (In fact, you can get a long way in Egyptian Arabic without using any verbs at all.) Here are three examples from Dialogue 2:

fiih khawáaga náazil.   There's a foreigner getting off.

ínta Táali9 il-míina búkra.   You're going to the port tomorrow.

il-itnáyn labsíin baraníiT.   The two (of them) are wearing hats.

As with other adjectives, active participles can be made negative using **mish**:

húwwa mish láabis bádla.   He's not wearing a suit.

húmma mish nazlíin hína innahárda.   They're not getting off here today.

ána mish 9áarif/9árfa.   I don't know. (masc./fem.) (lit. 'I'm not knowing')

You can also sometimes use active participles with **líssa** to mean 'just':

ána líssa wáakil.   I've just eaten.

íHna líssa sharbíin.   We've just had a drink.

| ibrahíim líssa Táali9 il-míina. | Ibrahim has just gone (up) to the port. |

Note: you need to be careful with **líssa**. In combination with some active participles it means 'still' rather than 'just': **húwwa líssa náyim** = 'he's still sleeping' (rather than 'he's just slept'). You will need to note this on a case-by-case basis.

Exercise 8

Change these sentences following the example:

ínti mish názla hina? (ínta) ➔ **ínta mish náazil hina?**

1 húwwa láabis burnáyTa. (híyya)

2 húwwa Táali9 il-míina búkra. (húmma)

3 ínta 9áarif widáad? (ínti)

4 ána líssa wáakil. (íHna)

5 húwwa náazil síllim il-márkib. (híyya)

6 húwwa líssa sháarib. (húmma)

7 ána *masc.* láabis banTalóhn. (ána *fem.*)

8 ínta SáaHi? (íntu)

9 húwwa náayim. (húmma)

10 ána mish 9áarif. (íHna)

Language point

Expressing age

9ánd + *attached pronoun* is used to express the age of someone (or something):

9ánduh arba9íin sána.	He's forty years old. (*lit.* 'he has forty year')
9andáhaa itnáashar sána.	She's twelve years old.
9ándi Hawáali khamsíin sána.	I'm about fifty years old.

9ándak tamantáashar   Are you eighteen years old?
sána?
Remember that numbers above ten are followed by a singular noun
(see page 86). All the example sentences above involve ages more
than ten and so the number is followed by **sána** (year). Only numbers
3–10 are followed by a plural noun, in this case **siníin** ('years'):

íbni 9ánduh 9áshar siníin.	My son is ten years old.
bintína 9andáhaa khámas siníin.	Our daughter is five years old.

To ask about age you use **kaam sána?** ('how many years?'). The
question word **kaam** ('how many') is also followed by a singular noun,
following a similar rule to the numbers over ten.

9ándak kaam sána?	How old are you? *(masc.)*
9ándik kaam sána?	How old are you? *(fem.)*
9ánduh kaam sána?	How old is he?
bintúku 9andáhaa kaam sána?	How old is your daughter?
il-wiláad 9andúhum kaam sána?	How old are the children?

 Exercise 9

Ask and answer questions about how old people are, using the
information provided. Follow the pattern in the example.

> **bíntak** (6) ➜ **bíntak 9andáhaa kaam sána?**
>   **9andáhaa sitt(i) siníin.**

1 **bíntak** (13)

2 **ibnúku** (3)

3 **íntu** (ána = 22 / híyya = 21)

4 **ínti** (40)

5 **góhzik** (about 45)

6 **wiláadik** (áHmad = 9 / láyla = 14)

7 **ábu gáabir** (82)

8 **ukht Hásan** (17)

Exercise 10 (Audio 1; 56)

Ibrahim is picking up a woman visitor at the airport. Listen to Widaad describing to Ibrahim what she looks like. Listen once for the general meaning; then listen again and try to draw a picture of the woman described, or make notes in English about her appearance if you prefer.

Exercise 11

Read this paragraph where Ibrahim describes himself and fill in the gaps in the English translation:

**ána Tawíil wi-rufáyya9 wi-9ándi khámsa wi-9ishríin sána.
shá9ri íswid wi-'uSáyyar wi-9aynáyya búnni. ána láabis bádla
kóHli wi-'amíiS ákhDar wi... áah w-ána bi-shánab.**

*I'm tall and _____ and I'm _____ years old. My hair is
_____ and short and my _____ are brown. I'm _____
a dark blue _____ and a _____ shirt and... ah, and I
have a _____.*

Now make up a similar paragraph about yourself. Substitute your characteristics using the vocabulary in this unit. Remember to change **láabis** to **lábsa** if you are a woman.

Learning with a friend or in a class?
Download ideas to practise describing people.

‏اب‎ The Arabic script

The following pair of Arabic letters share the same shape and, in spoken Egyptian Arabic, also often share the same pronunciation:

‏د‎   the letter **daal**, pronounced 'd' as in 'dad'

‏ذ‎   the letter **dhaal**, in Egyptian Arabic also pronounced 'd' as in 'dad' or sometimes 'z' as in 'zeal' (but more formally pronounced as a voiced 'th' as in 'that')

These two letters are non-joining letters. They will *not* join to the letter after:

$$ذ + ب = ذب$$
$$ش + د = شد$$
$$ن + ا + د + ي = نادي$$
$$ب + د + ل = بدل$$
$$ل + ذ + ي + ذ = لذيذ$$

Exercise 12

These English names all begin with 'd'. Can you read them written in Arabic script?

1 ‏داني‎

2 ‏دافيد‎

3 ‏دونالد‎

4 ‏دوروثي‎

5 ‏دايزي‎

6 ‏ديريك‎

Unit Seven
kída áHsan
That's better

In this unit you will learn about:

- comparing things
- buying tickets
- means of transportation
- expressing likes and dislikes
- agreeing and disagreeing
- recognizing these Arabic letters: ز ر

Dialogue 1

il-akl fi faránsa lazíiz (Audio 2; 1)

Gaber is telling Hassan about his honeymoon.

1	Which two countries do they talk about?
2	Where is Gaber going for his honeymoon?

GÁABIR:	íHna rayHíin faránsa fi shahr il-9ásal.
HÁSAN:	yá9ni mish rayHíin il-maksíik?
GÁABIR:	la', lagháyna l-maksíik la'annáhaa bi9íida, áb9ad min faránsa bi-kitíir. ána ma baHíbbish iT-Tayaráan iT-Tawíil.
HÁSAN:	wála ána. faránsa 'urayyíba ... á'rab min il-maksíik. kída áHsan fí9lan.
GÁABIR:	wi-kamáan il-akl fi faránsa lazíiz.
HÁSAN:	9ándak Ha'. il-akl il-lazíiz muhímm(a) gíddan.
GÁABIR:	ahámm(a) Háaga fi shahr il-9ásal!

GABER:	We're going to France for (our) honeymoon.
HASSAN:	So you're not going to Mexico?
GABER:	No, we cancelled Mexico because it's a long way, a lot further than France. I don't like long flights.
HASSAN:	Me neither. France is near ... nearer than Mexico. That's better actually.
GABER:	And also food in France is delicious.
HASSAN:	You're right. Delicious food is very important.
GABER:	The most important thing on honeymoon!

 ## Vocabulary

ráayiH (*fem.* ráyHa *pl.* rayHíin)	going (to); an active participle which doesn't need an additional following word meaning 'to'
shahr il-9ásal	honeymoon
il-maksíik*	Mexico
lagháyna	we cancelled
la'ánn	because
bi9íid	a long way/far
ma baHíbbish	I don't like
Tayaráan	flying/flight
wála ána	me neither/nor I
'uráyyib	near
fí9lan	actually/really
akl	food
lazíiz	delicious
9ándak Ha'	you're right ('you have right')
muhímm	important
gíddan	very
Háaga (*pl.* Haagáat)	thing; aHámm(a) Háaga = the most important thing

Note: countries are usually feminine.

Cultural point

Marriage in Egypt still tends to follow a traditional pattern. Islamic marriages can have several stages, with a ceremony attached to each. Initially, the groom asks for the bride's hand in marriage. If accepted, he'll lock hands with the bride's father and together they will recite the opening verse of the Qu'ran, known as the **fátHa**. This will later be followed by an engagement, including the exchange of rings and gifts. Only after the final **katb il-kitáab** ('signing of the book') and the following wedding party, **il-fáraH**, would the couple be officially married. Christian Coptic marriage customs can be similarly extended and ceremonies very elaborate, with the couple sitting on ceremonial 'thrones' and 'crowned'.

Generally newly-weds will depart on their honeymoon (**shahr il-9ásal**) straight after the ceremony. However, some more religious Coptic Christians follow a tradition of fasting for three days in isolation between the wedding ceremony and starting their married life together.

If you're lucky enough to be invited to an Egyptian wedding, you should take a small gift for the bride and groom.

Download additional vocabulary and phrases connected with marriage.

Language points

Generalization

When talking in general terms, Arabic uses the singular with **il**:

ma baHíbbish **iT-Tayaráan iT-Tawíil.**	I don't like long flights ['the long flying'].
il-akl fi faránsa lazíiz.	['the'] Food in France is delicious.

la´ánn + attached pronoun

la'ánn ('because') can be followed by a noun or an attached pronoun (see page 30):

lagháyna l-maksíik **la'annáhaa bi9íida.**	We cancelled Mexico because it's *(fem.)* a long way.
íHna rayHíin faránsa **la'ánn il-akl lazíiz.**	We're going to France because the food is delicious.
ána mish 9áwwiz shay **la'ánni líssa sháarib.**	I don't want tea because I have just had a drink.

Exercise 1

Practice joining **la'ánn** with the appropriate attached pronoun, as in the example:

la'ánn + ána ➜ la'ánni ... ('because I ...')

1 **la'ánn + ínta**

2 **la'ánn + húwwa**

3 **la'ánn + íHna**

4 **la'ánn + ínti**

5 **la'ánn + húmma**

6 **la'ánn + híyya**

7 **la'ánn + íntu**

Exercise 2

Now join the two sentences using **la'ánn** plus the appropriate attached pronoun, as in the example:

lagháyna l-maksíik. híyya bi9íida. →
lagháyna l-maksíik la'annáhaa bi9íida.

1 íHna rayHíin faránsa. híyya 'urayyíba.

2 il-akl áHsan fi faránsa. húwwa lazíiz gíddan.

3 íHna mish rayHíin amríika. ána ma baHíbbish iT-Tayaráan iT-Tawíil.

4 lagháyna k-kabíina. híyya Sughayyára.

5 húwwa mish 9áwwiz bilíila. húwwa líssa wáakil.

6 ínta mish miHtáag tilifóhn. ínta wálad Sugháyyar.

7 il-wiláad mish 9awzíin kóhla. húmma líssa sharbíin.

8 íntu hína. íntu 9awzíin máyya?

Language point

Comparatives from simple adjectives

Comparisons are made by using a special form of the adjective, equivalent to the English '-er' or 'more' as in 'big<u>ger</u>', '<u>more</u> important'. This form is called the *comparative*.

Arabic is a 'triliteral' language, meaning the vocabulary is largely based on root meanings conveyed by three consonants (non-vowels) in a particular order. Ignore all the vowels (including **ayy**) of a simple adjective and you can usually identify the root letters:

kibíir (big); root letters = **k** / **b** / **r**

rufáyya9 (thin); root letters = **r** / **f** / **9**

When you have a simple adjective with three different root consonants, these consonants are put into a particular pattern to form the comparative: add the sound **a** before the first root and another **a** between the second and third roots:

<u>a</u> + k + b + <u>a</u> + r = **ákbar** (bigger)

<u>a</u> + r + f + <u>a</u> + 9 = **árfa9** (thinner)

The second and third root letters can sometimes be the same. In this case they usually (but not always) join to become a double letter in the comparative, with the stress moving to the second syllable:

laziíz (delicious); root letters = l / z / z

alázz (more delicious)

Note: the comparative ágdad (newer) from the adjective gidíid (new) behaves regularly with the double letters remaining separate.

If the final root letter is **w** or **y**, then this drops out altogether.

Hílw (nice/sweet); root letters = H / l / w

áHla (nicer/sweeter)

gháali (expensive); root letters = gh / l / y

ághla (more expensive)

 ■ Some common comparatives **(Audio 2; 2)**

Listen to the adjectives with their comparatives and repeat the pattern.

Adjective	Comparative
kibíir (big)	ákbar (bigger/older *for people*)
gamíil (beautiful)	ágmal (more beautiful)
Sugháyyar (small)	áSghar (smaller/younger)
'uráyyib (near)	á'rab (nearer)
bi9íid (far)	áb9ad (further)
'adíim (old)	á'dam (older *for things*)
'uSáyyar (short)	á'Sar (shorter)
Tawíil (tall/long)	áTwal (taller/longer)
rufáyya9 (thin)	árfa9 (thinner)
tikhíin (fat)	átkhan (fatter)
Hílw (nice/sweet)	áHla (nicer/sweeter)
laziíz (delicious)	alázz (more delicious)
muhímm (important)	ahámm (more important)
gidíid (new)	ágdad (newer)

And the important irregular comparative:

kwáyyis (good)	áHsan (better)

Note: the sounds **sh**, **kh** and **gh** are single consonants in Arabic, represented by one letter of the Arabic alphabet. So the adjective **tikhíin** (fat) has the root **t/kh/n**, and **Sugháyyar** (small) has the root **S/gh/r**.

Cultural point

If you are familiar with names such as Ahmad (meaning 'most praiseworthy'), Ashraf ('noblest') or Akram ('most generous'), you will already know the Arabic comparative pattern. Most names of Arabic origin carry a meaning. This is interesting in its own right, but can also help you remember Arabic word patterns. Other names reflect different patterns, for example Nasser is the active participle **náaSir** ('conquering' or 'conquerer'), and Mokhtar is the adjective **mukhtáar** ('chosen') derived from the verb **yikhtáar** ('to choose').

Exercise 3

Without looking at the section above, give the feminine and comparatives for these adjectives and say what they mean, as in the example:

rufáyya9 ➜ **rufayyá9a, árfa9** (thin, thinner)

1 **tikhíin**

2 **kibíir**

3 **bi9íid**

4 **Tawíil**

5 **lazíiz**

6 **gháali**

7 **'uSáyyar**

8 **gidíid**

9 **kwáyyis**

10 **Hilw**

Using comparatives

Comparatives can be used in sentences to make comparisons. The equivalent in Arabic to the English word 'than' (as in 'thinner than') is **min**, which literally means 'from':

bínti áTwal min íbni.	My daughter is taller than my son.
faránsa á'rab min il-maksíik.	France is nearer than Mexico.
il-banafsígi áHla min il-áSfar.	The purple (one) is nicer than the yellow (one).
il-tufféaH ághla min it-tiin leh?	Why are the apples more expensive than the figs?

You can add attached pronouns (see page 30) to the word **min** to produce the meaning 'than me/you/him', etc. Notice how the final **n** of **min** can double when an attached pronoun is added:

ána áTwal mínnak.	I'm taller than you.
híyya ákbar mínni.	She's older than me.

To give the meaning of 'much', **bi-kitíir** ('by a lot') is added at the end of the comparison:

faránsa á'rab min il-maksíik bi-kitíir.	France is much nearer than Mexico.
il-9arabíyya di ághla bi-kitíir.	This car is much more expensive.

To express the superlative ('the ... est/the most ...'), simply add the comparative in front of the thing being described:

ahámm(a) Háaga	the most important thing
ákbar kabíina	the biggest cabin
aghla 9arabíyya	the most expensive car
á'rab bank	the nearest bank

Exercise 4

How do you say these in Arabic?

1 Gaber is shorter than Hassan.

2 Mexico is further than France.

3 This car is much smaller.

4 We'd like the biggest one, please.

5 Where's the nearest airport?

6 Our children are taller than us.

7 Her brother is younger ['smaller'] than her.

8 But I am older ['bigger'] than him.

9 The figs are much sweeter today.

10 That's better.

Exercise 5 (Audio 2; 3)

Play a game of one upmanship. Your friend is talking about himself, but everything he says, you go one better, like this:

> **ána Tawíil.** (I'm tall.) ➔
> **ána áTwal mínnak.** (I'm taller than you.)
>
> **úkhti Hílwa.** (My sister's pretty.) ➔
> **úkhti áHla min úkhtak.** (My sister's prettier than your sister.)

Follow the prompts on the recording to continue boasting.

Download extra lists of useful adjectives and comparatives.

Dialogue 2

árkhaS Háaga eh? **(Audio 2; 4)**

A female tourist is asking about tickets to Luxor from an agent.

Which means of transport does the tourist prefer?

IS-SÁYHA:	bikáam tazkárit lú'Sur ráayiH gáyy min fáDlik?
IL-WAKÍILA:	biT-Tayyáara wála bil-'aTr HaDrítik?
IS-SÁYHA:	árkhaS Háaga eh?
IL-WAKÍILA:	il-otobíis! bass ir-ríHla Tawíila wi-mish murííHa 'áwi.
IS-SÁYHA:	wiT-Tayyáara?
IL-WAKÍILA :	iT-Tayyáara ghálya, ághla min il-'aTr bi-kitíir. il-'aTr dáraga úula sí9ruh ma9'úul. HaDrítik 9áwza kaam tazkára?
IS-SÁYHA:	taláata ... itnáyn kubáar wi-Tifl wáaHid. fiih takhfiiDáat lil-aTfáal?
IL-WAKÍILA:	áywa, il-aTfáal bi-nuSS is-si9r.
IS-SÁYHA:	Táyyib. khallíina fil-'aTr áHsan.

TOURIST:	*How much is a return ticket to Luxor, please?*
AGENT:	*By plane or by train, Madam?*
TOURIST:	*What's the cheapest [thing]?*
AGENT:	*The bus! But the journey is long and not very comfortable.*
TOURIST:	*And the plane?*
AGENT:	*The plane is expensive, much more expensive than the train. First class in the train is a reasonable price. How many tickets do you want?*
TOURIST:	*Three ... two adults and a child. Are there discounts for children?*
AGENT:	*Yes, children are half price.*
TOURIST:	*OK. Let's stick with the train, it's better.*

Vocabulary

tazkára (*pl.* **tazáakir**)	ticket
ráayiH gáyy	return (ticket); literally 'going coming'
Tayyáara (*pl.* **Tayyaráat**)	plane
'aTr (*pl.* **'uTuráat**)	train
árkhaS	cheapest/cheaper; from **rakhíiS** (cheap)
otobíis (*pl.* **otobiisáat**)	bus/coach
ríHla (*pl.* **riHláat**)	journey
'áwi	very
gháali (*fem.* **ghálya**)	expensive
ághla	more expensive/most expensive
dáraga úula	first class
sí9r (*pl.* **as9áar**)	price
ma9'úul	reasonable
kubáar	adults
Tifl (*pl.* **aTfáal**)	child
takhfíiD (*pl.* **takhfiiDáat**)	discount
khallíina (fi)	let's stick (to)/let's stay (with)

Cultural point

There is a well-established rail network in Egypt connecting many of the major towns. Train travel is generally cheap and is a good way of seeing more of the Egyptian countryside. One of the most popular tourist routes is the line to Luxor, about 750 km south of Cairo. The sleeper train travels along the Nile valley to Luxor, from where cruise boats sail regularly to and from Aswan.

 Language point

Means of transport

bil- (**bi** + **il**, 'by the') is used to talk about means of transportation. Remember that the **i** of **il** can be assimilated by the sound of the following letter (see Unit 2):

bil-'aTr	by train
bil-otobíis	by bus
biT-Tayyáara	by plane
bil-márkib	by boat
bit-taks	by taxi

 ## Exercise 6

Make questions about the price of a ticket to different destinations by various means of transportation, as in the example.

iskindiríyya → **bikáam tazkárit iskindiríyya bil-'aTr?**

1 ig-gíiza   5 iz-zamáalik

2 aswáan   6 lú'Sur

3 is-sways   7 il-maksíik

4 faránsa   8 sharm ish-shaykh

Language point

Plural patterns

As you have seen in previous units, there are two types of plural in Arabic: *external* (-íin and -áat) and *internal* (altering vowels within words). When you start learning Arabic the plurals can seem complicated and random, but slowly you will spot patterns emerging. Here are some tips.

■ External -áat plural

This is probably the most common plural in Arabic. We have seen that the other external plural -íin can only be used to refer to groups of people (e.g. **mudarrisíin** 'teachers'). However, the external plural -áat is used with many Arabic words. These fall into three main categories:

1 Many feminine words ending in -a. Note that the singular ending -a is removed before the plural ending -áat is added:

Singular	Plural
Háaga (thing)	**Haagáat**
ríHla (journey)	**riHláat**
Tayyáara (plane)	**Tayyaráat**
9arabíyya (car)	**9arabiyyáat**
khaala (maternal aunt)	**khaaláat**

2 Some masculine Arabic words, often (but not always) longer words that don't fit easily into internal patterns. Remember that if the singular already ends with a long **áa**, this will shorten before the plural ending -áat since the emphasis shifts to the end of the word:

Singular	Plural
takhfíiD (discount)	**takhfiiDáat**
maTáar (airport)	**maTaráat**
Hammáam (bathroom)	**Hammamáat**
takhaSSúS (speciality)	**takhaSSuSáat**
igtimáa9 (meeting)	**igtima9áat**

3   Most words of foreign origin:

Singular	Plural
otobíis (bus)	otobiisáat
isTábl (stable)	isTabláat
tilifóhn (telephone)	tilifohnáat
banTalóhn (pair of trousers)	banTalohnáat

As a rule of thumb, it is often worth trying -áat if you are unsure of an individual plural. You could be correct and, at worst, you will be communicating that your meaning is plural (a little like a child saying 'mouses' instead of 'mice').

■ Arabic roots and common internal plural patterns

Internal plurals are generally used with shorter, more basic words that have three identifiable consonants (which can include **9** or the glottal stop '). Internal plurals are based on the three root consonants, which can usually be indentified by stripping out the short and long vowels from the singular word:

Tifl (child)   ➔   root = **T** / **f** / **l**

9ílba (packet/tin)   ➔   root = **9** / **l** / **b**

SáaHib (friend)   ➔   root = **S** / **H** / **b**

So, for the first example (**Tifl**) we can say that the first root consonant (C^1) is **T**, the second (C^2) is **f** and the third (C^3) is **l**.

An internal plural is formed from these root consonants with particular patterns of vowels. Some plurals can be grouped because they follow the same vowel pattern (in much the same way as 'mouse/mice' could be grouped with 'louse/lice', and 'foot/feet' with 'tooth/teeth').

There are a fair number of plural patterns in general circulation, but some are more common than others.

Here are four of the more common internal plural patterns.

1 $ac^1c^2\acute{a}ac^3$

Singular	Plural
Tifl (child)	**aTfáal**
si9r (price)	**as9áar**
SáaHib (friend)	**aS-Háab**

2 $c^1ic^2ac^3$

Singular	Plural
9ílba (box/tin)	**9ílab**
gázma (shoe/pair of shoes)	**gízam**
bádla (suit)	**bídal**

3 $c^1uc^2\acute{u}uc^3$

Singular	Plural
bayt (house)	**buyúut**
bank (bank)	**bunúuk**
far9 (branch)	**furúu9**

4 $c^1ic^2\acute{a}ac^3$

Singular	Plural
kalb (dog)	**kiláab**
gamal (camel)	**gimáal**
gabal (mountain)	**gibáal**

Note: It will take time to be comfortable with these and other internal plurals. Initially some of the patterns will seem very similar. However, slowly and with practice, you will come to recognize and use them.

Exercise 7 (audio online; WEB05)

Practise external and internal plurals. Cover the plural column in the table above and see if you can say them out loud looking only at the singular. (There is an additional downloadable audio file to help you remember the plurals quickly and fluently.)

Exercise 8 (Audio 2; 5)

Listen to a man buying travel tickets for his family and fill in the information chart below.

Information

Destination: ....

Means of transport: ....

Number of tickets: ....

Number of adults: ....

Number of children: ....

Discounts for children?: ....

Exercise 9 (Audio 2; 6)

Now it's your turn to buy tickets. You want tickets for two adults and one child to travel by bus to Port Said. Prepare what you might want to say and then join in the conversation, following the prompts on the recording.

Language point

Animals

Prepare for Dialogue 3 by looking at these Arabic words for animals. There are some more unusual plurals, so for the moment it's best to try and learn them individually:

kalb (*pl.* **kiláab**)	dog
'óTTa (*pl.* **'óTaT**)	cat
Husáan (*pl.* **HiSína**)	horse

Humáar (*pl.* Himíir)	donkey
faar (*pl.* firáan)	mouse
bá'ara (*pl.* bá'ar)	cow
báTTa (*pl.* baTT)	duck
kharúuf (*pl.* khirfáan)	sheep
árnab (*pl.* aráanib)	rabbit

Exercise 10 (audio online; WEB06)

Test yourself on the animals and their plurals. Cover the Arabic column in the list above and see if you can remember them. (There is an additional downloadable audio file to help you remember the plurals quickly and fluently.)

Exercise 11

Zakareyya's on his way to market with animals and food to sell. He's standing by the river bank planning how to cross in his small boat which only has limited space. He will definitely have to make more than one crossing.

Which of these pairs do you think he can leave safely together on the bank without risking losing one or the other?

1 ik-kalb wis-sabáanikh?

2 il-'óTTa wik-kalb?

3 il-Humáar wit-tufáaH?

4 il-bá'ara wiz-zaytúun?

5 il-bámya wil-'óTTa?

6 il-báTTa wil-árnab?

7 il-bá'ara wis-sabáanikh?

8 il-'óTTa wil-lában?

Download an additional list of animals.

Dialogue 3

il-'óTaT áHsan min ik-kiláab (**Audio 2; 7**)

Gaber and Hassan do not agree about household pets!

Which three animals do they mention?

GÁABIR:	ána baHíbb ik-kiláab. abúya 9ánduh tálat kiláab wuulf.
HÁSAN:	yaa sáatir! ána ma baHíbbish ik-kiláab. íHna 9andína 'óTTa siyáami. il-'óTaT áHsan min ik-kiláab.
GÁABIR:	il-'óTaT di maalháash fáyda.
HÁSAN::	izzáay? di mufíida 'áwi. bi-tímsik il-firáan wi-niDíifa zayy il-full.
GÁABIR:	firáan? ik-kiláab bi-tímsik Haraamíyya, mish firáan!

GABER:	*I like dogs. My father has three German Shepherd dogs.*
HASSAN:	*God help us! I don't like dogs. We have a Siamese cat. Cats are better than dogs.*
GABER:	*Those cats, they're useless.*
HASSAN :	*How come? They're very useful. They catch mice and are clean as anything.*
GABER:	*Mice? Dogs catch thieves, not mice!*

Vocabulary

kalb wuulf (*pl.* kiláab wuulf)	German Shepherd dog (*lit.* 'wolf dog')
yaa sáatir!	God help us!
'óTTa siyáami (*pl.* 'óTaT siyáami)	Siamese cat
maalháash fáyda	they're useless (*lit.* 'they have no use')
izzáay?	how (come)?
mufíid	useful
bi-tímsik	they catch
niDíif zayy il-full	clean as anything (*lit.* 'clean as Jasmine')
Haráami (*pl.* Haraamíyya)	thief/burglar

Language point

Agreeing and disagreeing

Here are some useful phrases for expressing your opinion:

(ána) baHíbb	I like
(ána) ma baHíbbish	I don't like
(ána) muwáafi'/muwáf'a	I agree (*masc./fem.*)
(ána) mish muwáafi'/ mish muwáf'a	I don't agree (*masc./fem.*)
9ándak Ha'/9ándik Ha'	you're right (*masc./fem.*)
ma 9andáksh(i) Ha'/ ma 9andakíish Ha'	you're not right (*masc./fem.*)
fí9lan	actually/really
ána kamáan	me too
wála ána	me neither/nor I

Exercise 12

Make these sentences negative, as in the example.

ána baHíbb ik-kiláab. → ána ma baHíbbish ik-kiláab.

1 ána baHíbb il-bámya.

2 ána baHíbb iz-zaytúun.

3 ána muwáafi'.

4 fí9lan 9ándak Ha' yaa ibrahíim.

5 áywa, 9ándik Ha' yaa widáad.

6 ána baHíbb il-fuul bil-laymúun.

7 ána kamáan.

Exercise 13 (audio online; WEB07)

What do you think? Look at the six statements below and decide if you agree or disagree with them, and how you might say that in Arabic. (There is an additional downloadable audio file to help you with your responses.)

1 ána baHíbb il-HiSína.

2 ána baHíbb il-'óTaT.

3 ána ma baHíbbish iz-zaytúun.

4 il-Himíir mufíida.

5 il-firáan maalháash fáyda.

6 il-akl fi faránsa alázz min il-akl fi ingiltára.

Learning with a friend or in a class?
Download ideas to practise expressing your opinion.

ايب
ت
The Arabic script

The following pair of Arabic letters share the same shape and are non-joining letters:

ر   the letter **ray**, pronounced as a slightly trilled 'r'

ز   the letter **zay**, pronounced as the 'z' in 'zebra'

Be careful not to confuse the shape of these two letters with that of **daal** (د) and **dhaal** (ذ) which you met in the last unit. The letters **ray** and **zay** have a straighter shape and sit *below* the line, rather than *on* the line as **daal** and **dhaal** do.

Now look at how some words you know that feature these letters are written in Arabic script:

ráayiH (going to) = رايح

gidíid (new) = جديد

ruzz (rice) = رز

árnab (rabbit) = أرنب

zayy (like/similar to) = زي

Exercise 14

Can you match the names to how they are written in Arabic script?

a	Widaad	1	جابر
b	Dina	2	وداد
c	Zidane	3	رشدي
d	Rushdi	4	زينب
e	Gaber	5	زيدان
f	Zeinab	6	دينا

Unit Eight
muráaga9a
Review

In this unit you will review the language covered so far,
before moving on to the second half of the course. If you
have difficulty completing one of these review exercises,
go back to the unit that deals with that language point
and re-read the explanations and dialogues.

 Exercise 1

Say where these people are from, as in the example:

Ahmed → áHmad min maSr. húwwa máSri.

1 Widaad   4 Holly

2 Pierre   5 Ronny

3 Maria   6 Jack

Exercise 2

Khalid is introducing the rest of his family. Look at the family portrait and read the description, filling in the gaps.

ána kháalid wi-di 9ílti. ána 9ándi ukht Sughayárra ismáhaa

_____ . híyya _____ khámas siníin. wi-9ándi akh ísmuh

_____ wi-húwwa _____ táman _____ . abúyaa

_____ walíid wi-9ánduh shánab kibíir. úmmi _____ móna

wi-híyya áHsan umm!

Can you write a similar description about your family?

Exercise 3

Make these sentences negative, as in the example:

híyya min maSr. → híyya mish min maSr.

1 il-9arabíyya fíihaa takíif.
2 húwwa 9áwwiz bilíila.
3 ána miHtáag gázma lish-shughl.
4 húwwa min faránsa.
5 ána baHíbb iT-Tayaráan iT-Tawíil.
6 fiih faar taHt ik-kúrsi.
7 híyya lábsa fustáan ábyaD.
8 íHna nazlíin wusT il-bálad bil-otobíis.

Exercise 4 (Audio 2; 8)

Listen to Widaad describing a hotel room to a client. Decide which of the facilities below the room offers.

1 takíif
2 tarabáyza
3 tilifizyóhn
4 siríir kibíir
5 rádyo
6 kúrsi muríiH
7 kombyúutir bil-internet

Exercise 5

Now make seven sentences describing the room in Exercise 4, as in the example.

1 fiiháa takíif.

Exercise 6

Look at the notes for Ibrahim's pick-up tomorrow:

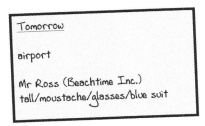

Tomorrow

airport

Mr Ross (Beachtime Inc.)
tall/moustache/glasses/blue suit

Describe to Ibrahim where he's going tomorrow, who he's picking up and what the visitor looks like. Start like this:

búkra ínta ráayiH ...

Exercise 7 (Audio 2; 9)

Listen to a group of friends ordering lunch in a restaurant. Make a note of what they order, as in the example:

	Meal	Drink
Man	**kebab and green salad**	
Woman 1		
Woman 2		

Exercise 8

Say these numbers in Arabic

13	6
5	27
72	18
14	39
44	100
140	250

Exercise 9

Can you remember what these words mean and give their plurals?

1 'amíiS

2 tilifizyóhn

3 Tába'

4 lohn

5 shóhka

6 bádla

7 rigl

8 naDDáara

9 takhfíiD

10 raghíif

Exercise 10

Use the adjectives in brackets to complete the sentences, changing them to feminine or comparative if necessary, as in the example.

ána ísmi nádya hiláal w-ána min iz-zamáalik fi maSr. 9ándi ukht

wi-akh. úkhti, sámya, _Tawíila_ (Tawíil) 'áwi, _____ (Tawíil) mínni

bi-kitíir. bass ána _____ (kibíir) mínhaa fis-sinn. akhúya, Táari',

9ánduh khamastáashar sána. húwwa _____ (rufáyya9) wi-

_____ ('uSáyyar) min sámya. abúna muHáami fi máktab

_____ (kibíir) fiz-zamáalik – wi-ummína mumassíla t-tilifizyóhn.

Unit Nine
Hayáati
My life

In this unit you will learn about:

- days of the week
- time
- describing your routine
- present/future tense of verbs
- recognizing these Arabic letters: م ع غ

Days of the week (Audio 2; 10)

Other than Friday and Saturday, the names of the days of the week are similar to the numbers one to five, starting with Sunday ('Day One'). Listen and repeat the days of the week and the example sentences.

il-Hadd	Sunday
il-itnáyn	Monday
it-taláat	Tuesday
il-árba9	Wednesday
il-khamíis	Thursday
ig-gúm9a	Friday
is-sabt	Saturday
innahárda il-árba9.	Today is Wednesday.
búkra il-khamíis.	Tomorrow is Thursday.
bá9da búkra ig-gúm9a.	The day after tomorrow is Friday.

Sometimes the word **yohm** ('day') is prefixed: **yohm il-Hadd** (Sunday), **yohm ig-gúm9a** (Friday), etc.

áHmad gayy yohm it-taláat.	Ahmed is coming on Tuesday.
il-maHáll maftúuH yohm il-Hadd.	The shop is open on Sunday.

Note: There is no equivalent of the English 'on' with days of the week.

 Cultural point

Friday (**ig-gúm9a**) is the main holiday (**agáaza**) for most Egyptians as it is the Muslim holy day. Many offices and schools also close on Saturday or Thursday, making a two-day weekend. Some schools and businesses close on Sunday.

 Download more information about public holidays in Egypt.

 Exercise 1 (audio online; WEB08)

There's an additional downloadable audio file for you to help you practise the days of the week.

 Exercise 2

Now complete the sentences, as in the example.

   innahárda is-sabt. búkra il-Hadd.

1 **innahárda it-taláat. búkra ...**

2 **búkra ig-gúm9a. innahárda ...**

3 **búkra is-sabt. bá9da búkra ...**

4 **áHmad gayy yohm ig-gúm9a. innahárda il-khamíis. áHmad gayy ...**

5 **innahárda il-khamíis. bá9da búkra ...**

6 **bá9da búkra il-árba9. búkra ...**

7 **innahárda il-árba9. búkra ...**

8 **búkra il-itnáyn. innahárda ...**

9 **iT-Tayáara gáyya yohm il-Hadd. innahárda ig-gúm9a.**
   iT-Tayáara gáyya ...

10 **bá9da búkra il-Hadd. innahárda ...**

Dialogue 1

yohm ig-gúm9a agáaza (Audio 2; 11)

Widaad is discussing the week ahead with Ibrahim.

1   What day is it today?
2   What day is the Japanese group arriving?
3   When are they going to Khan el-khalili?

WIDÁAD:	yaa ibrahíim, ísma9 ... búkra il-khamíis w-ínta Táali9 il-maTáar 9asháan místir nadíim min far9 9ammáan.
IBRAHÍIM:	is-sáa9a kaam iT-Tayáara?
WIDÁAD:	is-sáa9a khámsa S-SubH.
IBRAHÍIM:	yaa sáatir! bádri 'áwi!
WIDÁAD:	ma9lésh yaa ibrahíim, yohm ig-gúm9a agáaza. bass ínta mashgúul min is-sabt 9asháan il-fawg il-yabáani.
IBRAHÍIM:	rayHíin fáyn?
WIDÁAD:	is-sabt rayHíin il-ahráam bádri, Hawáali is-sáa9a sítta wi-nuSS ... wi-ba9d iD-Duhr kúlluh fil-mátHaf il-máSri. il-Hadd 9andúhum Hagz fi máT9am filfíla is-sáa9a wáHda ílla rub9 wi-rayHíin khaan il-khalíili ba9d il-gháda.
IBRAHÍIM:	khaan il-khalíili? záHma wil-murúur wíHish 'áwi hináak!

WIDAAD:	*Ibrahim, listen ... tomorrow is Thursday and you're going to the airport for Mr Nadim from the Amman branch.*
IBRAHIM:	*What time is the plane?*
WIDAAD:	*Five o'clock in the morning.*
IBRAHIM:	*My Goodness! [That's] very early!*
WIDAAD:	*Never mind Ibrahim, Friday's a holiday. But you're busy from Saturday because of the Japanese group.*
IBRAHIM:	*Where are they going?*
WIDAAD:	*On Saturday they're going to the pyramids early, about half past six ... and all afternoon at the*

IBRAHIM:

Egyptian Museum. Sunday they have a reservation in Filfila restaurant at quarter to one and they're going to Khan el-Khalili after lunch.
Khan el-khalili? It's crowded and the traffic is really terrible there!

Vocabulary

far9 (*pl.* furúu9)	branch
iS-SubH	(in) the morning
bádri	early
ma9lésh	never mind
agáaza (*pl.* agazáat)	holiday
mashgúul	busy
fawg (*pl.* afwáag)	group (of tourists)
il-ahráam	the pyramids (at Giza)
Hawáali	about/approximately
ba9d iD-Duhr	(in) the afternoon
mátHaf (*pl.* matáaHif)	museum
Hagz	reservation
máT9am (*pl.* maTáa9im)	restaurant
ba9d	after; before = 'abl
gháda	lunch; breakfast = fiTáar; dinner = 9ásha
záHma	crowded
murúur	traffic
wíHish	terrible/awful

 Language point

Telling the time

Arabic uses **is-sáa9a** ('the hour') to express the time:

is-sáa9a kaam?   What's the time?
                            (*lit.* 'the hour how many?')

is-sáa9a kaam iT-Tayáara?   What time is the plane?

is-sáa9a wáHda	one o'clock (*lit.* 'the hour one')
is-sáa9a itnáyn	two o'clock
is-sáa9a taláata	three o'clock
is-sáa9a arbá9a	four o'clock
is-sáa9a khámsa	five o'clock
is-sáa9a sítta	six o'clock
is-sáa9a sába9	seven o'clock
is-sáa9a tamánya	eight o'clock
is-sáa9a tís9a	nine o'clock
is-sáa9a 9áshara	ten o'clock
is-sáa9a Hidáashar	eleven o'clock
is-sáa9a itnáashar	twelve o'clock
(is-sáa9a) taláata wi-nuSS	half past three
(is-sáa9a) khámsa wi-rub9	quarter past five
(is-sáa9a) tís9a wi-tilt	twenty past nine (*lit.* 'nine and a third')
(is-sáa9a) Hidáashar wi 9áshara	ten past eleven
(is-sáa9a) sítta ílla rub9	quarter to six (*lit.* 'six less a quarter')
(is-sáa9a) itnáashar ílla tilt	twenty to twelve (*lit.* 'twelve less a third')
(is-sáa9a) tamánya ílla khámsa	five to eight

There is no equivalent of the English 'on', 'at' or 'in' when expressing time:

iT-Tayáara is-sáa9a khámsa S-SubH.	The plane is [at] five o'clock [in] the morning.

is-sabt rayHíin il-ahráam.	[On] Saturday they're going to the pyramids.
9andúhum Hagz fi máT9am filfíla is-sáa9a wáHda ílla rub9.	They have a reservation in Filfila restaurant [at] quarter to one.

 Exercise 3

is-sáa9a kaam?
Say what time it is.

1   2   3

4   5   6

7   8

 Download an extra activity and additional vocabulary for telling the time.

 Exercise 4 **(Audio 2; 12)**

You're going to play the role of a manager in a tourist office briefing your assistant about the arrival of a group. Look back at Dialogue 1 and the vobabulary and then listen to the recording. Follow the prompts on the recording to take part in the conversation.

Language point

Nouns of place

Arabic has a special pattern for words that decribe the place where something happens, and these are called *nouns of place*. For example, from the root **kh/b/z** ('baking') you get **mákhbaz** (bakery, 'place of baking') and from the root **s/g/d** ('kneeling in prayer') you get **másgid** (mosque, 'place of kneeling').

The pattern is to add **má-** to the root and then **a**, or less commonly **i**, between the second and third root consonants ($maC^1C^2aC^3$ or $maC^1C^2iC^3$). In addition, nouns of place sometimes include the feminine ending **-a**, for example **madrása** (school, 'place of studying') from the root **d/r/s** ('studying') .

There are many nouns of place and recognizing the pattern will help you build your vocabulary. Here is a list of some of the most common:

máktab (office, place of writing) root = **k/t/b**

máSna9 (factory, place of manufacture) root = **S/n/9**

madrása (school, place of studying) root = **d/r/s**

máT9am (restaurant, place of eating) root = **T/9/m**

mátHaf (museum, place of precious things) root = **t/H/f**

máTbakh (kitchen, place of cooking) root = **T/b/kh**

maghsála (laundry, place of washing) root = **gh/s/l**

maktába (library/bookshop, place of writing) an alternative meaning from the root = **k/t/b**

The plural pattern for most nouns of place is $maC^1áaC^2iC^3$, e.g.

mátHaf ➜ **matáaHif** (museums)

madrása ➜ **madáaris** (schools)

Exercise 5

Give the meanings and the plurals for these nouns of place.

1 madrása   5 másgid

2 maghsála   6 máktab

3 máT9am   7 máTbakh

4 mátHaf   8 mákhbaz

Exercise 6

rayHíin fayn? *Where are they going?*

You're a tour guide and are being asked about a group's itinerary. Look at the notes and say where they are going and when, as in the example.

Monday/pyramids/6:00 ➔ **(yohm)** **il-itnáyn** **rayHíin** **il-ahráam is-sáa9a sítta.**

1 Tuesday/Egyptian Museum/10:00

2 Wednesday/Nefertiti Restaurant/1:30

3 Thursday/Alexandria/7.15

4 Friday/Mohammed Ali mosque/4.30

5 Saturday/Khan el-khalili/5:00

6 Sunday/airport/8.45

Dialogue 2

ána muDîifa fi maSr liT-Tayaráan (Audio 2; 13)

Samya, a flight attendant for EgyptAir, is talking about her weekly routine.

1   **Which days does she fly to Amman?**
2   **Does she work on Tuesdays?**

SÁMYA: ána muDîifa fi maSr liT-Tayaráan wi-sákna fi maSr il-gidîida.

is-sáa9a khámsa wi-nuSS(i) báSHa wi-báakul Háaga khafíifa wi-bákhrug min il-báyt is-sáa9a sítta wi-rub9. báwSal il-maTáar is-sáa9a sáb9a biZ-ZabT.

il-itnáyn wil-árba9 wis-sabt bi-nisáafir 9amáan, wil-khamíis wil-Hadd bi-nisáafir aswáan marritáyn – márra S-SubH wi-márra D-Duhr.

it-taláat agáaza wi-barúuh in-náadi ba9d iD-Duhr Hawáali is-sáa9a khámsa bál9ab basketball má9a aS-Háabi wi-má9a náadya bint(i) 9ámmi.

ig-gúm9a bá'9ud fil-bayt áakul w-anáam!

SAMYA: *I'm a flight attendant for Egypt Air and I live in Heliopolis.*

At half past five I get up, eat something light and I leave the house at quarter past six. I arrive at the airport at seven o'clock exactly.

On Monday, Wednesday and Saturday we travel to Amman, and on Thursday and Sunday we go down to Aswan twice – once in the morning and once in the afternoon.

Tuesday is a holiday and I go to the club in the afternoon about five o'clock and play basketball with my friends and with Nadia, my cousin.

On Friday I stay at home and eat and sleep!

Vocabulary

sáakin (fi) (fem. sákna; pl. sakníin)	live (in); **sáakin** is an active particle (lit. 'living') and tends to be used for a specific neighbourhood. If referring to a country, city or region then the alternative active participle **9áayish** (fem. **9áysha**; pl. **9ayshíin**) is generally used: **ána 9áayish fi maSr** (I live in Egypt)/ **íHna 9áyshíin fis-sways** (we live in Suez)
maSr ig-gidíida	an area of Cairo (lit. 'new Egypt'); also known as 'Heliopolis'
khafíif	light (opposite of 'heavy')
biZ-ZabT	exactly
márra	once
marritáyn	twice
náadi (pl. nawáadi)	club
SáaHib (fem. SáHba; pl. aS-Háab)	friend
bint(i) 9ámmi	my cousin; lit. 'daughter of my (paternal) uncle'. There is no single word for 'cousin'. You need to express the relationship in terms of the son or daughter of maternal or paternal aunt or uncle, giving you eight different relationships. (See Unit 2 for family members.)

Language points

Verbs: introduction

Arabic only has two tenses: present/future and past. From this point of view it is straightforward.

This unit will cover the present/future tense. The past tense will be covered later in the course.

Try to gradually master the basic principles of the verbs first – the variations will come as you progress. Remember, too, that the verbs 'am', 'are' and 'is' are generally not needed in Arabic, and that you can sometimes use an active participle instead of a verb.

Verbs: present/future

How to form the present/future

The basic present/future tense is formed by adding prefixes to a present stem. Three parts of the verb (**ínti**, **íntu** and **húmma**) also include suffixes.

Here is the present/future for the verbs 'to play' and 'to go out'. There is no infinitive in Arabic (equivalent of the English 'to play'), so the **húwwa** ('he') part of the verb is used when referring to a verb in general: **yíl9ab** ('to play'), **yúkhrug** ('to go out'), etc.

	Prefix/suffix	yíl9ab *(stem = l9ab)*
ána (I)	a-	ál9ab
ínta (you, *masc.*)	ti-	tíl9ab
ínti (you, *fem.*)	ti-/i	til9ábi
húwwa (he)	yi-	yíl9ab
híyya (she)	ti-	tíl9ab
íHna (we)	ni-	níl9ab
íntu (you, *pl.*)	ti-/u	til9ábu
húmma (they)	yi-/u	yil9ábu

	Prefix/suffix	yúkhrug *(stem = khrug)*
ána (I)	a-	ákhrug
ínta (you, *masc.*)	tu-	túkhrug
ínti (you, *fem.*)	tu-/i	tukhrúgi
húwwa (he)	yu-	yúkhrug
híyya (she)	tu-	túkhrug
íHna (we)	nu-	núkhrug
íntu (you, *pl.*)	tu-/u	tukhrúgu
húmma (they)	yu-/u	yukhrúgu

Verbs fit into one of the two patterns above, the difference being the vowel on the prefix. The prefix vowelled with **i** (**ti-**, **yi-**, **ni-**) is more common in Egyptian Arabic.

Look at these verbs with the present stem underlined:

yú<u>khrug</u>	to go out/leave
yí<u>l9ab</u>	to play
yi<u>rúuH</u>	to go (to)
yí<u>gi</u>	to come (to)
yí<u>9mil</u>	to do
yú<u>'9ud</u>	to stay/sit down
yí<u>shrab</u>	to drink
y<u>áakul</u>	to eat
yí<u>SHa</u>	to wake up
yi<u>náam</u>	to sleep
yí<u>wSal</u>	to arrive
yi<u>sáafir</u>	to travel (to)

If the stem *starts* with a vowel, for example **áakul**, the prefixes are shortened to **y-**, **t-**, and **n-**:

yáakul	he eats
táakul	you *(masc.)* eat/she eats
náakul	we eat

If the stem *ends* with a vowel, e.g. **yíSHa**, **yígi**, the final vowel is removed before any suffix is added:

tíSHi	you *(fem.)* wake up
yígu	they come

Using a verb for invitations or suggestions

The basic present verb can be used as an invitation or suggestion. You've already met examples of this in Unit 3:

táakul Ta9míyya? Would you like to eat falafel? *(to a male)*

tishrábi shay? Would you like to drink tea? *(to a female)*

Here are some more examples:

tíl9ab basketball? Would you like to play basketball? *(to a male)*

tirúuHi il-mátHaf? Would you like to go to the museum? *(to a female)*

tu'9údu fil-bayt? Would you like to stay in the house? *(to a group)*

nirúuH in-náadi? Shall we go to the club?

ági búkra? Shall I come tomorrow?

Exercise 7

Make suggestions and invitations as in the example.

we go/tomorrow? → **nirúuH búkra?**

1 you *(fem.)* play/basketball?

2 you *(masc.)* go/the club?

3 we come/today?

4 he stay/house?

5 you *(pl.)* drink/ tea?

6 I sleep/after lunch?

7 they eat/falafel?

8 you *(pl.)* come/the club?

9 we drink/water?

10 I go out/after breakfast?

Using a verb for describing routine

In Dialogue 2, Samya uses verbs to describe her daily routine ('I wake up'/'I play basketball', etc.). When a verb is used to describe routine it is usually preceded by the sound **bi-**.

bi-níl9ab	we play
bi-yirúuH	he goes
bi-tukhrúgu	you *(pl.)* go out

The **bi-** is shortened to **b-** before the part of the verb for **ána**:

| báSHa | I wake up |
| bákhrug | I go out |

You don't necessarily need a pronoun (**ána**, **ínta**, etc.) with a verb as the prefix (and suffix) will make the subject clear:

bákhrug min il-báyt is-sáa9a sítta wi-rub9.	I leave the house at quarter past six.
il-khamíis wil-Hadd bi-nisáafir aswáan.	Thursday and Sunday we travel to Aswan.
ig-gúm9a bi-yirúuh in-náadi má9a aS-Háabuh.	On Friday he goes to the club with his friends.

However, you will sometimes hear the subject pronoun used for emphasis, or for clarification between the identical **ínta** and **híyya** parts of the verb.

| húwwa bi-yíl9ab basketball
bass ána bál9ab tennis. | He plays basketball but
I play tennis. |
| híyya bi-tú'9ud fil-bayt
má9a ummáhaa? | Does she stay at home with
her mother? |

Exercise 8

Change the subject of these sentences, as in the example.

>   **bákhrug is-sáa9a sítta. (húwwa) ➔ bi-yúkhrug is-sáa9a sítta.**

1   **báSHa is-sáa9a khámsa wi-nuSS. (húwwa)**

2   **bi-tíl9ab basketball? (ínti)**

3 **bi-tíwSal il-maTáar is-sáa9a sáb9a biZ-ZabT.** (ána)

4 **bi-yirúuH in-náadi má9a as-Háabuh.** (íHna)

5 **bi-túkhrug bádri.** (húmma)

6 **báakul Háaga khafíifa.** (ínta)

7 **barúuH in-náadi yohm is-sabt.** (híyya)

8 **bi-nígi hína ba9d il-gháda?** (íntu)

Exercise 9

Look back at the flight attendant's week in Dialogue 2. Imagine you are telling a friend about her routine. Start like this:

sámya muDíifa fi maSr liT-Tayaráan. is-sáa9a khámsa wi-nuSS bi-tíSHa...

Using a verb for talking about future plans

You can make the same verbs describe plans for the future by adding **Ha-** (or **H-** for the **ána** part of the verb):

íbni Ha-yináam ba9d il-gháda.	My son will sleep after lunch.
HarúuH in-náadi búkra.	I'll go to the club tomorrow.
Ha-ní9mil eh fil-agáaza?	What will we do in the holiday?
il-wiláad Ha-yawSálu is-sáa9a sáb9a.	The children will arrive at seven oclock.

Exercise 10

How do you say the following in Arabic using **Ha-** or **H-**:

1 Tomorrow I'll wake up early.

2 On Friday we'll travel to Amman.

3 On Saturday Samya will go to the club.

4 Will you *(pl.)* come with your friends?

5 The children will sleep after dinner.

6 I'll eat something light at five o'clock.

7 Will you *(fem.)* eat in the house?

8 My husband will leave the office at half past seven.

Download extra activities to practise Arabic present/future verbs.

 Exercise 11 (audio online; WEB09)

 Here is your diary for tomorrow. Imagine you are explaining your movements to a partner or friend. Try to speak out loud to improve your confidence. (There's an additional downloadable model audio file.)

is-sáa9a tamánya Hákhrug min il-bayt wi-...

> 8.00 leave house
> 8.30 arrive office
> 11.00 go to airport
> 12.45 lunch at the Nile restaurant
> 2.20 go to Marwan's school
> 6.30 leave office
> 7.15 basketball with friends at club

Dialogue 3

 ínti bi-tidrísi eh? (**Audio 2; 14**)

Back to the student radio quiz. The announcer is finding out a bit more about the contestants.

| 1 | Which student is studying chemistry? |
| 2 | Which hotel is Kamal training in? |

IL-MUZÍI9:	móna, ínti bi-tidrísi eh?
MÓNA:	ána bádris fi 9ulúum iskindiríyya, takháSSuS kímya.
IL-MUZÍI9:	w-ínta yaa kamáal bi-tídris eh?
KAMÁAL:	ána fi má9had il-fanáadi', wi-batmárran fi fúndu' ish-sheraton.
IL-MUZÍI9:	9aZíim. w-ínti yaa samíira?
SAMÍIRA:	ána 9áysha fi buur sa9íid wi-baHáDDar majistáyr lugháat sharqíyya fi gám9it il-qanáah.
IL-MUZÍI9:	mashaa'alláah yaa samíira ... musta9idíin lil-as'íla yaa shabáab?
IT-TALÁATA:	musta9idíin!

| BROADCASTER: | *Mona, what are you studying?* |

MONA:	*I'm studying in the faculty of sciences at Alexandria, speciality chemistry.*
BROADCASTER:	*And you, Kamal, what are you studying?*
KAMAL:	*I'm in the Hotel Institute, and I train at the Sheraton Hotel.*
BROADCASTER:	*Great. And you Samira?*
SAMIRA:	*I live in Port Said and I'm preparing a masters in Eastern Languages at the University of the Canal.*
BROADCASTER:	*That's great, Samira ... Ready for the questions you guys?*
ALL THREE:	*Ready*

Vocabulary

yídris	to study
9ulúum	sciences. When referring to a particular faculty in a college or university, Egyptians often simply put the subject in front of the name of the university: **9ulúum iskindiríyya** = [faculty of] sciences [at] Alexandria; **tigáarit asyúut** = [faculty of] commerce [at] Asyut.
takháSSuS (*pl.* **takhaSSuSáat**)	speciality (subject); major (at university)
má9had (*pl.* **ma9áahid**)	institute
fúndu' (*pl.* **fanáadi'**)	hotel; **má9had il-fanáadi'** = hotel institute
yitmárran	to train
9aZíim!	great!
yiHáDDar	to prepare
majistáyr	masters (degree); from the French 'magistère'
lúgha (*pl.* **lugháat**)	language
shárqi (*fem.* **sharqíyya**)	Eastern
gám9a (*pl.* **gam9áat**)	university; **gám9it il-qanáah** = 'University of the Canal' – a well-known university in the Suez Canal region
mashaa'alláah	literally 'what God wishes', used to express approval or admiration
musta9íd	ready
su'áal (*pl.* **as'íla**)	question
yaa shabáab	you guys (literally 'you youths')

Cultural point

Egypt is well known for its extensive network of universities and vocational colleges. There are 17 public universities and about the same number of private universities, as well as over 50 technical institutes. Every Egyptian is entitled to free higher education – an entitlement that has put pressure on the system as the population grows and aspirations increase. Nevertheless, some of the most respected international doctors, academics and engineers are still the product of Egyptian state-funded higher education.

 ## Exercise 12 (Audio 2; 15)

Listen to Samira talking about her daily routine. Fill in the missing times in the table below as you listen. (*Note:* 'to go home' = **yiráwwaH il-bayt**; 'generally' = **9umúuman**)

Activity	Time
Wake up 7.00ᴀᴍ	
Drink tea....................................	
Leave house............................	
Arrive at university..................	
Sandwich break	
Go home	
Go to club with friends	

  ## Exercise 13 (audio online; WEB10)

An Arabic friend is asking you some questions about your daily routine. Firstly, work out the questions and think about how you might reply. Then go to the recording to answer your friend's questions. (Note the feminine versions of the questions are in brackets)

- **bi-tíSHa (bi-tíSHi) is-sáa9a kaam?**
- **bi-tíshrab (bi-tishrábi) eh iS-SubH?**

- bi-túkhrug (bi-tukhrúgi) min il-bayt is-sáa9a kaam?
- bi-táwSal (bi-tawSáli) is-sáa9a kaam?
- bi-táakul (bi-tákli) eh fil-gháda?
- bi-tiráwwaH (bi-tirawwáHi) il-bayt is-sáa9a kaam?
- 9umúuman bi-tí9mil (bi-ti9míli) eh ba9d il-9ásha?

Now take part in the conversation with your friend on the recording.

Learning with a friend or in a class?
Download ideas to practise talking about your daily routine.

Pronunciation

The letter **9ayn** (ع) is a sound distinctive to Arabic. Since there is no English equivalent, this course uses the number **9** to represent this letter.

To say **9ayn**, tighten your throat and say 'ah' while pushing up air from your stomach. It will take time to hear the sound and longer to be able to produce it, but to Arabs it is a consonant like any other and you should try to master it.

Exercise 14 (Audio 2; 16)

Listen and repeat these words you have met. They all contain the letter **9ayn**. Concentrate on reproducing this sound.

9áshara (ten)

arbá9a (four)

9ándi (I have)

bi9íid (far)

9ayn (eye)

muzíi9 (broadcaster)

rub9 (quarter)

shá9r (hair)

تِ اب   The Arabic script

The Arabic **m** (**miim**) looks like a small circle with a tail:

مـ   **miim**, pronounced 'm' as in 'milk'

When joined to the next letter, the tail disappears, leaving just the small circular shape:

(Egyptian) **máSri** مصري

(crowded) **záHma** زحمة

(name) **ism** اسم

miim is a common prefix in Arabic. For example, the nouns of place you have learnt in this unit all begin with **miim**:

(mosque) **másgid** مسجد

(restaurant) **máT9am** مطعم

(school) **madrása** مدرسة

(laundry) **maghsála** مغسلة

The guttural letter **9ayn** shares its shape with the letter **ghayn**. The two letters are only distinguished by a dot above the **ghayn**:

ع   the letter **9ayn**, the famous Arabic guttural sound – see pronunciation on page 157

غ   the letter **ghayn**, pronounced as a throaty 'r' like the French 'r' in 'rue'

These two letters change shape significantly when they are joined to other letters.

joined to the letter after: ...ـع

joined on both sides: ...ـعـ...

joined to the letter before: ع...

Here are some words from this unit that feature the letters ع and غ:

عشرة 9áshara (ten)

أربعة arbá9a (four)

لغة lúgha (language)

طالع Táali9 (heading for/going up)

غداء gháda (lunch)

Unit Ten
baHíbb Sayd is-sámak
I like fishing

In this unit you will learn about:

- describing your pastimes
- making sentences negative
- giving advice
- electronic communication
- recognizing these Arabic letters: ف ق

Hobbies (Audio 2; 17)

Egyptian Arabic often refers to sports and pastimes using terms adopted from English, but some traditional pastimes retain the Arabic term. Listen to this list of some popular hobbies and the example sentences:

il-iskwáash	squash
it-ténnis	tennis
ig-golf	golf
il-basketball	basketball
ik-kúra	football/soccer
Sayd is-sámak	fishing
rukúub il-khayl	horse riding
il-muusíiqa	music
il-'iráaya	reading

baHíbb il-'iráaya.	I like reading.
ma baHíbbish ik-kúra.	I don't like football.

Note: **Sayd is-sámak** literally means 'hunting fish'. If you just use **Sayd** by itself you are talking about hunting in general.

Download a list of additional pastimes and hobbies.

Exercise 1 (Audio 2; 18)

Now say whether you like or dislike certain pastimes using **baHíbb** (I like) or **ma baHíbbish** (I don't like). Follow the prompts on the recording.

Dialogue 1

hiwayáatak eh? **(Audio 2; 19)**

At the radio quiz the announcer is finding out about the contestants'
hobbies and leisure activities.

---

1   Which of the contestants likes fishing?
2   Who likes squash?
3   Who likes surfing the Internet?

IL-MUZÍI9:	móna, ínti hiwayáatik eh?
MÓNA:	ána baHíbb ál9ab iskwáash. ána káabtin faríi' ik-kullíiya. wi-kamáan baHíbb il-muusíiqa wi-riwayáat nagíib maHfúuZ.
IL-MUZÍI9:	w-ínta yaa kamáal? hiwayáatak eh?
KAMÁAL:	baHíbb ál9ab kúra w-ána gháawi l-internet. kull yohm láazim á'9ud saa9táyn taláata 'udáam ik-kombyúutir. ma bakhrúgsh min il-bayt 'áblima aSábbaH 9ála k-kombyúutir.
IL-MUZÍI9:	haa! haa! w-ínti yaa samíira?
SAMÍIRA:	lil-ásaf dilwá'ti ma 9andíish wa't l-hiwáayti – Sayd is-sámak má9a bába wi-Hásan akhúya. kull yohm gúm9a húmma bi-yiTlá9u iS-Sayd w-ána bá'9ud azáakir.
IL-MUZÍI9:	ma9lésh yaa samíira. bá9d il-majistáyr múmkin tiSTáadi sámak il-baHr kúlluh!

BROADCASTER:	*Mona, what are your hobbies?*
MONA:	*I like playing squash. I'm the captain of the college team. And I also like music and the novels of Naguib Mahfouz.*
BROADCASTER:	*And you, Kamal? What are your hobbies?*
KAMAL:	*I like playing football and I'm keen on the Internet. Every day I have to sit for two or three hours in front of the computer. I don't leave the house before I say good morning to the computer.*
BROADCASTER:	*Ha! Ha! And you Samira?*
SAMIRA:	*Unfortunately now I don't have time for my hobby – fishing with Dad and Hassan, my brother. Every Friday they go off fishing and I stay and study.*
BROADCASTER:	*Never mind Samira. After the masters degree you can catch all the fish in the sea!*

Vocabulary

hiwáaya (*pl.* **hiwayáat**)	hobby
káabtin	captain (of a sports team)
faríi' (*pl.* **fíra'**)	team
kullíiya (*pl.* **kulliiyáat**)	college/faculty
riwáaya (*pl.* **riwayáat**)	novel
gháawi (*fem.* **gháwya**)	keen on
kull	every/all; **kull yohm** = every day; **kull yohm gúm9a** = every Friday; **kúlluh** = all of it/them
kombyúutir (*pl.* **kombyuutiráat**)	computer
'áblima	before (+ verb; *lit.* 'before what'); after + verb = **bá9dima**
yiSábbaH	to say good morning to; to greet in the morning
lil-ásaf	unfortunately
dilwá'ti	now
wa't	time
yizáakir	to study
yiSTáad	to fish/to hunt
baHr (*pl.* **biHúur**)	sea

Cultural point

Naguib Mahfouz

Naguib Mahfouz, who died in 2006 at the age of 94, is probably the best-known modern Egyptian author. Famous for his gritty style and dramatic tales set in the backstreets of old Cairo, he was the first Arab to win the Nobel Prize for Literature in 1988. A distinctive feature of his literary style is the inclusion of Egyptian spoken dialect in the dialogue where previous writers had mainly used the formal standard Arabic. This use of the colloquial helps create a more realistic portrait of the characters and setting. The novels of Naguib Mahfouz have been translated into many languages and made into films popular throughout the Arab world. Amongst his best-known works are **il-liSS wik-kiláab** (*The Thief and the Dogs*), **zuqáaq il-Mídaq** (*Midaq Alley*) and **awláad Haarítna** (*Children of our Alley*).

 Language point

Talking about likes and dislikes

■ Talking in general

We have already seen that Arabic often uses the definite
article **il-** when talking in general. This is also usually the case with
sports and pastimes:

baHíbb ig-golf.	I like golf.
baHíbb il-muusíiqa.	I like music.
ma baHíbbish ir-riwayáat.	I don't like novels.

Remember that **il-** is dropped from the *first* word of an **iDáafa**
construction (see Unit 3), although the construction as a whole
remains definite:

ma baHíbbish rukúub il-khayl.	I don't like horse riding.
móna bi-tiHíbb riwayáat nagíib maHfúuZ.	Mona likes the novels of Naguib Mahfouz.

■ **bi-yiHíbb** + verb

The verb **bi-yiHíbb** ('to like') can be followed by another verb with the
same subject:

baHíbb ál9ab iskwáash.	I like playing squash. (*lit.* 'I like I play squash')
kamáal bi-yiHíbb yi'9úd 'udáam ik-kombyúutir.	Kamal likes sitting in front of the computer. (*lit.* 'Kamal likes he sits...')

Note: when a sport follows the verb **yíl9ab** (to play), you don't generally
include the article **il-**: **baHíbb il-iskwáash** (I like squash) but **baHíbb**
ál9ab iskwáash (I like playing squash).

Exercise 2

Look at the pastimes and make sentences as in the example:

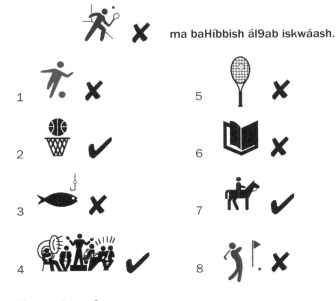

ma baHíbbish ál9ab iskwáash.

1 ✗

2 ✓

3 ✗

4 ✓

5 ✗

6 ✗

7 ✓

8 ✗

Exercise 3

Now try to say four or five things about your own hobbies, using Exercise 2 as a model.

Language point

Modifying words

There are a number of useful words which can be used before a present verb to modify the meaning. Amongst the most common are:

■ **láazim** (have to/must)

láazim a'9úd saa9táyn taláata.	I have to stay/sit for two or three hours.
íbni láazim yizáakir innahárda.	My son must study today.

- **múmkin** (can/be allowed to)

múmkin tiSTáadi sámak.	You *(fem.)* can go fishing.
múmkin nirúuH in-náadi?	Can we go to the club?

- **il-mafrúuD** (should/supposed to)

il-mafrúuD táakul Háaga.	You *(masc.)* should eat something.
il-mafrúuD yúkhrug dilwá'ti.	He's supposed to go out now.

- **Darúuri** (need to/must)

Darúuri níSHa is-sáa9a sáb9a.	We need to get up at seven o'clock.
il-wiláad Darúuri yináamu bádri.	The children must sleep early.

Notice how the modifying words themselves don't change according to the subject, but the following verb does.

Exercise 4

How would you say the following in Arabic?

1 I must go now.

2 Can we go fishing today?

3 They need to get up at half past six.

4 You *(fem.)* should drink something.

5 Mona has to study for two or three hours.

6 Can the childen play football today?

7 You *(pl.)* can play golf in the club.

8 My father needs to sleep early.

9 Can I stay in the house?

10 You *(masc.)* should study every day.

Language point

Forming the negative

There are two principal ways of forming the negative. The uses outlined below are guidelines, but be aware that the colloquial language is flexible and you may hear other combinations.

■ **ma ... (i)sh**

Uses:

1 With present verbs (and past verbs presented in Unit 12):

baHíbb/ma baHíbbish   I like/I don't like

bi-yúkhrug/ma bi-yukhrúgsh he goes out/he doesn't go out

2 With certain phrases, such as **fiih** ('there is/are'), and **9and** ('have/has'):

fiih/ma fíish   there is/there isn't

9andáhaa/ma 9andaháash she has/she doesn't have

Note: the stress can move to the following syllable when using **ma ... (i)sh** for the negative, for example **bi-yúkhrug** (he goes out) but **ma bi-yukhrúgsh**; **9ándi** (I have) but **ma 9andíish** (I don't have).

■ **mish**

Uses:

1 With simple non-verbal sentences:

húwwa mudárris./   He's a teacher./
húwwa mish mudárris.   He isn't a teacher.

íHna fik-kullíiya./   We're in the college./
íHna mish fik-kullíiya. We're not in the college.

2 With adjectives and active participles:

il-'amíiS kibíir./   The shirt is big./
il-'amíiS mish kibíir. The shirt isn't big.

ána máSri./   I'm Egyptian./
ána mish máSri.   I'm not Egyptian.

húmma naymîin dilwá'ti./	They're sleeping now./
húmma mish naymîin dilwá'ti.	They're not sleeping now.
ána gháawi Sayd is-sámak./	I'm keen on fishing./
ána mish gháawi Sayd is-sámak.	I'm not keen on fishing.

3 With modifying words:

láazim á'9ud./	I have to sit down./
mish láazim á'9ud.	I don't have to sit down.
Darúuri túkhrug./	You (masc.) need to go out./
mish Darúuri túkhrug.	You don't need to go out.
múmkin niSTáad hína./	We can fish here./
mish múmkin niSTáad hína.	We can't fish here.

4 With future verbs using **Ha-**:

Ha-yíwSal búkra?/	Will he arrive tomorrow?/
mish Ha-yíwSal búkra?	Won't he arrive tomorrow?
Ha-yígu l-bayt./	They'll come to the house./
mish Ha-yígu l-bayt.	They won't come to the house.

 Exercise 5 (audio online; WEB11)

This downloadable audio exercise is designed to improve your oral fluency forming negatives.

 Exercise 6

Make these sentences negative, as in the example.

baHíbb it-ténnis. → ma baHíbbish it-ténnis.

1 bi-niHíbb rukúub il-khayl.
2 móna gháwya Sayd is-sámak.
3 9ándik wa't l-hiwáaytik?
4 fiih shibbáak ganb is-siríir.
5 láazim nirúuH il-mádrasa.
6 múmkin ál9ab má9ak?
7 bi-yiHíbb riwayáat nagíib maHfúuZ.
8 it-taláat barúuH in-náadi.

9 búkra kamáal Ha-yíl9ab iskwáash.

10 Darúuri áTla9 il-maTáar.

Exercise 7 (Audio 2; 20)

A friend is checking out your lifestyle and hobbies, but has got many of the details wrong. Listen to the prompts on the recording and correct your friend's mistakes.

Download extra activities to practise forming negatives.

Exercise 8

A friend of yours has been told he's overweight. Give him some advice using the picture prompts and either **il-mafrúuD...** (You should...) or **mish láazim...** (You mustn't...), as in the example.

 → mish láazim táakul kayk.

1

2

3

4

5

6

7

Can you think of any more advice for your friend using the Arabic you have learnt so far in this course?

Learning with a friend or in a class?
Download ideas to practise giving advice.

Dialogue 2

il-far9 ig-gidíid (**Audio 2; 21**)

Widaad's manager, Madam Dina, is explaining her company's plans
for a new branch.

1	**Where is Nile Travel intending to open the new branch?**
2	**What two ways can people book at the moment?**
3	**When does Madam Dina think the new branch will be ready?**

MADÁAM DÍINA: shírkit in-niil lis-siyáaHa náwya tíftaH far9 gidíid fi
                  sharm ish-shaykh. il-Huguuzáat fi maktábna bitáa9
                  miidáan il-úubraa, wil-Huguuzáat fi mawqí9na 9ála
                  l-internet, kitíir gíddan wi-bi-tizíid Hawáali 9ishríin fil-
                  míyya kull sána. tag-híiz il-far9 ig-gidíid ma bi-
                  yaakhúdsh wa't. muhándis id-diikór bitáa9na saríi9
                  wi-múmkin yikhállaS shúghluh 'áblima yibtídi il-
                  múusim. ána ráyHa sharm ish-shaykh wi-Hashúuf
                  makáan munáasib w-ána hináak.

MADAM DINA: *The Nile Travel Company is intending to open a new*
                  branch in Sharm el-sheikh. Bookings in our office
                  in Opera Square, and booking on our website on
                  the Internet, are very good [literally 'very many']
                  and increase by about 20 per cent every year. The
                  preparation of the new branch won't take time. Our
                  interior designer is fast and he can finish his work
                  before the season starts. I'm going to Sharm
                  el-sheikh and I'll look for [literally 'see'] a suitable
                  place while I'm there.

Vocabulary

shírka (*pl.* **shirkáat**)	company/business
náawi (*fem.* **náwya;**	intending to
pl. **nawyíin**)	
yíftaH	to open
far9 (*pl.* **furúu9**)	branch (of company, of tree, etc.)
Hagz (*pl.* **Huguuzáat**)	booking/reservation

miidáan (*pl.* mayaadíin)	(town) square; miidáan il-úubraa = Opera Square, a well-known square in central Cairo
mawqí9 (*pl.* mawáaqi9)	site, website; noun of place from root w/q/9 (to place/to site)
yizíid	to increase
fil-míyya	per cent (*lit.* 'in the hundred')
tag-híiz	preparation
yáakhud	to take; stem starts with a vowel – see yáakul (to eat) Unit 9.
wa't (*pl.* aw'áat)	time (duration)
muhándis id-diikór	interior designer
saríi9	fast
yikhállaS	to finish; yikhállaS shúghluh = to finish his work
yibtídi	to start, to begin
múusim (*pl.* mawáasim)	season (e.g. tourist season, apricot season)
yishúuf	to see; this is a flexible verb. Here it means 'to look for' but it can be used with the meaning of 'to think about' or 'to consider'
makáan (*pl.* amáakin)	place, location
munáasib (*fem.* munásba)	suitable

Cultural point

Electronic communication in Egypt

The Internet and social media are as popular in Egypt as they are in the rest of the world. Newspapers and magazines have their own sites, as do other companies and tourist-orientated businesses. Although English is widely used, many tweeters, bloggers and surfers communicate in Arabic, either by making use of Arabic-script applications or by using Latin-script spellings. The use of Latin script to spell Arabic, together with the incorporation of many English words, has developed a life of its own and is sometimes known as **9arabíizi** (a combination of **9árabi** and **inglíizi**) or **9árabi bil-inglíizi** (Arabic in English). Some Arab linguists fear this trend will have a detrimental affect on more traditional Arabic writing skills.

# Language points

Simultaneous events

Arabic uses **wi-**, literally 'and', to express events that happen simultaneously, where in English we would use 'while':

Hashúuf makáan munáasib w-ána hináak.	I'll look for a suitable place while I'm there.
láazim tishúuf kháalak w-ínta fi iskindiríyya.	You must see your aunt while you're in Alexandria.
múmkin yi9míl il-Hagz wi-húwwa 'áa9id fil-bayt.	He can make the booking while he's sitting at home.
bi-náakul w-íHna wa'fíin.	We eat (while) standing up.

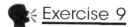## Exercise 9

How do you say the following in Arabic?

1 We'll look for a suitable place while we're there.

2 I must see my aunt while I'm in Egypt.

3 He can finish his work while he's in the office.

4 Kamal eats while sitting in front of the computer.

5 You *(fem.)* can drink the cola while standing up.

6 Madam Dina intends to look for a new office while she's in Sharm el-sheikh.

Exercise 10

Here is the text of Madam Dina's speech. Fill the gaps with the words in the box and then check your answer with the recording of Dialogue 2 or the answer section.

shúghluh	hináak	Hashúuf
shírkit	Hawáali	il-múusim
mawqí9na	sána	muhándis
far9	kitíir	miidáan

_____ in-niil lis-siyáaHa náwya tíftaH _____ gidíid fi sharm ish-shaykh. il-Huguuzáat fi maktábna bitáa9 _____ il-úubraa, wil-Huguuzáat fi _____ 9ála l-internet, _____ gíddan wi-bi-tizíid _____ 9ishríin fil-míyya kull _____. tag-híiz il-far9 ig-gidíid ma bi-yaakhúdsh wa't. _____ id-diikór bitáa9na saríi9 wi-múmkin yikhállaS _____ 'áblima yibtídi _____. ána ráyHa sharm ish-shaykh wi-_____ makáan munáasib w-ána _____.

Language point

Summary of plurals

Now that you have met more Arabic words and their plurals, you should be able to see patterns emerging. Here is a summary of the main plural patterns you have met so far in this course, with examples:

■ External plural -íin (only used for people)

  muhándis (teacher) ➜ *pl.* **muhandisíin**

  máSri (Egyptian) ➜ *pl.* **maSriyyíin**

■ External plural -áat

  banTalóhn (trousers) ➜ *pl.* **banTalohnáat**

  otobíis (bus) ➜ *pl.* **otobiisáat**

  agáaza (holiday/vacation) ➜ *pl.* **agazáat**

  ríHla (journey) ➜ *pl.* **riHláat**

■ Internal plural $aC^1C^2áaC^3$

  sí9r (price) ➜ *pl.* **as9áar**

  SáaHib (friend) ➜ *pl.* **aS-Háab**

  lohn (colour) ➜ *pl.* **alwáan**

  fawg (group) ➜ *pl.* **afwáag**

■ Internal plural $C^1uC^2úuC^3$

far9 (branch) → *pl.* furúu9

bank (bank) → *pl.* bunúuk

bayt (house) → *pl.* buyúut

■ Internal plural $C^1iC^2áaC^3$

kalb (dog) → *pl.* kiláab

gamal (camel) → *pl.* gimáal

■ Internal plural $C^1íC^2aC^3$

bádla (suit) → *pl.* bídal

gázma (shoe) → *pl.* gízam

9ílba (packet/box/tin) → *pl.* 9ílab

■ Internal plural $maC^1áaC^2iC^3$ (nouns of place)

má9had (institute) → *pl.* ma9áahid

mátHaf (museum) → *pl.* matáaHif

madrása (school) → *pl.* madáaris

mawqí9 (site) → *pl.* mawáaqi9

■ Other internal plurals

Tába' (plate) → *pl.* Tubáa'

su'áal (question) → *pl.* as'íla

shóhka (fork) → *pl.* shúwak

óhDa (room) → *pl.* ówaD

óTTa (cat) → *pl.* óTaT

raghíif (loaf) → *pl.* raghífa

HuSáan (horse) → *pl.* HiSína

'amíiS (shirt) ➜ *pl.* 'umSáan

fustáan (dress) ➜ *pl.* fasatíin

náadi (club) ➜ *pl.* nawáadi

siríir (bed) ➜ *pl.* saráayir

makáan (place/location) ➜ *pl.* amáakin

Try to learn the plural for each word when you learn the singular. You can write the singular on the front of a small card and the plural and English meaning on the back. Shuffle the cards and then put them with the singular showing. Try to remember what the word means and say its plural. Put those you get right on one side and those you don't on another. Keep shuffling and testing yourself until you can get them all right.

Exercise 11

Can you remember the meanings and plurals of these words?

1 máktab

2 far9

3 másgid

4 agáaza

5 náadi

6 SáaHib

7 kombyúutir

8 su'áal

9 hiwáaya

10 máT9am

11 lúgha

12 bádla

13 'amíiS

14 kalb

15 makáan

16 mudárris

Singular and plural in sentences

Verbs, adjectives, participles, pronouns and particles match the gender of a singular noun. For example, in the following sentence from Madam Dina's speech, the participle **náwya** and the verb **tíftaH** are feminine because the subject **shírka** (company) is feminine:

> **shírkit in-niil lis-siyáaHa náwya tíftaH far9 gidíid.**
> The Nile Travel Company is intending to open a new branch.

If she had used a masculine subject, such as **máT9am** (restaurant), the active participle and verb would have been masculine:

> **máT9am in-niil náawi yíftaH far9 gidíid.**
> The Nile restaurant is intending to open a new branch.

In the plural, the situation is less clear-cut. In general, all non-human plurals (objects, ideas, etc.) are considered *grammatically feminine singular*. Non-human plurals are referred to using:

1. *feminine singular pronouns* (**híyya/di**)

> **il-gízam di bitáa9tak?**   Are these your shoes?
>
> **áywa bitáa9ti.**   Yes, they're mine.

2. *feminine singular adjectival endings* (**-a**)

> **il-makáatib naDíifa.**   The desks are clean.
>
> **kull il-madáaris bi9íida 9an**   All the schools are far from
> **baytína.**   our house.

3. *feminine singular personal/possessive endings* (**-haa**)

> **il-'umSáan di kibíira.**   These shirts are big.
> **ána 9áawiz áSghar mínhaa.**   I want smaller ones
>   (*lit.* 'smaller than them').

4. *feminine singular verbs* (**ti-/tu-**):

> **il-Huguuzáat bi-tizíid Hawáali** Bookings increase by about
> **9ishríin fil-míyya kull sána.**   20 per cent every year.

The plural forms are generally reserved for people:

il-mudarrisíin mashguulíin.	The teachers are busy.
aS-Háabna Ha-yisáfru yohm is-sabt.	Our friends will travel on Saturday.

The treatment of non-human plurals as feminine singular is an absolute rule in formal Arabic. However, there is more flexibility in the spoken dialect. You may hear people using either the feminine singular (híyya/di, etc.) or the plural (húmma/duul, etc.) to refer to plural objects. As a learner it is simpler to stick using the feminine singular while being aware of variations.

Exercise 12

Make these sentences plural and give the meaning, as in the example. You can use the bilingual glossary at the end of the book to check the plurals of words.

il-bayt da kibíir. (This house is big.)
→ il-buyúut di kibíira. (These houses are big.)

1 il-far9 da gidíid.

2 il-9arabíyya di Sughayyára.

3 il-makáan da mish munáasib.

4 il-Hagz mawgúud 9ála k-kombyúutir.

5 il-maT9ám bi9íid 9an miidáan il-úubraa.

6 iT-Tayáara bi-tíwSal yohm ig-gúm9a.

7 il-máktab ig-gidíid Ha-yáakhud wa't.

8 il-'amíiS Sugháyyar. ána 9áawiz ákbar mínnuh.

9 il-bank hináak wil-mátHaf 'uddáamuh.

10 il-má9had Ha-yíftaH búkra.

11 il-óhDa fíihaa tilifizyóhn wi-siríir muríiH.

12 ik-kalb bi-yiHíbb il-láHma wil-'óTTa bi-tiHíbb il-lában.

Download a list of some additional useful plurals.

اب تـ The Arabic script

ف   the letter **faa**, pronounced 'f' as in 'fall'

ق   the letter **qaaf**, formally 'q' produced from the back of
            the throat, but usually pronounced as a glottal stop in
            Egyptian Arabic. This glottal stop is similar to the sound
            made when the word 'butter' is pronounced with a
            Cockney accent, dropping the 'tt'. An apostrophe (') is
            used to represent this sound.

These two letters have a similar shape but **qaaf** has a more rounded
tail, only evident when not joined to the letter following:

فندق fúndu' (hotel)   **فوج** fawg (group)

فريق faríi' (team)   **قميص** 'amííS (shirt)

وقت wa't (time)   **قاعد** 'áa9id (sitting)

Note that the **qaaf** cannot be always be dropped in Egyptian dialect.
A few words retain the formal pronunciation, for example:

قريـة qárya (village)   **موقع** máwqi9 (site)

An Arabic stop sign features the letters **qaaf** and **faa**, spelling **qif** (stop!).

Unit Eleven

9ála Tuul!

Straight on!

In this unit you will learn about:

- places around town
- understanding directions
- giving instructions
- different types of verbs
- recognizing this Arabic letter: و
- how long vowels are written in the Arabic script

Asking directions (Audio 2; 22)

A useful expression for asking directions is:

... **mináyn?**	How do I get to ...?
	(*lit.* '... from where?')
il-mátHaf mináyn?	How do I get to the museum?
il-maHáTTa mináyn?	How do I get to the station?

You could also add:

law samáHt!	Excuse me! (*to a male*)
law samáHti!	Excuse me! (*to a female*)

Exercise 1 (Audio 2; 23)

Practise asking directions to different places around town. Follow the prompts on the recording.

Dialogue 1

ma tikhaafíish yaa madáam (Audio 2; 24)

Ibrahim phones Widaad in the office to talk about Mr Laurence's plans.

> **1   Which two places does Mr Laurence want to visit?**
> **2   Does Widaad think it's a good idea for him to go by himself?**

IBRAHÍIM:	aló? áywa yaa madáam, ána ibrahíim. da "mister Laurence" 9áawiz yínzil wusT il-bálad li-wáHduh.
WIDÁAD:	leh yaa ibrahíim?
IBRAHÍIM:	bi-yi'úul 9áawiz yirúuH miidáan it-taHríir 9asháan yizúur il-mátHaf wi-ba9dáyn 9áawiz yínzil maHáTTit ramsíis 9asháan yíHgiz fi 'aTr lú'Sur.
WIDÁAD:	il-mátHaf wil-maHáTTa? akháaf laytúuh yaa ibrahíim.
IBRAHÍIM:	ma tikhafíish yaa madáam. ána HawSíf luh is-sikka kwáyyis.

IBRAHIM:	*Hello? Yes, Madam. This is Ibrahim. This Mr Laurence wants to go down to the city centre by himself.*

WIDAAD:	Why, Ibrahim?
IBRAHIM:	He says he wants to go to Tahrir Square to visit the museum and then he wants to go to Ramsis station to reserve [tickets] on the Luxor train.
WIDAAD:	The museum and the station? I'm afraid in case he gets lost, Ibrahim.
IBRAHIM:	Don't worry Madam. I'll describe the route to him well.

Vocabulary

wusT il-bálad	city centre/downtown
li-wáHduh	by himself; **li-wáHdi** = by myself, **li-waHdáhaa** = by herself, etc.
yi'úul	to say
yizúur	to visit
ba9dáyn	then
maHáTTa (*pl.* **maHaTTáat**)	station
yikháaf	to be afraid/to be worried; **akháaf laytúuh** = I'm afraid in case he gets lost
ma tikhafíish	don't worry (*fem.*)
yíwSif	to describe
síkka (*pl.* **síkak**)	route/way

Other places around town

It's always a good idea to remember important places around town. Here are some others you might need:

síinima (*pl.* **siinimáat**)	cinema
másraH (*pl.* **masáariH**)	theatre
bank (*pl.* **bunúuk**)	bank
maHáll (*pl.* **maHalláat**)	shop/store
sifáara (*pl.* **sifaráat**)	embassy
suu' (*pl.* **aswaa'**)	market/souq
mustáshfa (*pl.* **mustashfayáat**)	hospital

kúbri (*pl.* **kabáari**)	bridge
sháari9 (*pl.* **shawáari9**)	street
sháari9 in-niil	Nile Street
isháara (*pl.* **isharáat**)	(traffic) lights

Download a list of additional places around town.

Exercise 2

Ask for directions to these places, as in the example.

→ **law samáHt, il-kúbri mináyn?**

1 
2 
3 
4 
5 
6 

How would you ask a woman the same questions?

Exercise 3

Imagine you want to visit these places. Make sentences as in the example. Use **9áawiz** if you are male and **9áwza** if you are female, followed by one of these three verbs: **arúuH** '(I) go'; **azúur** '(I) visit'; **áakul fi** '(I) eat in'. There could be more than one correct answer.

theatre/centre of town
→ **ána 9áawiz/9áwza arúuH il-másraH fi wusT il-bálad.**

1 bank/Nile Street

2 Nefertiti Hotel/Tahrir Square

3 Nile Restaurant/Mosaddaq Street

4 Station/Ramsis Square

5 Egyptian Museum/centre of town

6 American Embassy/'Garden City' (an area of Cairo)

7 my (maternal) aunt/hospital

8 Filfila Restaurant/Tala'at Harb Street

Language points

Types of verbs

■ Regular verbs

Regular verbs are those that have three different, consistently pronounced, root consonants. In the most basic type of regular verb, the three root consonants are separated in the present/future tense by a vowel between the second and third root letters:

yíHgiz to reserve; root = H/g/z

yúkhrug to go out; root = kh/r/g

yínzil to go down/get off; root = n/z/l

■ Irregular verbs

Most irregularities occur when **waaw, yaa** or the glottal stop **hamza** is one of the root letters. These letters can mutate into a vowel sound causing a change in the verb stem pattern.
    There are three main types of irregular verbs:

1 The first type of irregular verb features a present stem starting with a long vowel (because the first root is **hamza**), e.g.

yáakul to eat; present stem = **áakul**; root = **hamza/k/l**

yáakhud to take; present stem = **áakhud**; root = **hamza/kh/d**

The present/future prefix is shortened to **y-**, **t-**, **n-**, etc., for example **yáakul** (he eats); **táakul** (she eats); **náakhud** (we take). There is no need to add a prefix at all for 'I': **áakul** (I eat); **áakhud** (I take).

Note: the initial long vowel in verbs such as **yáakhud** shortens when a suffix is added and the second vowel drops out altogether, e.g. **tákhdi** (you *fem.* take), rather than **táakhudi**; **yáklu** (they eat), rather than **yáakulu**.

2 The second type of irregular verb features a present stem with a long vowel in the middle (because the middle root is **waaw** or **yaa**). These verbs are known as *hollow verbs*, e.g.

yirúuH to go; present stem = **ruuH**; root = **r/w/H**

yizúur to visit; present stem = **zuur**; root = **z/w/r**

yizíid to increase; present stem = **ziid**; root = **z/y/d**

yináam to sleep; present stem = **naam**; root = **n/w/m**

Note: the stress in hollow verbs shifts to the long vowel, e.g. **yirúuH** (to go/he goes); compare with **yínzil** or **yúkhrug**.

3 The third type of irregular verb features a present stem ending with a vowel (because the final root is **waaw** or **yaa**). These verbs are known as *defective verbs*, e.g.

yíSHa to wake up; present stem = **SHa**; root = **S/H/w**

yíb'a to become; present stem = **b'a**; root = **b/'/y**

In a defective verb, the final vowel of the present stem is removed before any suffix is added, e.g. **yíSHa** (to wake up/he wakes up); **yíSHu** (they wake up); **tíSHi** (you *fem.* wake up).

Exercise 4

What are these irregular verbs in Arabic?

1 he visits

2 we go

3 you *(masc.)* wake up

4 it *(fem.)* becomes

5 you *(pl.)* eat

6 it *(masc.)* increases

7 they visit

8 he takes

9 you *(fem.)* sleep

10 I take

11 they wake up

12 you *(pl.)* go

13 we sleep

14 you *(pl.)* visit

15 it *(fem.)* increases

Download a list of additional useful irregular verbs.

Exercise 5

Change the sentences you created in Exercise 3 to refer to different subjects, as in the example:

íHna → íHna 9awzíin nirúuH il-másraH fi wusT il-bálad.

1 húwwa

2 húmma

3 híyya

4 íntu

5 widáad

6 gáabir

7 íHna

8 il-wiláad

Exercise 6 (Audio 2; 25)

Listen to this conversation between Hassan and Gaber about their plans for the day and tick the places each of them wants to go, as in the example.

	Hassan	Gaber
Hospital		
Bank		
French Embassy		
Station		
Cinema		
Market	✔	
Music Shop		

Dialogue 2

il-mátHaf wil-maHáTTa mináyn (Audio 2; 26)

Ibrahim explains to Mr Laurence how to find his way to the museum and Ramsis Station via the Cairo Tower.

1	Which of the two destinations is near the Hilton Hotel?
2	Which is near a fuul (beans) and falafel sandwich shop?

IBRAHÍIM: HawSíf lak il-mátHaf wil-maHáTTa mináyn.

il-áwwil íTla9 kúbri sítta oktúubir w-ínzil ba9d il-burg. khallíik dúghri 9ála k-korníish wi-khud shimáal 9and il-Hilton. Ha-tiláa'i l-mátHaf 9ála l-yimíin.

bin-nísba lil-maHáTTa khallíik fi sháari9 ramsíis 9ála Tuul li-gháayit il-miidáan náfsuh. khálli báalak, mádkhal il-maHáTTa ba9d táani isháara taHt ik-kúbri, ganb maHáll kibíir bi-yibíi9 sandawitsháat fuul wi-Ta9míyya ísmuh 'ábu wárda'.

IBRAHIM: *I'll describe to you how you get to the museum and the station.*

First go up the 6th of October Bridge and come down after the Tower. Keep straight on along the corniche and take a left at the Hilton. You will find the museum on your right-hand side.

As regards the station, keep straight on in Ramsis Street until the square itself. Be careful, the entrance of the station is after the second set of lights under the bridge, near a big shop selling bean and falafel sandwiches called 'Abu Warda'.

Vocabulary

il-áwwil	first/firstly
kúbri sítta oktúubir	6th of October Bridge
burg (*pl.* **abráag**)	tower; here referring to the Cairo Tower, a well-known landmark (see photo)
korníish	corniche
yiláa'i	to find
bin-nísba li	as regards/in relation to
li-gháayit	until/up to
náfsuh	itself/himself; **náfsi** = myself, **nafsáhaa** = herself, etc.
khálli báalak (*fem.* **báalik**)	be careful/watch out
mádkhal (*pl.* **madáakhil**)	entrance; noun of place from root **d/kh/l** (to enter), exit = **mákhrag** from root **kh/r/g** (to go out)
yibíi9	to sell

Note: See page 188 for vocabulary connected with giving directions.

Phrases for giving directions

khallíik *(fem.* khallíiki)	keep/stay *(lit.* 'keep yourself')
shimáal	left
yimíin	right
dúghri/9ála Tuul	straight on
khud *(fem.* khúdi)	take
áwwil (sháari9)	the first (street)
táani (isháara)	the second (traffic lights)
táalit (kúbri)	the third (bridge)
9ála sh-shimáal	on the left
9ála l-yimíin	on the right

Language points

Giving instructions (the imperative)

To give instructions or orders, you need to use a form of the verb known as the *imperative.*

■ Regular and defective verbs

For regular verbs and defective verbs (ending in a vowel), the imperative is formed by taking the 'you' part of the verb and simply removing the initial **t-**.

tínzil you *(masc.)* go down → ínzil go down! *(to a male)*

tinzíli you *(fem.)* go down → inzíli go down! *(to a female)*

tinzílu you *(pl.)* go down → inzílu go down! *(to a group)*

tíTla9 you *(masc.)* go up → íTla9 go up! *(to a male)*

tiTlá9i you *(fem.)* go up → íTlá9i go up! *(to a female)*

tiTlá9u you *(pl.)* go up ➜ iTlá9u go up! *(to a group)*

túkhrug you *(masc.)* go out ➜ úkhrug go out! *(to a male)*

tukhrúgi you *(fem.)* go out ➜ ukhrúgi go out! *(to a female)*

tukhrúgu you *(pl.)* go out ➜ ukhrúgu go out! *(to a group)*

tíSHa you *(masc.)* wake up ➜ íSHa wake up! *(to a male)*

tíSHi you *(fem.)* wake up ➜ íSHi wake up! *(to a female)*

tíSHu you *(pl.)* wake up ➜ íSHu wake up! *(to a group)*

■ Other irregular verbs

For irregular verbs that have a long vowel in the middle (*hollow*) or that start with a long vowel, the initial **t-** *and* the following vowel are removed for the imperative:

tirúuH you *(masc.)* go ➜ ruuH go! *(to a male)*

tirúuHi you *(fem.)* go ➜ rúuHi go! *(to a female)*

tirúuHu you *(pl.)* go ➜ rúuHu go! *(to a group)*

tibíi9 you *(masc.)* sell ➜ bii9 sell! *(to a male)*

tibíi9i you *(fem.)* sell ➜ bíi9i sell! *(to a female)*

tibíi9u you *(pl.)* sell ➜ bíi9u sell! *(to a group)*

táakhud you *(masc.)* take ➜ khud take! *(to a male)*

tákhdi you *(fem.)* take ➜ khúdi take! *(to a female)*

tákhdu you *(pl.)* take ➜ khúdu take! *(to a group)*

Note: the middle vowel in the feminine and plural reappears in the imperative, e.g. **tákhdi** (you *fem.* take) becomes **khúdi** (take!), **táklu** (you *pl.* eat) becomes **kúlu** (eat!).

There is one imperative in Dialogue 2 which is from a different type of verb: **khálli** (keep/stay!). You can just recognize this for the moment; more details of this type of verb will be given in Unit 13.

Exercise 7
How do you give these instructions in Arabic?

1 Go! *(to a group)*

2 Go down! *(to a female)*

3 Sleep! *(to a group)*

4 Eat! *(to a male)*

5 Go out! *(to a group)*

6 Go up! *(to a female)*

7 Wake up! *(to a female)*

8 Take! *(to a group)*

9 Sell! *(to a male)*

10 Eat! *(to a female)*

11 Drink! *(to a group)*

12 Visit! *(to a male)*

13 Reserve! *(to a female)*

14 Go up! *(to a group)*

15 Sell! *(to a female)*

Exercise 8
Change these into instructions and give the meaning, as in the example.

tiTla9 kúbri sítta oktúubir. → íTla9 kúbri sítta oktúubir.

(Go up 6th of October Bridge.)

1 tiTlá9u is-síllim.

2 tinzíli bá9d táani isháara.

3 tukhrúgu min il-bayt is-sáa9a sáb9a.

4 tákhdi áwwil sháari9 shimáal.

5 tirúuH il-mádrasa asháan ibrahíim.

6   tishrábi Háaga sáa9a?

7   tináamu bádri.

8   tákli Háaga 'ábl il-mádrasa?

9   tibíi9u il-9arabíyya.

10 tizúur il-máTHaf?

Negative instructions

A negative instruction is made in one of two ways. Make a special note that both ways use the *present* verb rather than the imperative.

■ ma- … -sh

Add **ma-** and **-sh** either side of the present verb:

ma tinzílsh!	don't go down! *(to a male)*
ma tukhrugísh!	don't go out! *(to a female)*
ma takhdúsh!	don't take! *(to a group)*

   Notice that the word stress moves to the last syllable in this type of negative instruction.

■ baláash …

Add **baláash** in front of the present verb. The instructions above would then become:

baláash tinzíl!	don't go down! *(to a male)*
baláash tukhrúgi!	don't go out! *(to a female)*
baláash tákhdu!	don't take! *(to a group)*

Exercise 9

Now make the instructions in Exercise 8 negative using both alternatives, as in this example.

   ma tiTlá9sh kúbri sítta oktúubir. / baláash tíTla9 kúbri sítta oktúubir.

Download extra activities to practise giving instructions.

Exercise 10 (Audio 2; 27)

Listen to the directions on the recording and mark the position of these buildings around town. Write the correct number in each box on the plan.

1 il-bank   2 il-mátHaf   3 il-maHáTTa
4 is-sifáara il-amriikíyya   5 is-síinima

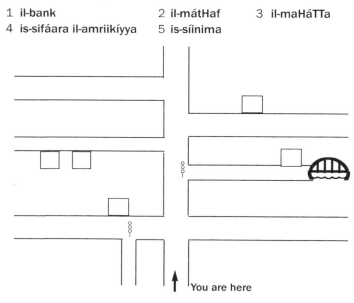

You are here

Exercise 11

Now try to describe in your own words to a passer-by how to get to the places in Exercise 10, using your completed plan. Compare what you said against the directions on the recording for Exercise 10.

Exercise 12 (Audio 2; 28)

You are going to give someone directions to your office. Follow the prompts on the recording. You will hear a model answer after the pause, but don't forget that your answer could be phrased slightly differently.

Learning with a friend or in a class?
Download ideas to practise asking and giving directions.

The Arabic script

ا ب
ت

Here is a letter that does not share its shape with any other:

و   the letter **waaw** can be a consonant pronounced 'w' as in 'window' or a long vowel pronounced **uu** as in 'b<u>oo</u>t' or **oh** as in 't<u>oe</u>' or 'b<u>oa</u>t'

waaw is a non-joining letter and so doesn't change its shape whatever its position in a word:

واحد   **wáaHid** (one)

قوي   **'áwi** (very)

Vowels in Arabic script

Short vowels (**a**, **i**, etc.) are not normally written as part of the script (see Arabic script section, Unit 2). The fluent experienced reader is expected to know them.

Long vowels are shown in the script. The three letters **waaw**, **álif** and **yaa** are used to form the long vowels:

و = **uu** or **oh**, e.g. يروح **yirúuH** (to go); يوم **yohm** (day)

ا = **aa**, e.g. ينام **yináam** (to sleep); غاوي **gháawi** (keen on)

ي = **ii** or **ay**, e.g. عصير **9aSíir** (juice); بيت **bayt** (house)

Exercise 13

Can you read these words you have met in this unit?

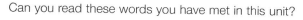

4 سينما   1 شمال

5 يزور   2 يمين

6 شارع   3 دوغري

Unit Twelve

inbasáTt fi faránsa?

Did you enjoy yourself in France?

In this unit you will learn about:

- how to talk about past events
- months of the year
- calendar dates
- recognizing these Arabic letters: ك ه

Dialogue 1

9imíltu eh hináak? **(Audio 2; 29)**

Hassan is asking Gaber about his recent honeymoon.

---

1   Which city did he go to?
2   What did he enjoy most?

HÁSAN: izzáyyak yaa 9aríis? inbasáTt fi faránsa?
GÁABIR: 'áwi, 'áwi.
HÁSAN: wiSíltu ímta?
GÁABIR: wiSílna yohm is-sabt.
HÁSAN: wi-widáad? líssa bi-tikháaf min iT-Tayyaráat?
GÁABIR: áywa, bass khádit musákkin min id-duktúur.
HÁSAN: fí9lan? wi-9imíltu eh hináak?
GÁABIR: rúHna amáakin kitíira – matáaHif, wi-burg 'Eiffel', wi-nizílna fi márkib 9ála nahr is-'Seine'. Hilw in-nahr. shúfna kull Háaga min il-márkib – ik-kanáayis il-'adíima, wil-mabáani ig-gamíila, tamaasíil dáhab ...
HÁSAN: wi-káltu kwáyyis?

GÁABIR: ána kalt sámak lazíiz wi-maHáar, láakin widáad ma
            bi-tiHíbbish is-sámak, fa-kálit láHma wi-firáakh wi-
            Haagáat   zayy   kídda.   wi-Táb9an   garrábna
            il-Halawiyáat – áHsan Halawiyáat fid-dúnya!
HÁSAN: yaa saláam yaa síidi. wi-eh kamáan?
GÁABIR: in-naas hináak Táb9an bi-yishrábu in-nibíit il-faran-
            sáawi il-mashhúur, bass íHna shiríbna masharíib
            mun9ísha gíddan ma9múula min in-ni9náa9 wi-
            rummáan.
HÁSAN: ni9náa9 wir-rummáan? – da eh ig-gamáal da?!
GÁABIR: áywa, áakhir gamáal, bass khalláaS, rigí9na dilwá'ti.

HASSAN: *How are you, bridegroom? Did you enjoy yourself in*
            France?
GABER: *Very much.*
HASSAN: *When did you arrive (back)?*
GABER: *We arrived on Saturday.*
HASSAN: *And Widaad? Is she still afraid of aeroplanes?*
GABER: *Yes, but she got a sedative from the doctor.*
HASSAN: *Really? And what did you do there?*
GABER: *We went to lots of places – museums, and the Eiffel*
            Tower and we went out on a boat on the River Seine.
            The river's lovely. We saw everything from the boat
            – the old churches, and the beautiful buildings, the
            golden statues ...
HASSAN: *Did you eat well?*
GABER: *I ate some delicious fish and oysters but Widaad*
            doesn't like fish so she ate meat and chicken and
            things like that. And of course we tried the patisserie
            – the best in the world!
HASSAN: *My goodness. And what else?*
GABER: *People there of course drink the famous French wine,*
            but we drank very refreshing drinks made from mint
            and pomegranate.
HASSAN: *Mint and pomegranate? Oh! How marvellous!*
GABER: *Yes, marvellous indeed! But it's over. We're back now*
            ('we've returned now').

Vocabulary

musákkin	sedative; painkiller
(pl. musakkináat)	
fí9lan?	really?
kiníisa (pl. kanáayis)	church
mábna (pl. mabáani)	building
timsáal (pl. tamaasíil)	statue
dáhab	gold; **tamaasíil dáhab** = statues [of] gold
maHáar	oysters
láHma	meat
firáakh	chicken (meat)
Halawiyáat	patisserie/pastries
id-dúnya	the world
mashhúur	famous
mashrúub (pl. masharíib)	drink
naas	people
mun9ísh	refreshing
ma9múul min	made from
ni9náa9	mint
rummáan	pomegranate
da eh il-gamáal da?!	how marvellous! (lit. 'what's this beauty?'); the endorsement **áakhir gamáal** means 'the ultimate (in) beauty' i.e. there's nothing more beautiful
khalláaS	(it's) over/finished

Note: for past verbs, see the Language Points below.

Language points

Past tense: regular verbs

When talking about completed actions, Arabic uses the past tense. This is formed by adding endings to a past stem.

In basic regular verbs, the past stem is formed by taking the three root letters and separating them with short vowels, most commonly **i**.

yínzil (to go down/get off)	root = **n/z/l**	past stem = **nizil**
yíshrab (to drink)	root = **sh/r/b**	past stem = **shirib**
yíwSal (to arrive)	root = **w/S/l**	past stem = **wiSil**
yírga9 (to return)	root = **r/g/9**	past stem = **rigi9**

The following table shows the past endings and an example for the verb **yínzil** with the past stem **nizil**:

	Ending	**yínzil** *(to go down/get off)* *(past stem = **nizil**)*
ána (I)	-t	nizílt
ínta (you, *masc.*)	-t	nizílt
ínti (you, *fem.*)	-ti	nizílti
húwwa (he)	—	nízil
híyya (she)	-it	nízlit
íHna (we)	-na	nizílna
íntu (you, *pl.*)	-tu	nizíltu
húmma (they)	-u	nízlu

Note that for **húwwa** there is no ending, and that **ána** and **ínta** are the same in the past. Pay attention also to how the word stress moves for the different parts of the verb. For **híyya** and **húmma**, where the stress falls on the first syllable, the second vowel of the stem drops out altogether.

wiSílna yohm is-sabt.	We arrived on Saturday.
shírbu masharíib mun9ísha.	They drank refreshing drinks.
rigí9t imbáariH.	I returned yesterday.
gáabir nízil wusT il-bálad.	Gaber went downtown.

Note: There's no direct equivalent of the English 'we have returned' or 'he has arrived'. The past tense is used for this meaning also.

Exercise 1

How do you say the following in Arabic?

1 I arrived

2 she returned

3 they went down/got off

4 you *(masc.)* drank

5 you *(pl.)* arrived

6 we returned

7 you *(fem.)* went down/got off

8 they returned

9 he drank

10 I went down/got off

Past tense: irregular verbs

■ Verbs starting with a vowel (**hamza** as first root letter)

The initial vowel of these verbs is generally dropped for the past stem, leaving just the second and third root letters separated by **a**.

    yáakul (to eat)   root = '/k/l   past stem = **kal**

    yáakhud (to take)   root = '/kh/d   past stem = **khad**

In other respects, these verbs are regular.

	Ending	yáakul *(to eat)* *(past stem =* **kal***)*
ána (I)	-t	kalt
ínta (you, *masc.*)	-t	kalt
ínti (you, *fem.*)	-ti	kálti
húwwa (he)	—	kal
híyya (she)	-it	kálit
íHna (we)	-na	kálna
íntu (you, *pl.*)	-tu	káltu
húmma (they)	-u	kálu

■ Hollow verbs (with **waaw** or **yaa** as middle root)

Hollow verbs have two past stems, a long **aa** in the middle for **húwwa**, **híyya** and **húmma**, and a short **u** or **i** for the other parts of the verb:

yirúuH (to go)	root = r/w/H	past stem = raaH/ruH
yizúur (to visit)	root = z/w/r	past stem = zaar/zur
yibíi9 (to sell)	root = b/y/9	past stem = baa9/bi9
yizíid (to increase)	root = z/y/d	past stem = zaad/zid

	Ending	**yirúuH** *(to go)* (raaH/ruH)	**yibíi9** *(to sell)* (baa9/bi9)
ána (I)	-t	ruHt	bi9t
ínta (you, *masc.*)	-t	ruHt	bi9t
ínti (you, *fem.*)	-ti	rúHti	bí9ti
húwwa (he)	—	raaH	baa9
híyya (she)	-it	ráaHit	báa9it
íHna (we)	-na	rúHna	bí9na
íntu (you, *pl.*)	-tu	rúHtu	bí9tu
húmma (they)	-u	ráaHu	báa9u

■ Defective verbs (with **waaw** or **yaa** as final root)

The past stem of a defective verb ends with a vowel, but it varies from verb to verb. The final vowel is also unstable and sometimes drops out or changes to **y** as in the example below. Here is a table showing the verb **yíSHa** (to wake up), with the past stem **SíHi**:

	Ending	**yíSHa** *(to wake up)* (past stem = **SíHi**)
ána (I)	-t	SiHít
ínta (you, *masc.*)	-t	SiHít
ínti (you, *fem.*)	-ti	SiHíti
húwwa (he)	—	SíHi
híyya (she)	-it	SíHyit
íHna (we)	-na	SiHína
íntu (you, *pl.*)	-tu	SiHítu
húmma (they)	-u	SíHyu

Here are the verbs in Dialogue 1 with their past stems. Some are new
verbs and some you have met already in the present/future form.

yíwSal/wíSil	to arrive
yáakhud/khad	to take
yí9mil/9ámal	to do
yirúuH/raaH (ruHt)	to go
yínzil/nízil	to go down/get on
yishúuf/shaaf (shuft)	to see
yáakul/kal	to eat
yíshrab/shírib	to drink
yírga9/rígi9	to return
yinbísiT/inbásaT*	to enjoy
yigárrab/gárrab*	to try

* Note: the final two verbs are varieties with additions to the root.
  More detail will be given of these types of verb in Unit 13.

Verbs are given in the glossary as above, with both the present and
past for reference.

Exercise 2

How do you say the following in Arabic?

1 I ate

2 she went

3 they woke up

4 it *(fem.)* increased

5 you *(pl.)* saw

6 we took

7 you *(fem.)* sold

8 they visited

9 you *(masc.)* woke up

10 I went

11 he saw

12 you *(pl.)* woke up

13 it *(masc.)* increased

14 I visited

15 we sold

Exercise 3

Read this description of what Widaad and Gaber did yesterday and put the verbs in brackets in the correct past form to fill in the gaps, as in the example.

imbáariH widáad wi-gáabir ___nízlu___ (yínzil) wusT il-bálad. il-áwwil

gáabir _____ (yirúuH) maHáll il-muusíiqa láakin widáad _____

(yirúuH) il-mustáshfa wi-_____ (yizúur) kháalhaa. wi-ba9dáyn

húmma l-itnáyn _____ (yishúuf) film gidíid wi-_____ (yáakul)

sámak fi máT9am 9ála k-korníish.

Exercise 4 (Audio 2; 30)

Imagine you went on a boat trip on the Nile yesterday and a friend is asking about your day. Follow the prompts on the recording to answer her questions.

Download an additional list of useful past verbs and extra activities.

Language point

Negative of the past tense

The past is made negative by using **ma** ... **-(i)sh**:

shírib / ma shiríbsh	he drank / he didn't drink
wiSílt / ma wiSíltish	I arrived / I didn't arrive
ríg9it / ma rig9ítsh	she returned / she didn't return
shúfna / ma shufnáash	we saw / we didn't see

Remember that the stress may shift when adding the negative **ma** ... **-(i)sh**.

 Exercise 5 (audio online; WEB12)

Download an additional audio activity to practise negative verbs in the past and how to pronounce them. Follow the prompts.

 Exercise 6

Match the questions with the correct answers.

1 9amáltu eh fi wusT il-bálad?
2 kalt sámak fil-máT9am?
3 abúki raaH fayn?
4 li9íbti il-iskwáash má9a náadya?
5 widáad nízlit is-suu' ímta?
6 shuft il-film ig-gidíid?

a raaH li d-duktúur.
b Hawáali is-sáa9a tís9a.
c la', li9íbt má9a sáara.
d zúrna l-mátHaf.
e la', líssa ma shuft(u)húush.
f la', kalt firáakh.

Exercise 7

Leila had a list of things to do yesterday, but didn't get round to doing all of them. Make sentences about what she did and didn't do as in the example.

1 **ma raaHítsh il-bank imbáariH.**

1 Go to bank ✗
2 Visit Nadia in hospital ✔
3 Finish novel ✗
4 Go downtown ✔
5 Play squash with Zeinah ✗
6 Take dress to tailor ✗
7 Go to station ✔

Exercise 8

Say something about what you did and didn't do yesterday, using as many different verbs as possible, for example:

zurt úmmi imbáariH.   I visited my mother yesterday.

ma rúHtish il-bank.   I didn't go to the bank.

Learning with a friend or in a class?
Download ideas to practise talking about what you did yesterday.

Dialogue 2

i9áara fi gám9it 'Edinburgh' (Audio 2; 31)

An Egyptian university lecturer describes the year he and his family spent on secondment in Scotland.

1 **In which month did they arrive in Edinburgh?**
2 **How long did they spend in Scotland?**
3 **Did they enjoy their stay?**

IL-USTÁAZ: ána ustáaz fi kullíiyit iT-Tibb, gám9it il-qáahira. is-sána ílli fáatit ruHt i9áara fi gám9it 'Edinburgh'. saafírna, ána wi-9ílti iskutlánda fi oghúsTus wi-laa'ína shá''a fi wusT 'Edinburgh', 'urayyíba min ig-gám9a. il-awláad ráahu l-madrása fi sibtámbir wi-'a9ádna hináak 9áshar shuhúur li-gháayit niháayit is-sána id-diraasíyya fi yúunio. rigí9na maSr fi yúulio. inbasáTna fi 'Edinburgh' w-iHtimáal nírga9 táani fil-mustá'bal.

THE PROFESSOR: *I'm a professor in the Faculty of Medicine, University of Cairo. Last year I went on secondment to Edinburgh University. We travelled, I and my family, to Scotland in August and we found a flat in the centre of Edinburgh near the university. The children went to school in September and we stayed there ten months until the end of the school year in June. We returned to Egypt in July. We enjoyed Edinburgh and we might return in the future.*

Vocabulary

ustáaz (*pl.* asátza)	professor; a word which also means 'Mr'
iT-Tibb	medicine/the study of medicine
kullíiyit iT-Tibb	the faculty of medicine
is-sána ílli fáatit	last year (*lit.* 'the year which has passed')
i9áara (*pl.* i9aaráat)	secondment (*lit.* 'lending')
iskutlánda	Scotland
hináak	there
shá''a (*pl.* shú'a')	flat/apartment
awláad	children, slightly more formal pronunciation of **wiláad**; plural of **wálad**, meaning 'boy' but used generally to mean 'children'
shahr (*pl.* shuhúur)	month
niháaya	end/finish
is-sána id-diraasíyya	the academic year
iHtimáal	possibility; **iHtimáal** + present verb = may/might; this is another modifying word that can be used like **láazim**, etc. (see Unit 10)
táani	again (*lit.* 'second time' – see Unit 11)
il-mustá'bal	the future

 Download a list of additional educational vocabulary.

Language point

Months of the year (Audio 2; 32)

The months of the year commonly used in Egypt sound similar to their English equivalents. Listen and repeat them on your recording.

yanáayir	January
fibráayir	February
máaris	March
abríil	April
máayo	May
yúunio	June
yúulio	July
oghúsTus	August
sibtámbir	September
oktúubir	October
nofámbir	November
disámbir	December

Cultural point

The Islamic calendar

The Western calendar has been widely adopted for everyday and administrative purposes. However, the Islamic, or **hígra**, calendar is also used, particularly for religious events and feasts. There are 12 months in the **hígra** calendar, based on the cycle of the moon. This means a lunar **hígra** year lasts 354 or 355 days. The Islamic months don't have a fixed season and move 10 to 11 days every year against the solar calendar.

Year zero of the Islamic calendar is 622ᴀᴅ, when the prophet
Muhammed fled from Mecca to the city of Medina (**higra** means
'flight'). Newspapers often give the date in both the lunar **higra**
calendar and the Western solar calendar. The two best-known months
of the **higra** calendar are **ramaDáan**, the month of fasting and prayer,
and **zuu l-Higga**, the month of the annual **Hagg** (pilgrimage) to Mecca

The fast during the Islamic month of **ramaDáan** is traditionally broken at
sunset with milk and dates (**lában wi-tamr**).

 Download a full list of the months of the Islamic calendar.

 Exercise 9 (audio online; WEB13)

Review the list on page 205. Then download an additional audio
activity to test yourself on the months of the year.

 Exercise 10 (Audio 2; 33)

A student is describing how she took a year off and went around the
world. Listen to the description of the places she visited and write
the appropriate months next to the countries she visited.

1 England   5 Japan

2 France   6 China

3 Italy   7 India

4 USA   8 Egypt

Language point

Dates

When describing the date, you can use the ordinary numbers directly in front of the name of the month:

itnáyn fibráayir	February 2nd
khámsa máaris	March 5th
arba9táashar yúunio	June 14th
tamantáashar oghúsTus	August 18th
sáb9a wi-9ishríin sibtámbir	September 27th
talatíin disámbir	December 30th

Note: look back at Unit 5 if you need to review the numbers.

For the first day of the month, the date can be expressed using **wáaHid** ('one') or **áwwil** ('the first'):

wáaHid yanáayir/	January 1st
áwwil yanáayir	

The Arabic for 'birthday' is **9iid miláad**, meaning 'festival of birth'. So 'my birthday' is **9iid miláadi** ('festival of my birth'), 'his birthday' is **9iid miláaduh** ('festival of his birth'), etc.

ána ándi arba9íin sána.	I'm forty years old.
9iid miláadi itnáyn wi-9ishríin yúunio.	My birthday is June 22nd.

íbni ánduh 9áshar siníin.	My son is ten years old.
9iid miláaduh áwwil máayo.	His birthday is May 1st.

Note: look back at Unit 6 to remind yourself of what you've learnt about expressing age.

Exercise 11

How old are these people and when are their birthdays? Look at the picture and word prompts and describe their ages and birthdays, as in the example.

 gamíila/6 → gamíila 9andáhaa sítt siníin.
9iid miláadhaa khámsa máaris.

1 manSúur/8   2 bashíir/30

3  fáTma/10   4 áHmad/43

5  núura/17   6 sáara/25

7 muHámmad/15 8 wisáam/12

 # Exercise 12

Can you say how old you are and when your birthday is? How about your friends and family?

The Arabic script

ا ب
ت

There are now only two letters of the alphabet you have not met. These are both distinctive and don't share their shapes with any other letters:

ه   the letter **haa**, pronounced 'h' as in 'hat'

ك   the letter **kaaf**, pronounced 'k' as in 'kettle'

These two letters change their shapes significantly depending on how they are joined:

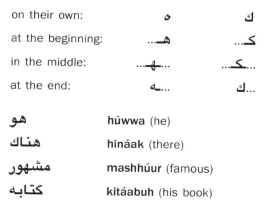

on their own:	ه	ك
at the beginning:	...ﻫ	...ﻛ
in the middle:	...ﻬ...	...ﻜ...
at the end:	...ﻪ	...ك

هو	**húwwa** (he)
هناك	**hináak** (there)
مشهور	**mashhúur** (famous)
كتابه	**kitáabuh** (his book)

The feminine ending ة, known as **taa marbúuTa** ('tied up **taa**'), is written like a final **haa** with two dots above. It is found only at the end of words, and is usually pronounced -a, but changes to -it when followed by a possessive ending or another noun – see Units 2 and 3 for more details.

بداية	**bidáaya** (beginning)
بداية الموسم	**bidáayit il-múusim** (the beginning of the season)
كلية	**kullíiya** (college/faculty)
كلية الطب	**kullíiyit iT-Tibb** (the faculty of medicine)

Exercise 13

Can you match the Arabic months of the year with their English equivalents?

a	January	يونيو	1
b	March	فبراير	2
c	December	أكتوبر	3
d	April	أغسطس	4
e	October	أبريل	5
f	November	يناير	6
g	May	ديسمبر	7
h	June	نوفمبر	8
i	February	يوليو	9
j	July	سبتمبر	10
k	August	مارس	11
l	September	مايو	12

You have now covered the basic Arabic alphabet. There is a full list of the letters of the alphabet on pages 8–9, and you can also download the complete table of Arabic letters in all their positions. Try reading the dialogues in the Arabic script supplement, alongside the transcription if necessary.

Download a complete table of Arabic letters in all their positions.

Unit Thirteen
min zamáan
A long time ago

In this unit you will learn about:
- comparing past and present
- higher Arabic numbers and dates
- the verb 'to be' in the past
- forms of the verb
- how to read Arabic numbers

Dialogue 1

zamáan ma kaansh fiih kull da (Audio 2; 34)

Widaad is talking to Mr Laurence on the way to the pyramids in Giza.

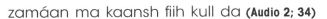

1   What can you see today along the Pyramids Road?
2   Was it the same in the past?

WIDÁAD: da sháari9 il-háram – dáyman záHma! shuft kull
il-9arabiyyáat wil-mabáani wil-maTáa9im wil-maHalláat?
zamáan ma kaansh fiih kull da. kaan fiih ghayTáan barsîim
wi-nakhl wi-Himîir. ána fákra lámma kunt Sughayyára kaan
9ándi SáHba káanit 9áysha hína ganb it-tír9a fi bayt gamíil
háadi. bass dilwá'ti fi makáan báythaa Ha-tiláa'i khámas
9imaráat!

gíddi 'aal li in fit-talatiináat wil-arba9iináat kaan fiih
mu9áskar tába9 ig-gaysh il-ingilíizi, hináak fi S-SaHrá 9and
ábul-hohl. Táb9an il-ingilíiz míshu min zamáan, min sánat

alf w-tis9umíyya arbá9a wi-khamsíin, láakin líssa fiih
isTabláat li-gháayit dilwá'ti win-naas tí'dar tírkab khayl
hináak 9andúhum.

WIDAAD: *This is the Pyramids Road – it's always crowded! Did you*
see all the cars, buildings, restaurants and shops? A long
time ago there wasn't all of this. There were fields of
clover, palm trees and donkeys. I remember when I was
young I had a friend [who] was living here near the canal,
in a beautiful peaceful house. But now in the place of her
house you'll find five apartment blocks!

My grandfather told me that in the thirties and forties
there was a camp belonging to the English army, there in
the desert by the Sphinx. Of course, the English left a long
time ago, from 1954, but there are still stables until now
and people ride horses there [with them].

Vocabulary

dáyman	always
zamáan/min zamáan	a long time ago
ghayT (*pl.* **ghayTáan**)	field
barsíim	clover (a common animal feed)
nakhl	palm trees
fáakir (*fem.* **fákra;** *pl.* **fakríin**)	remember(ing); an active participle used with a verbal meaning – see Unit 6
lámma	when; used in a sentence rather than a question (compare with **ímta?** – when?)
tír9a (*pl.* **tíra9**)	canal (small irrigation channel)
háadi	peaceful/quiet
fi makáan	in the place of
9imáara (*pl.* **9imaráat**)	apartment building/block of flats
min ... (+ period of time)	... ago
gidd	grandfather; **gídda** = grandmother
in	that; **'aal li in** = he told me that
mu9áskar	military camp; encampment
tába9	belonging to/relating to; similar to **bitáa9** but less personal
gaysh (*pl.* **giyúush**)	army
SaHrá	desert
ábul-hohl	the Sphinx
yímshi/míshi	to go (away); to walk
isTábl (*pl.* **isTabláat**)	stable
yí'dar/'ídir	to be able/can; followed directly by another verb in the present tense: **in-naas ti'dar tírkab khayl** = people can ride horses
yírkab/ríkib	to ride
khayl	horses

🔍 Language points

Numbers above 100 (audio online; WEB14)

Here are the numbers from 100. There is an additional downloadable
audio file to help you with the pronunciation:

míyya	one hundred
mitáyn	two hundred
tultumíyya	three hundred
rub9umíyya	four hundred
khumsumíyya	five hundred
suttumíyya	six hundred
sub9umíyya	seven hundred
tumnumíyya	eight hundred
tis9umíyya	nine hundred
alf	one thousand
alfáyn	two thousand
milyóhn	one million
tultumíyya wi-sittíin	three hundred and sixty
tis9umíyya khámsa wi-9ishríin	nine hundred and twenty-five
alf wi-suttumíyya	one thousand six hundred

Years in dates

The year in a date is usually expressed by saying the number prefixed
by **sánat** ('year of'):

1954 = **sánat alf wi-tis9umíyya arbá9a wi-khamsíin**
('the year of one thousand, nine hundred and fifty-four')

1450 = **sánat alf wi-rub9umíyya wi-khamsíin**

2002 = **sánat alfáyn w-itnáyn**

2015 = **sánat alfáyn wi-khamastáashar**

Notice that you need to say the complete number in Arabic dates and cannot break the year into two numbers as often happens in English ('nineteen fifty-four', 'fourteen fifty', etc.).

You can also talk about decades within a century ('the thirties', 'the seventies', etc.) by adding the plural **-áat** to the number. Pay attention to how the stress shifts when the plural ending is added.

it-talatiináat.   the thirties (from **talatatíin**, thirty)

is-saba9iináat   the seventies (from **saba9íin**, seventy)

Exercise 1

How would you say these dates in Arabic?

1	**1960**	6	**1885**
2	**2004**	7	**2019**
3	**1990**	8	**1972**
4	**1570**	9	**2009**
5	**2020**	10	**2034**

Download additional practice of higher numbers and dates.

Language points

The verb 'to be': yikúun/kaan

Although the verb 'to be' (**yikúun/kaan**) is usually omitted in the present tense, it is essential in the past and the future.

húwwa ga9áan.	He's hungry.
kaan ga9áan.	He was hungry.
Ha-yikúun ga9áan.	He will be hungry.
ínti gáhza?	Are you *(fem.)* ready?
kúnti gáhza?	Were you ready?

Ha-tikúuni gáhza?	Will you be ready?
ána mish fil-bayt.	I'm not in the house.
ma kúntish fil-bayt.	I wasn't in the house.
mish Hakúun fil-bayt.	I won't be in the house.

■ How to form the verb **yikúun/kaan**

yikúun/kaan is a hollow verb formed in a similar way to **yirúuH/raaH**
('to go' – see Unit 11 and Unit 12). This table shows the complete verb:

	Present/future	*Past*
ána (I)	akúun	kunt
ínta (you, *masc.*)	tikúun	kunt
ínti (you, *fem.*)	tikúuni	kúnti
húwwa (he)	yikúun	kaan
híyya (she)	tikúun	káanit
íHna (we)	nikúun	kúnna
íntu (you, *pl.*)	tikúunu	kúntu
húmma (they)	yikúunu	káanu

Exercise 2

How do you say these in Arabic?

1 We were hungry.

2 They weren't in the house.

3 I'll be in the bank.

4 My grandfather was Egyptian.

5 We won't be there.

6 Will you (*pl.*) be in Cairo tomorrow?

7 The desert was peaceful.

8 My daughter will be busy.

9 The fields were large.

10 Weren't you (*masc.*) in [the] school?

Some other uses of yikúun/kaan

■ After modifying words

As well as being used with **Ha-** for the future, **yikúun** is also used after modifying words such as **láazim** (have to), **múmkin** (can), and so on (see Unit 10). Remember that you must use the appropriate form to agree with the subject.

il-bayt láazim yikúun háadi. The house must be peaceful.

iHtimáal yikúunu ga9aníin. They might be hungry.

■ As a second verb

yikúun is used as a second verb after expressions such as 'want' or 'like', again in the appropriate form to agree with the subject.

bínti 9áwza tikúun hína lámma l-wiláad yíSHu.	My daughter wants to be here when the children wake up.
ána baHíbb akúun mashghúul.	I like to be busy.
íntu 9awzíin tikúunu áwwil naas yudkhúlu?	Do you *(pl.)* want to be the first people to go in?

■ Before **fiih** and **9and**

kaan or **ma kaansh** is used in front of standard phrases such as **fiih** ('there is/are') and **9and** ('to have') to make them refer to the past.

kaan fiih ghayTáan barsíim.	There were fields of clover.
ma kaansh fiih kull da.	There wasn't all of this.
kaan 9ándi SáHba.	I had a (female) friend.
kaan fiih mu9áskar.	There was a camp.

Ha-yikúun ('will be') can be used in a similar way to refer to the future:

Ha-yikúun fiih Háfla hína búkra.	There'll be a party here tomorrow.
mish Ha-yikúun fiih akl.	There won't be any food.
Ha-yikúun 9andúhum tiin?	Will they have figs?

Exercise 3

Rephrase these sentences following the prompts, as in the example.

> **húwwa fil-bayt.** → **iHtimáal yikúun fil-bayt.**

1 **íHna fil-madrása.** → **láazim…**

2 **íbni hína.** → **íbni 9áwwiz…**

3 **húmma min aswáan.** → **iHtimáal…**

4 **húwwa mumássil.** → **múmkin…**

5 **ána l-áwwil.** → **baHíbb…**

6 **íHna ga9aníin.** → **mish 9awzíin…**

 ## Exercise 4

Put these sentences and questions into the past, as in the example.

> **fiih nakhl kitíir.** → **kaan fiih nakhl kitíir.**

1 9ándi SáaHib 9áayish hína.

2 fiih mátHaf fi wusT il-bálad.

3 húmma muhandisíin?

4 ma fiish bank ganb is-síinima.

5 9andína 9aSíir tufffáaH.

6 íHna mashghuulíin.

7 9ándak SáaHib hináak?

8 ma 9andíish 9arabíyya.

 ## Exercise 5

Now put the sentences and questions in Exercise 4 into the future tense, for example.

> **fiih nakhl kitíir.** → **Ha-yikúun fiih nakhl kitíir.**

Exercise 6

Look at this scene now and 100 years ago. Make as many sentences as you can about the changes that have happened, using the example as a model.

min míʼit sána kaan fiih nakhl kitíir, bass dilwáʼti fiih 9imaráat.
(A hundred years ago there were many palm trees, but now there are apartment buildings.)

Exercise 7

Think about where you live or a town you know well and the changes that have happened over the past 100 years. Try to make five or six sentences in Arabic explaining these changes.

Language point

Compound tenses with kaan

The verb **kaan** can also be used to form compound tenses, turning 'is doing' into 'was doing', 'does' into 'used to do' and 'going to do' into 'was going to do'. Here are the three main compound tenses.

■ **kaan** + active participle – past continuous ('was ...ing')

kaan láabis 'amíiS ákhDar.	He was wearing a green shirt.
kúnti gáyya hína?	Were you (*fem.*) coming here?

■ **kaan** + present – past habitual ('used to')

kúnna bi-níl9ab kúra kull yohm.	We used to play football every day.
ma kaanúush bi-yiStáadu fit-tír9a.	They didn't used to fish in the canal.

■ **kaan** + future – past intention ('was going to')

káanit Ha-tizáakir bass ma káansh fiih wa't.	She was going to study but there wasn't time.
ma kúntish Hanáam bass kunt ta9báan.	I wasn't going to sleep but I was tired.

 Exercise 8

How would say these in Arabic?

1 We used to fish in the canal.

2 My sister was wearing a red dress.

3 Were they coming to the party?

4 Were you (*fem.*) sleeping?

5 I used to play tennis every day.

6 Didn't you *(masc.)* used to ride horses?

7 My son was going to play football but he was tired.

8 We were going to study but we were busy.

Download additional practice of the verb **yikúun/kaan**.

Dialogue 2

káanit ríHla gamíila **(Audio 2; 35)**

A visitor to Upper Egypt is recounting his holidays there.

1	**How did he travel to Luxor this year?**
2	**How did he travel to Luxor last year?**
3	**Where did he go from Aswan by bus this year?**

SAAYIH: íHna saafírna lú'Sur biT-Tayyáara, wi-ba9dáyn khádna filúuka min lú'Sur li-'aswáan. káanit ríHla gamíila fi n-niil. il-marákbi Tábakh lináa sámak wi-ruzz. lámma wiSílna aswáan rúHna ábu símbel bil-otobíis.

is-sána ílli fáatit rúHna lú'Sur bi-táksi min il-ghardá'a. khádna is-síkka ílli bi-tirúuH min safáaga. il-mishwáar khad luh Hawáali tálat saa9áat láakin íHna inbasáTna li'ánn is-sawwáa' kaan mishághghal agháani afláam zamáan. ána baHíbb il-afláam il-'adíima áktar min il-afláam ig-gidíida li'ánn afláam zamáan mitkallífa wi-ma9múula bi-zímma.

VISITOR: *We travelled to Luxor by plane, and then we took a felucca from Luxor to Aswan. The journey was beautiful on the Nile. The boatman cooked us fish and rice. When we arrived in Aswan, we went to Abu Simbel by bus.*

Last year we went to Luxor by taxi from Hurghada. We took the route that goes from Safaga. The [whole] distance took about three hours but we enjoyed ourselves because the driver was playing songs from old films. I like old films more than new films because the films from the past are lavish and made with integrity.

Vocabulary

filúuka (*pl.* faláayik)	felucca; sailing boats that ply the River Nile. They are mostly for cargo, but can be hired by passengers.
marákbi (*pl.* marakbíyya)	boatman
yúTbukh/Tábakh	to cook
mishwáar (*pl.* mashawíir)	distance/errand; a flexible word used for errands, or travel to another town, e.g. shopping trip
sawwáa' (*pl.* sawwa'íin)	driver
yishághghal/shághghal	to operate/to play (a DVD, etc.); **kaan mishághghal** = he was playing
ughníyya (*pl.* agháani)	song
film (*pl.* afláam)	film/movie
mitkállif	lavish/costing a lot
zímma	integrity/honesty

Cultural point

Abu Simbel

Abu Simbel was originally the name of a site on the banks of the Nile in Southern Egypt where two huge temples had been cut into the rock in the reign of Ramsis II. During the 1960s the temples were the subject of a massive rescue effort to save them from being submerged by Lake Nasser, created when the Aswan Dam was built. In a series of operations, the temples were moved to the desert south-west of Aswan and can now be visited by plane or bus.

Language points

who/which: ílli

Arabic only uses the word **ílli** ('who/which') when referring to a definite noun (e.g. 'the girl'). When the meaning is indefinite (e.g. 'a girl') **ílli** is omitted:

ána shuft il-bint ílli káanit rákba HuSáan.	I saw the girl who was riding a horse.
ána shuft bint káanit rákba HuSáan.	I saw a girl who was riding a horse.

Here are two examples from the dialogues in this unit:

is-sána ílli fáatit	last year (*lit.* 'the year which has passed')
kaan 9ándi SáHba káanit 9áysha hína.	I had a friend who was living here.

Attached pronouns with verbs

The attached pronouns that are used on the end of nouns and prepositions (see Units 2 and 4) can also be used with verbs. The only change is that **-i** ('my') changes to **-ni** ('me') on the end of a verb:

maHmúud záarni imbáariH.	Mahmoud visited me yesterday.
ána ma shuftuhúmsh fil-máktab.	I didn't see them in the office.
ma fiish masharíib fit-taláaga. khallasnáhaa.	There's no drinks in the fridge. We finished them.*

*Remember plurals of objects will use the feminine singular, in this case the attached pronoun **-haa**.

■ Shifting stress patterns **(Audio 2; 36)**

An issue with adding attached pronouns is that the word stress often changes. Shifting stress is a feature generally of Egyptian Arabic, but particularly with personal endings and negatives. You could compare this to the changing stress on the English *phótograph, photógrapher, photográphic.*

Look carefully at the following examples and listen to the recording.
Try to copy the stress patterns.

ána shúft Hásan.	I saw Hassan.
ána shúftuh.	I saw him.
ána ma shuftuhúush.*	I didn't see him.
íHna simí9na l-akhbáar.	We heard the news.
íHna simi9náhaa.	We heard it.
íHna ma simi9naháash.	We didn't hear it.
ínti bi-tákli ruzz.	You (fem.) eat rice.
ínti bi-taklíih.	You eat it.
ínti ma bi-taklihúush.	You don't eat it.

*Note: you could also hear a shorter version of this: **ána ma shuftúush.**

You will pick up these stress patterns with time and practice. It is
more a question of ear than firm rules.

Exercise 9 (audio online; WEB15)

Download an additional audio activity to practise shifting stress
patterns. Look at the sentences and questions below and think
about how you would rephrase them using an attached pronoun,
and then how you would make the result negative. Then go to the
recording and follow the prompts.

1 **íHna shúfna samíira.** (We saw Samira.)

2 **ána báakul gíbna kull(i) yohm.** (I eat cheese every day.)

3 **il-wiláad khallásu l-9aSíir.** (The children finished the juice.)

4 **widáad záarit gáabir imbáariH.** (Widaad visited Gaber yesterday.)

5 **il-markábi Tábakh samak.** (The boatman cooked fish.)

6 **ínta shuft il-mudarrisíin?** (Have you seen the teachers?)

Language point

Forms of the verb

You may have already noticed that certain verbs have additional letters around the three root consonants, for example the verb **yishághghal** (to operate/to play) has the root **sh/gh/l** but the middle root **gh** is doubled; **yinbísiT** (to enjoy) has an additional **n** sound before the root **b/s/T**. When verbs have these additional letters they are referred to as *forms of the verb*. 'Forms' in this context simply means variations. Verbs in different 'forms' with the same root consonants usually have related meanings.

There are ten 'forms' altogether, including the basic verbs which are counted as the first form. Western Arabic scholars generally refer to the forms of the verb using Roman numerals, i.e. form I (basic verbs), form II, form III, form IV, etc. Form IX is very rare and form IV is uncommon in Egyptian Arabic, leaving seven significant variations.

■ How the forms vary

Here are forms with examples in the present and past tenses. Form IV is included in grey for completeness. Some of these examples are already familiar and you can use them to remember the patterns. The short vowels vary slightly between forms and tenses, but the main features of each form are shown in the right-hand column of the table.

	Present/Past	Main features
Form II	yikhállaS/khállaS (to finish; root **kh/l/S**)	doubling of middle root
Form III	yisáafir/sáafir (to travel; root **s/f/r**)	long **áa** after first root
Form IV	yún9ish/án9ash (to refresh; root **n/9/sh**)	á before first root in past
Form V	yitmárran/itmárran (to train; root **m/r/n**)	additional **t** before first root; doubling of middle root
Form VI	yit'áabil/it'áabil (to meet up; root **'/b/l**)	additional **t** before first root; long **áa** after first root
Form VII	yinbísiT/inbásaT (to enjoy; root **b/s/T**)	additional **n** before first root
Form VIII	yishtághal/ishtághal (to work; root **sh/gh/l**)	additional **t** between first and second root
Form X	yistáhlik/istáhlak (to consume; root **h/l/k**)	additional **st** before first root

The subject prefixes and endings and the attached pronouns
remain the same for all types of verb:

il film kaan Tawíil, láakin íHna khallaSnáah.	The film was long, but we finished it.
ána basáafir iskindiríyya fish-shíta li'annáha hádya.	I travel to Alexandria in winter because it's quiet.
láazim titmárran kull yohm tálat sa9áat.	You *(masc.)* have to train every day for three hours.
it'aabílna 9and baab in-náadi is-sáa9a itnáyn.	We met up at the door of the club at two o'clock.
il-wiláad bi-yinbísTu hína 9alasháan fiih khayl.	The children enjoy it here because there are horses.
ána bashtághal bil-layl fi máT9am maksíiki.	I work at night in a Mexican restaurant.
istáhlaku kull il-máyya fil-biir.	They consumed all the water in the well.

Exercise 10

How would you say these in Arabic?

1 We've finished the bread.

2 Did her sister enjoy [herself]?

3 My father works at night in a small restaurant.

4 The children met up at the cinema after school.

5 I train every day in the club.

6 Why did they travel to Alexandria yesterday?

7 We need to work on Sunday.

8 Did you *(pl.)* consume all the fish this year?

■ Meaning patterns

Particular forms of the verb can be associated with particular variations in meaning. For example, form II often makes the meaning causitive or transitive (carrying out an action on someone/something else). A good example of this is the root **kh/l/S**, generally associated with 'finishing' or 'completing'. The basic verb is intransitive, but by doubling the middle root to make it form II the meaning becomes transitive:

yíkhlaS/khíliS	to finish
il-film khíliS.	The film has finished.
yikhállaS/khállaS	to finish *something*
ána khalláSt il-lában.	I've finished the milk.

Certain meanings are associated with each form, although these are not always obvious in individual verbs. Here is a some other meaning patterns that you may find useful:

Form	Meaning patterns
Form II	• carrying out an action on someone/ something else • doing something intensely or repeatedly
Form III	• trying to do something • doing something with someone else
Form V	• doing something to or for yourself; (reflexive of form II)
Form VI	• doing something together/collaborating in doing something
Form VII	• doing something to or for yourself; (reflexive of form I)
Form VIII	• similar to form VII
Form X	• asking to do something • considering something/someone to be

There are usually two to four verb forms that are possible with a particular root, but there may be up to five or six, or indeed none at all. Although the forms may at first seem irrelevant and complicated (after all, you can just learn the verbs individually), they can help you. If you recognize the root and the form of the verb, you can have a guess at the meaning even if you have never met that particular word.

Forms of the verb: participles

In the same way that active participles can be formed from basic verbs (e.g. **ráayiH/9áarif**), so they can also be made from the forms of the verb. They are largely predictable and are formed by using the prefix **mu-** (or sometimes **mi-**) with the present tense pattern. These active participles have the meaning of doing something, and may also be used for the person who carries out the action, e.g.

yishághghal (to operate, form II) ➜ **mishághghal** operating

yisáafir (to travel, form III) ➜ **musáafir** travelling/traveller

yistáhlik (to consume, form X) ➜ **mustáhlik** consuming/consumer

Exercise 11

Can you identify the original verb, form and root letters associated with these participles, as in the example? Try to guess at the meaning of the original verb.

mustáhlik (consumer) ➜ **yistáhlik** root **h/l/k** (form X), *to consume*

1 **muHáasib** (accountant)

2 **mumássil** (actor)

3 **mitkállif** (lavish/costing a lot)

4 **mistá9gil** (urgent/express)

5 **mudárris** (teacher)

6 **mustá9mil** (using/user)

7 **musákkin** (tranquillizer/painkiller)

8 **mitgáwwiz** (married)

9 **mukhtálif** (differing/different)

Download additional information about forms of the verb.

Exercise 12

Here is the text of the second half of Dialogue 2 again, this time in the wrong order. Without looking back, try to put the sentences and phrases into the right order.

1   ... li'ánn afláam zamáan mitkallífa wi-ma9múula bi-zímma.

2   ... li'ánn is-sawwáa' kaan mishághghal agháani afláam zamáan.

3   ána baHíbb il-afláam il-'adíima áktar min il-afláam ig-gidíida...

4   il-mishwáar khad luh Hawáali tálat saa9áat ...

5   is-sána ílli fáatit rúHna lú'Sur bi-táksi min il-ghardá'a.

6   khádna is-síkka ílli bi-tirúuH min safáaga.

7   ... láakin íHna inbasáTna ...

Exercise 13 (Audio 2; 37)

You are going to tell an Egyptian friend in Arabic about your holiday last year on the Red Sea coast. Look at the details below and prepare what you are going to say. Then turn on the recording and join in the conversation.

• travelled to Sharm el-sheikh (**sharm ish-shaykh**) by plane

• went with your family: wife or husband and three daughters

• fished in the Red Sea (**il-baHr il-áHmar**) and went out on a boat

• went to Taba (**Táaba**) by bus

• journey took about three hours but driver was playing an old film in the bus

• enjoyed holiday and might go back in the future

You will hear a model conversation on the recording after the exercise, but your responses could vary slightly.

Exercise 14

Think of a holiday you have enjoyed in the past and try to make up a short description of what you did. If possible, find an Egyptian to listen to your description and give you feedback.

Learning with a friend or in a class?
Download ideas to practise talking about your holiday.

The Arabic script

Numbers

Arabic has its own set of figures which are different but related to the ones used in English and other Latin-script languages. Here are the figures 0–9:

0	•
1	١
2	٢
3	٣
4	٤
5	٥
6	٦
7	٧
8	٨
9	٩

Unlike the rest of the Arabic script, numbers are written left to right (the same way as English):

١٤ (14)   ٩٠ (90)   ٢٠٤٥ (2045)

٣١ (31)   ١٥٦ (156)   ١٨٧٢ (1872)

Exercise 15

Can you work out the registration number of this car?

Exercise 16

What are these numbers? Say them out loud in Arabic.

a ٥   b ١٣   c ٢٠

d ٨٦   e ١٠٠   f ٢٥٠

g ١٣٤٤   h ١٩٩٧   i ٢٠٠٠

j ٢٠١٢   k ٢٠٢٠   l ٢٠٥٨

Unit Fourteen
máT9am in-niil
The Nile Restaurant

In this unit you will learn about:

- making restaurant reservations by phone
- making suggestions
- some typical Egyptian dishes

Dialogue 1

káanit ríHla gamíila (Audio 2; 38)

Gaber is phoning the Nile Restaurant to reserve a table.

1   **For how many people is the reservation?**
2   **What day of the week does he want the table?**
3   **Does he have any special requests?**

IL-METR:	máT9am in-niil, SabáaH il-khayr.
GÁABIR:	áywa, máT9am in-niil?
IL-METR:	áywa, SabáaH il-khayr yaa fándim.
GÁABIR:	SabáaH in-nuur. law samáHt 9awzíin níHgiz tarabáyza li-khámsa yohm ig-gúm9a ig-gáyya.
IL-METR:	taHt ámrak yaa fándim. láHZa ma9áaya min fáDlak … ig-gúm9a sittáashar HaDrítak?
GÁABIR:	áywa, maZbúuT. ig-gúm9a ig-gáyya 9ála Tuul.
IL-METR:	tarabáyza li-khámsa. b-ism miin HaDrítak?
GÁABIR:	b-ísmi ána. gáabir 9ábd il-waháab.
IL-METR:	gáabir 9ábd il-waháab. HaDrítak Ha-tisharráfna is-sáa9a kaam in sháa' alláah?
GÁABIR:	wáHda wi-nuSS, itnáyn. bá9d Saláat ig-gúm9a kída.
IL-METR:	áhlan bi-HaDrítak yaa fándim.
GÁABIR:	miin ma9áaya?
IL-METR:	ána metr ábu s-su9úud.
GÁABIR:	áhlan biik yaa metr. ba'úulak eh, wiHyáatak ána 9áwwiz tarabáyza Hílwa 9ála n-niil 9ála Tuul.
IL-METR:	in sháa' alláah yaa beh bass HaDrítak 9áarif Táb9an yohm ig-gúm9a bi-yíb'a záHma shuwáyya ma9lésh.
GÁABIR:	la', yaa ábu s-su9úud wiHyáatak. ma tiksafníish. ána Ha-yikúun ma9áaya gamáa9a agáanib. láazim ni'a99ádhum 9ála n-niil.
IL-METR:	in sháa' alláah yaa fándim.
GÁABIR:	khalláaS. ittafá'na yaa ábu s-su9úud. is-saláamu 9aláykum.
IL-METR:	má9a alf saláama yaa gáabir beh.

MAÎTRE D':	Nile Restaurant, good morning.
GABER:	Yes, Nile Restaurant?
MAÎTRE D':	Yes, good morning sir.
GABER:	Good morning. Please, we want to reserve a table for five next Friday.
MAÎTRE D':	At your service, sir. One moment please ... Friday the sixteenth sir?
GABER:	Yes, (that's) right. The Friday coming directly.
MAÎTRE D':	Table for five. In whose name, sir?
GABER:	In my name. Gaber Abd al-Wahaab.
MAÎTRE D':	Gaber Abd al-Wahaab. What time will you arrive sir, God willing?
GABER:	Half past one, two. After Friday prayers some time.
MAÎTRE D':	You're welcome, sir.
GABER:	Who's speaking?
MAÎTRE D':	I'm the maître d', Abu Al-Su'ud.
GABER:	Welcome to you, maître. I tell you what, please, I want a nice table directly overlooking the Nile.
MAÎTRE D':	God willing sir, but you know of course that Friday gets a little busy, sorry.
GABER:	No, Abu Su'ud. Don't disappoint me. I'll be with a group of foreigners. We must seat them overlooking the Nile.
MAÎTRE D':	God willing sir.
GABER:	OK. We've agreed Abu Su'ud. Goodbye.
MAÎTRE D':	Goodbye, Gaber, sir.

Cultural point

The head waiter is usually called **il-metr** in Egypt. This is a corruption of the French term *maître d'*. If a waiter looks like a senior figure you can address him using **yaa metr**! For more junior waiters, it's usual to use **garsón**, from the French *garçon*: **yaa garsón**!, or **áanisa** ('miss') for females: **yaa áanisa**!

Vocabulary

gáyy	next ('coming'); active participle from the verb **yíigi** (see Language point); **(yohm) il-itnáyn ig-gayy** = next Monday; **(yohm) ig-gúm9a ig-gáyya** = next Friday.
taHt ámrak	at your service (*lit.* 'under your command')
(*fem.* **taHt ámrik**)	
láHZa ma9áaya	one moment (*lit.* 'a moment with me')
maZbúuT	correct/right; here used with the meaning 'exactly'
yishárraf	to honour; a verb often used with the meaning of 'to honour us with your presence'. **Ha-tisharráfna is-sáa9a kaam?** (*lit.* 'You will honour us what time?') is a polite way of asking when someone will be arriving.
Saláat	prayers; **Saláat ig-gúm9a** is the main Friday prayers and sermon in the mosque.
miin ma9áaya?	who's speaking? (*lit.* 'who with me?'); another useful telephone phrase
wiHyáatak	please (*lit.* 'on your life')
(*fem.* **waHyáatik**)	
beh	sir; from the Turkish 'Bey'
shuwáyya	a little/somewhat
ma9lésh	sorry; never mind
yíksif/kásaf	to disappoint/to embarrass; **ma tiksifníish** = don't disappoint me
gamáa9a	group
(*pl.* **gamaa9áat**)	
agnábi (*pl.* **agáanib**)	foreigner
yi'á99ad/á99ad	to seat; **láazim ni'a99ádhum** = we must seat them
yittífi'/ittáfa'	to agree; **ittafá'na** = we have agreed (a closing remark similar to the English 'agreed')
is-saláamu 9aláykum	'peace on you'; the traditional greeting or leave-taking which has a number of possible replies, including **má9a alf saláama** ('with a thousand peaces') and **wa-9aláykum is-saláam** ('and peace on you')

Exercise 1

Reserve a table using the number of people and days of the week given, as in the example:

Next Monday for 3 ➜ **9awzíin níHgiz tarabáyza li-taláata yohm il-itnáyn ig-gayy.**

1 Next Tuesday for 5

2 Next Saturday for 4

3 Next Wednesday for 6

4 Next Friday for 2

5 Next Sunday for 8

6 Next Thursday for 15

Exercise 2

Match these key expressions from the dialogue to the situations.

miin ma9áaya?	**ittafá'na**	**láHZa ma9áaya**
SabáaH il-khayr yaa fándim	**ma9lésh**	**taHt ámrak**

1 You want to apologize.

2 You want someone to hold on a minute.

3 You want to signal that you are happy to do something.

4 You're not sure who you're talking to on the telephone.

5 You want to greet someone politely.

6 You want to express your agreement with someone.

Exercise 3 (Audio 2; 39)

Join in the conversation on the recording where you'll be reserving a table for yourself and two friends. You'll be prompted when it's your turn to speak.

Language point

yíigi (to come)

We have seen that the active participle **gayy** (*fem.* **gáyya**, *pl.* **gayyíin**) can mean both 'coming' or 'next'. It's worth looking in more detail at the complete verb **yíigi/geh** ('to come') as it is particularly irregular. Notice that the imperative ('come!') follows an entirely different pattern to the main verb.

	Present/ future	Past	Imperative ('come!')
ána (I)	**ági**	**gayt**	
ínta (you, *masc.*)	**tíigi**	**gayt**	**ta9áala!** (to a male)
ínti (you, *fem.*)	**tíigi**	**gáyti**	**ta9áali!** (to a female)
húwwa (he)	**yíigi**	**geh**	
híyya (she)	**tíigi**	**gat**	
íHna (we)	**níigi**	**gáyna**	
íntu (you, *pl.*)	**tíigu**	**gáytu**	**ta9áalu!** (to a group)
húmma (they)	**yíigu**	**gum**	

Ha-tíigu ímta?	When are you (*pl.*) coming?
bi-níigi kull yohm sabt.	We come every Saturday.
gum min sáa9a.	They came an hour ago.
bass samíira ma gatsh.	But Samira didn't come.
níigi nishúufak yohm ig-gúm9a ig-gáyya?	Shall we come to see you next ('the coming') Friday?
ta9áali hína yaa samíira!	Come here Samira!

Note: if you use **kull** (every) with a day of the week, **il-** is omitted: **kull yohm sabt** (every Saturday), **kull yohm khamíis** (every Thursday), etc.

Exercise 4

Can you say these in Arabic?

1 We'll come at eight o'clock.

2 My mother came yesterday.

3 Widaad is coming to see us next Friday.

4 Come here Hassan!

5 I come here every Thursday.

6 Do you *(masc.)* want to come to the club?

7 They came yesterday but I wasn't here.

8 You *(pl.)* must come now.

9 Gaber doesn't come here every Friday.

10 Come here children!

11 Why didn't you *(fem.)* come?

12 The engineer didn't come at six o'clock.

 Download additional activities using the verb yíigi/geh.

 Dialogue 2

 káanit ríHla gamíila **(Audio 2; 40)**

Hassan, Widaad, Samira and her English friend Jane are at the
restaurant trying to decide what to eat.

1	**Who orders the stuffed vine leaves?**
2	**Who orders the okra?**
3	**Who orders the fish**

WIDÁAD:	samíira, Ha-ti'akkíli SaHbítik eh?
SAMÍIRA:	*What do you want to eat, Jane?*
JANE:	*Something typically Egyptian!*
GÁABIR:	uTlubú lhaa muluukhíyya bil-aráanib.
WIDÁAD:	la' yaa gáabir, mish ma9'úul. il-9iyáal il-ingilíiz bi-yirábbu l-aráanib fil-buyúut zayy il-'óTaT wik-kiláab wil-Haagáat di 9andína.
SAMÍIRA:	Ha-ti'úul 9aláyna mutawaHHishíin law 'úlna láhaa Ha-ni'akkílik árnab.
WIDÁAD:	núTlub láhaa wára 9ínab másalan?

SAMÍIRA:	aah, wára 9ínab yíb'a gamíil. *Jane, have you tried stuffed vine leaves?*
JANE:	*Yes! Dolmades! We had it in Greece. It was good!*
SAMÍIRA:	OK. khalláaS. núTlub láhaa wára 9ínab má9a firáakh másalan aw láHma banáyh.
HÁSAN:	má9a kabáab áHsan 9alasháan ik-kabáab máSri aSíil.
WIDÁAD:	áywa, SaHH. w-ínti yaa samíira, Ha-táakli eh?
SAMÍIRA:	walláahi ána miHtáara bayn il-bámya wi-bayn il-bisílla.
WIDÁAD:	ána shakhSáyyan HáTlub bámya.
SAMÍIRA:	Tab khalláaS. áTlub ána l-bisílla, w-ána adawwá'ik bisillíti, w-ínti tidawwa'íini bamyítik!
GÁABIR:	ána miHtáar yaa gamáa9a. áakul sámak má'li walla firáakh?
HÁSAN:	íHna múmkin niná''i sámaka kibíira wi-ni'símhaa.
GÁABIR:	máashi. wi-Ha-núTlub gambári Táb9an.
HÁSAN:	Táb9an.
WIDÁAD:	huh? gaahzíin yaa gamáa9a núTlub?
HÁSAN/GÁABIR:	gaahzíin.
GÁABIR:	yaa metr. yaa ábu s-su9úud ... íHna gaahzíin.
WIDAAD:	*Samira ... What are you going to feed your friend?*
SAMIRA:	*What do you want to eat, Jane?*
JANE:	*Something typically Egyptian!*
GABER:	*Order (for) her molokheyya with rabbit.*
WIDAAD:	*No Gaber, (that's) not reasonable. English kids keep rabbits in their houses like cats and dogs and those kind of things we have.*
SAMIRA:	*She'll call us savages if we tell her 'we're going to give you a rabbit to eat'.*
WIDAAD:	*Let's order stuffed vine leaves for her, for example.*
SAMIRA:	*Yes, stuffed vine leaves would be nice. Jane, have you tried stuffed vine leaves?*
JANE:	*Yes! Dolmades! We had it in Greece. It was good!*
SAMIRA:	*OK. Decided. We'll order her stuffed vine leaves with chicken, for example, or pan-fried meat.*
HASSAN:	*With kebab is better because kebab is authentic Egyptian.*
WIDAAD:	*Yes, right. And you Samira, what are you going to eat?*
SAMIRA:	*Really I'm wavering between the okra and the peas.*
WIDAAD:	*Personally, I'm going to order the okra.*

SAMIRA:	OK, that settles it. I'll order the peas and I'll give you a taste of my peas, and you give me a taste of your okra!
GABER:	I'm wavering, everyone. Shall I eat the fried fish or the chicken?
HASSAN:	We can choose a large fish and share it.
GABER:	OK. And we'll order prawns of course.
HASSAN:	Of course.
WIDAAD:	So, is everyone ready to order?
HASSAN/GABER:	Ready.
GABER:	Maître d'! Abu S-Su'ud! We're ready.

Vocabulary

yi'ákkil/ákkil	to give (someone) food/to feed
yúTlub/Tálab	to order/to ask for; **utlubú lhaa** = order (pl.) for her
9áyyil (pl. 9iyáal)	kid
yirábbi/rábba	to keep (pets)/to breed/to bring up
yi'úul/'aal (9ála)	to say (of someone or something)
mutawáHHish (pl. mutawaHHishíin)	savage
máshwi (fem. mashwíyya)	grilled
másalan	for example
banáyh	pan fried; escalope
aSíil	authentic; original
walláahi	really (lit. 'by God')
miHtáar (bayn)	wavering (between)/undecided
bisílla	peas
shakhSáyyan	personally; from **shakhS** (person)
yidáwwa'/dáwwa	to give (someone) a taste
yaa gamáa9a	everyone/'you lot'
má'li (fem. ma'líyya)	fried
yiná''i/ná''a	to choose
yí'sim/'ásam	to share/to split
gambári	prawns
gáahiz (fem. gáahza; pl. gaahzíin)	ready

Cultural point

Egyptian cooking

A typical Egyptian restaurant meal consists of **láHma** (meat) or **sámak** (fish) – grilled, fried or in a sauce with vegetables. This is eaten with rice and bread.

The meat and vegetable dishes are often referred to by just the name of the vegetable, e.g. **bámya** (okra), **bisílla** (peas), **muluukhíyya** (a green, spinach-type vegetable). If you want the vegetables without the meat (usually lamb) you need to specify **min ghayr láHma** ('without meat').

The main course is usually preceded by **sálaTit TaHíina** (tahini dip), **sálaTa báladi** (local salad of finely chopped tomato, peppers and onions), **Túrshi** (pickles) and **9aysh** (bread).

Download some more information about Egyptian cooking.

Exercise 5 (Audio 2; 40)

Without looking at the transcript, listen again to Dialogue 2 and fill in the following chart, as in the example:

	kebab	chicken	fish	prawns	peas	okra	vine leaves
Jane		✔					✔
Samira							
Widaad							
Gaber							
Hassan							

Exercise 6

Now say what you're going to order as in the example:

chicken with salad ➔ **HáTlub firáakh má9a sálaTa.**

1 chicken with rice

2 okra with bread

3 grilled prawns

4 kebab with salad

5 chicken with peas

6 fried fish and prawns

7 molokheyya with rabbit

8 vine leaves and escalope

Language point

More about forms of the verb

■ Form II

Form II is one of the most common forms in Egyptian colloquial Arabic.
The dialogues in this unit have several examples of this type of verb.
Notice how the meaning becomes transitive when the root is put
into the form II pattern:

form I	yú'9ud/'á9ad	to sit (root = '/9/d)
form II	yi'á99ad/á99ad	to seat (someone else)

láazim nú'9ud 9ála n-niil.	We must sit overlooking the Nile.
láazim ni'a99ádhum 9ála n-niil.	We must seat them overlooking the Nile.

form I	yáakul/kal	to eat (root = '/k/l)
form II	yi'ákkil/ákkil	to feed (someone else)

akálti eh?	What did you *(fem.)* eat?
akkílti SaHbítik eh?	What did you *(fem.)* feed your friend?

Note: Be careful to pronounce the doubled middle root fully to
distinguish the verb from the basic form, particularly in the past tense.
Notice also how the stress can move when endings are added to the
core verb: **ákkil** (he fed) but **akkílti** (you fed); **ni'á99ad** (we seat) but
ni'a99ádhum (we seat them).

Other similar examples of verbs becoming transitive in form II are:

form I	yílbis/líbis	to dress yourself (root = l/b/s)
form II	yilábbis/lábbis	to dress someone else

form I	yífham/fíhim	to understand (root = f/h/m)
form II	yifáhhim/fáhhim	to explain ('make understand')

labbíst bínti fustáanhaa ig-gidíid.	I dressed my daughter in her new dress.

láazim tifahhímni.	You must *(masc.)* explain to me.
láazim tifahhimíini.	You must *(fem.)* explain to me.

■ Hollow verbs in the forms

Hollow verbs that have either the letter **waaw** or **yaa** as the middle
root letter are irregular in the basic form I (see page 199). However, in
form II they behave regularly and the doubled middle root reappears:

form I	yidúu'/daa'	to taste (root = **d/w/'**)
form II	yidáwwa'/dáwwa'	to give someone a taste

daa' il-bámya.	He tasted the okra.
dawwá'ni il-bámya.	He gave me a taste of the okra.

Hollow verbs also behave regularly in forms III, V and VI.

form III	yiHáawil/Háawil	to try/to attempt (root = **H/w/l**)
form V	yitgáwwiz/itgáwwiz	to get married (root = **g/w/z**)
form VI	yitDáayi'/itDáayi'	to get annoyed (root = **D/y/'**)

However, in the other forms of the verb, hollow verbs tend to display
their characteristic long vowel.

form VIII	yikhtáar/ikhtáar	to choose (root = **kh/y/r**)
form X	yistafíid/istafáad	to benefit (root = **f/w/d**)

Download additional information about forms of the verb.

Exercise 7

Can you say what these verbs mean, as in the example?

Haawílna ➜ we tried/we attempted

1 **baHáawil**

2 **labbísit**

3 **afahhímuh**

4 **itgawwízti**

5 **akkílna**

6 (ínta) **tikhtáar**

7 **istafáad**

8 'a99adúni

9 Ha-nidawwá'ik

10 bi-yitDáayi'

Exercise 8

Now choose one of the verbs from Exercise 7 to complete each sentence or question.

1 kunt fil-máT9am da wi- _____ ganb ish-shibbáak.

2 il-mudárris _____ láma shaaf iS-Súura.

3 ána láazim _____ il-film da.

4 samíira! ínti _____ áHmad ímta?

5 ána _____ akhállas ish-shughl.

6 ta9áali 9andína yohm ig-gúm9a wi- _____ ik-kabáab il-aSíil.

7 Hagíib lak 'amíiS ábyaD wi-'amíiS ázra' w-inta _____ .

8 abúhum _____ min ziyáarit il-bank

9 díina _____ bínthaa il-fustáan il-áSfar.

10 fil-Háfla _____ iD-duyúuf ruzz wi-sámak wi-gambári.

Exercise 9 (Audio 2; 41)

Imagine you are being taken to a restaurant in Cairo by some Egyptian friends. Of course, you can do better than Jane and discuss what you'd like to eat in Arabic! Look at the list in Exercise 5 and think about what you would like to order and then follow the prompts on the recording.

The final speaking exercise in this unit is a little different from other similar exercises since there is no correct answer. Just try to join in the conversation in the pauses using the language you have learnt so far.

Learning with a friend or in a class?
Download ideas to practise reserving tables and ordering food.

The Arabic script

Reading menus

Now that you have the basic Arabic script and numbers, you should be able to get the gist of menus and other simple lists and signs.

Exercise 10

Look at the menu below and see if you can work out how much the following cost:

1 stuffed vine leaves   5 molokheyya

2 okra   6 fried chicken

3 prawns   7 cola

4 fish with rice   8 lemon juice

Unit Fifteen
muráaga9a
Review

This final review gives you the chance to consolidate what you have learnt in this course, particularly Units 9–14. If you have difficulty completing one of these review exercises, go back to the unit that deals with that language point and re-read the explanations and dialogues. You will also find some tips on continuing your study of Egyptian Arabic.

Exercise 1

Fill in the gaps in this verb table.

Present	Past	English
_____	raaH	_____
yí9mil	_____	_____
_____	sáafir	_____
yáakul	_____	_____
_____	_____	to see
yíSHa	_____	_____
_____	_____	to come
_____	kaan	_____
yi'ákkil	_____	_____
_____	_____	to enjoy
yitmárran	_____	_____
_____	Háawil	_____
_____	_____	to consume
_____	wíSil	_____

Exercise 2

What day and time is it?

Friday → **yohm ig-gúm9a is-sáa9a taláata.**

1 Monday   5 Sunday

2 Thursday   6 Tuesday

3 Friday   7 Wednesday

4 Saturday   8 Next Friday

 Exercise 3

Can you say these in Arabic?

1 On Sunday I travelled to my grandfather's house by car.

2 We usually feed the horse at six o'clock.

3 Did you enjoy the holiday, children?

4 The town was quiet and beautiful.

5 I wake up every day at half past seven.

6 My (paternal) aunt will try to come on Tuesday.

7 Hassan trained for three hours in the club on Thursday.

8 The plane will arrive on Saturday at twenty past two.

9 They didn't see the restaurant next to the station.

10 What will you (*fem.*) do next Friday?

Exercise 4 (Audio 2; 42)

Listen to Gaber talking to a friend about a trip he took recently to the village where his grandparents live. Decide if the sentences below are true or false.

1 His grandfather's house is in a big city.

2 Gaber travelled there by train.

3 His grandparents have chickens, ducks and a horse.

4 The horse is called Mansour.

5 Gaber still rides the horse.

6 The grandparents' house was always quiet in the past.

7 Now the house is full of people.

8 The family tries to visit for feast days and special occasions.

Exercise 5

Try to match the Arabic phrases from the conversation to their English equivalents, for example 1e. Then listen again Exercise 4.

1	**mish zayy zamáan**	a	full of people
2	**ás-hal wi-ásra9**	b	horse riding
3	**il-a9yáad**	c	special occasions
4	**bálad sughayyára**	d	there's only ('there's nothing except')
5	**malyáan naas**	e	not like the past
6	**bi-yíSHu bádri**	f	a small village
7	**ma fiish ghayr**	g	the chickens and the ducks
8	**rukúub il-khayl**	h	whose name is Mansour
9	**il-munaasbáat is-sa9íida**	i	their life is simple
10	**il-firáakh wil-baTT**	j	they wake up early
11	**Hayáathum basíiTa**	k	easier and faster
12	**ílli ísmuh manSúur**	k	feast days

Exercise 6

Make these sentences and questions negative, as in the example.

> baHíbb ik-kúura. → ma baHíbbish ik-kúura.

1 áHmad bi-yiHíbb il-'iráaya.

2 rúHti il-bank leh?

3 láazim núkhrug is-sáa9a taláata.

4 húmma naymíin dilwá'ti.

5 Ha-yikúun fiih akl fil-Háfla.

6 il-wiláad inbásTu imbáariH?

7 ána basáafir aswáan fish-shíta.

8 fiih masharíib fit-taláaga.

9 samíira ríg9it min il-madrása.

10 khúdu áwwil sháari9 9ála l-yimíin.

Exercise 7

Can you remember what these words mean and give their plurals?

1 mátHaf   11 burg

2 agáaza   12 ghayT

3 kullíiya   13 náadi

4 muhándis   14 bank

5 shahr   15 ríHla

6 9imáara   16 mádkhal

7 bayt   17 madrása

8 maHáTTa   18 shá"a

9 film   19 fawg

10 HuSáan   20 agnábi

Exercise 8 (Audio 2; 43)

Now it's your turn to talk. A friend is asking you about a trip you've recently taken. Follow the prompts on the audio and answer her questions.

Exercise 9

You are directing people to places around town. Look at the map below and direct them to the correct location. Take care to use the appropriate instruction depending on whether you are talking to a male, a female or a group of people. (You'll find some example answers in the key, but your may vary slightly.)

1 Direct a man to the bank.
2 Direct a woman to the train station.
3 Direct a group to the cinema (next to the museum).
4 Direct a man to the hospital.
5 Direct a woman to the tower.
6 Direct a group to the airport.
7 Direct a man to the bridge.
8 Direct a group to the bus station (opposite the bank).

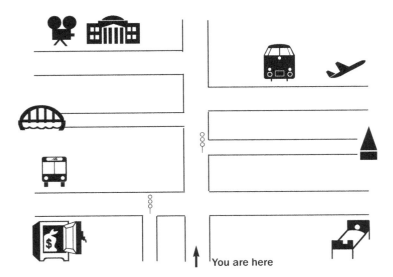

You are here

Exercise 10

Finally, try to talk about yourself including some detail about the following.

- your personal details (name/address/nationality, etc.)
- your family
- your occupation and where you work or study
- what you like doing in your spare time
- your daily routine
- what you did for your last holiday

Make notes and then record yourself if you can. You can play this to an Egyptian friend or teacher. If you're brave, you can post it online for comments. Try to be ambitious for this final project and include as much of the relevant vocabulary in this course as you can.

 # Hints for further study

You have now reached the end of *Colloquial Arabic of Egypt* and we hope you have enjoyed the course.

A visit to Egypt is obviously the best method of practising and improving your grasp of the language, but there are also other things you can do to help your fluency.

It is reasonably easy to find Egyptian soap operas, cartoons and films on the Internet, and some may have English subtitles. These popular programmes tend to use colloquial language, as opposed to news or current affairs which will generally be in the more formal Modern Standard Arabic.

Many large Western cities have Arabic shops and cafés where you may get a chance to practise your Egyptian Arabic. Egyptian newspapers also carry cartoons with captions in colloquial and, if you are already familiar with Standard Arabic, you can read novelists such as Naguib Mahfouz and Alaa Al-Aswany who include dialogue in colloquial.

Good luck! **HaZZ sa9íid!**

Stucture summary

This section summarizes the main grammar points in the course for easy reference.

1 Gender

All nouns are either masculine or feminine. Almost all feminine nouns end with an -a (and almost all masculine nouns do not):

fáraH *(masc.)*	wedding
rádyo *(masc.)*	radio
Súura *(fem.)*	photo/picture
kháala *(fem.)*	aunt (maternal)

The main exceptions are some feminine nouns which don't end in -a but refer to females, e.g. **umm** (mother), **bint** (daughter/girl), etc.

2 Articles

The definite article is **il**. There is no indefinite article ('a/an'):

bint	(a) girl
il-bint	the girl

If **il** follows a word ending in a vowel, the **i** is dropped, and the **l** sound elided with the preceding vowel:

ímta l-fáraH?	When's the wedding?
fiS-Sayf (= **fi** + **iS-Sayf**)	in the summer
wil-wiláad (= **wi** + **il-wiláad**)	and the children

■ Sun letters

Certain initial letters (known as *Sun letters*) cause the **l** sound of **il** to 'assimilate', for example:

Súura	(a) picture
iS-Súura	the picture
rádyo	(a) radio
ir-rádyo	the radio

The full list of Sun letters is as follows:

t, d, z, n, r, s, sh, k, S, T, D, Z, l, and sometimes g

3 Pronouns

■ Personal pronouns

ána	I
ínta	you (*masc. sing.*)
ínti	you (*fem. sing.*)
húwwa	he
híyya	she
íHna	we
íntu	you (*pl.*)
húmma	they

■ Attached pronouns

The attached pronouns can change slightly depending on whether the word they are attached to originally ends in a consonant or a vowel:

	After consonant	Example (**wiláad**)	After vowel	Example (**ábu**)
my	-i	wiláadi	-ya	abúya
your (*masc.*)	-ak	wiláadak	-k	abúk
your (*fem.*)	-ik	wiláadik	-ki	abúki
his	-uh	wiláaduh	-h	abúh
her	-haa	wiláadhaa	-haa	abúhaa
our	-na	wiláadna	-na	abúna
your (*pl.*)	-ku	wiláadku	-ku	abúku
their	-hum	wiláadhum	-hum	abúhum

When an attached pronoun is added to a feminine noun, the feminine ending -a usually changes to -t if the attached pronoun begins with a vowel, or to -it if the attached pronoun begins with a consonant:

Súura picture → **Súrtak** your *(masc.)* picture
→ **Suurítna** our picture

kháala (maternal) aunt → **khálti** my aunt
→ **khaalíthum** their aunt

bitáa9/bitáa9it (belonging to) can also be used with the attached pronouns:

ir-rádyo bitáa9i   the radio belonging to me;
                            i.e. my radio

iS-Súura bitaa9íthaa   the picture belonging to her;
                            i.e. her picture

The equivalent of the English verb 'to have' is expressed by using the word **9and** and the appropriate attached pronoun:

9ándi   I have
9ándak   you *(masc.)* have
9ándik   you *(fem.)* have
9ánduh   he has
9andáhaa   she has
9andína   we have
9andúku   you *(pl.)* have
9andúhum   they have

The attached pronouns can also be used with verbs. The only change is that -i ('my') changes to -ni ('me') on the end of a verb:

maHmúud záarni imbáariH.   Mahmoud visited me yesterday.

4 Plurals

Arabic plurals are divided into simple external endings and internal plurals that have to be learnt individually.

■ External plural -íin (only used for people)

   muhándis (teacher) → *pl.* muhandisíin

   máSri (Egyptian) → *pl.* maSriyyíin

■ External plural -áat

   banTalóhn (trousers) → *pl.* banTalohnáat

   agáaza (holiday/vacation) → *pl.* agazáat

■ Internal plural $aC^1C^2\acute{a}aC^3$

   SáaHib (friend) → *pl.* aS-Háab

   fawg (group) → *pl.* afwáag

■ Internal plural $C^1uC^2\acute{u}uC^3$

   bank (bank) → *pl.* bunúuk

   bayt (house) → *pl.* buyúut

■ Internal plural $C^1iC^2\acute{a}aC^3$

   kalb (dog) → *pl.* kiláab

   gamal (camel) → *pl.* gimáal

■ Internal plural $C^1\acute{i}C^2aC^3$

   bádla (suit) → *pl.* bídal

   gázma (shoe) → *pl.* gízam

■ Internal plural $maC^1\acute{a}aC^2iC^3$ (nouns of place)

   mátHaf (museum) → *pl.* matáaHif

   madrása (school) → *pl.* madáaris

■ Other internal plurals

Tába' (plate) ➜ *pl.* Tubáa'

su'áal (question) ➜ *pl.* as'íla

shóhka (fork) ➜ *pl.* shúwak

óhDa (room) ➜ *pl.* ówaD

óTTa (cat) ➜ *pl.* óTaT

raghíif (loaf) ➜ *pl.* raghífa

HuSáan (horse) ➜ *pl.* HiSína

'amíiS (shirt) ➜ *pl.* 'umSáan

fustáan (dress) ➜ *pl.* fasatíin

náadi (club) ➜ *pl.* nawáadi

siríir (bed) ➜ *pl.* saráayir

makáan (place/location) ➜ *pl.* amáakin

In general, all non-human plurals (objects, ideas, etc.) are considered *grammatically feminine singular*. Non-human plurals are referred to using:

1. *feminine singular pronouns* (híyya/di)

il-gízam di bitáa9tak?   Are these your shoes?

áywah bitáa9ti.   Yes, they're mine.

2. *feminine singular adjectival endings* (-a)

il-makáatib naDíifa.   The desks are clean.

kull il-madáaris bi9íida 9an   All the schools are far from
baytína.   our house.

3. *feminine singular personal/possessive endings* (-haa)

il-'umSáan di kibíira.   These shirts are big.
ána 9áawiz áSghar mínhaa.   I want smaller ones
                                 (*lit.* 'smaller than them').

4. *feminine singular verbs* (**ti-/tu-**):

| il-Huguuzáat bi-tizíid Hawáali | Bookings increase by about |
| 9ishríin fil-míyya kull sána. | 20 per cent every year. |

The plural forms are generally reserved for people:

5 Adjectives

Adjectives come *after* the noun and change according to the gender and number of what they are describing:

| bayt kibíir | a large house *(masc.)* |
| kabíina kibíira | a large cabin *(fem.)* |

Adjectives referring to people can often (but not always) be made plural by adding the external plural **-íin**:

maHámmad mawgúud?	Is Mohammed present/available?
widáad mawgúuda?	Is Widaad present/available?
il-wiláad mabsuuTíin?	Are the children happy?

To say, 'the new bed', rather than 'the bed is new', you need to add **il-** to the adjective as well as to the noun:

| is-siríir gidíid. | The bed is new. |
| is-siríir ig-gidíid | the new bed |

| il-9arabíyya 'adíima. | The car is old. |
| il-9arabíyya il-'adíima | the old car |

Some adjectives don't usually take the feminine ending by convention:

Sáyfi	for summer
shítwi	for winter
Haríimi	for ladies
rigáali	for men
búnni	brown
banafsígi	purple
laymúuni	lemon(y)

■ Colours

The basic colours have their own special feminine form.
However, the basic colours have a different feminine form which should be used when describing a feminine noun. Practice your pronunciation by repeating the models on the recording:

masculine	feminine	translation
áSfar	Sáfra	yellow
ázra'	zár'a	blue
áHmar	Hámra	red
ákhDar	kháDra	green
ábyaD	báyDa	white
íswid	sóhda	black

■ Comparitives and superlatives

Adjective	Comparative
kibíir (big)	ákbar (bigger/older for people)
gamíil (beautiful)	ágmal (more beautiful)
Sugháyyar (small)	áSghar (smaller/younger)
'uráyyib (near)	á'rab (nearer)
bi9íid (far)	áb9ad (further)
'adíim (old)	á'dam (older for things)
'uSáyyar (short)	á'Sar (shorter)
Tawíil (tall/long)	áTwal (taller/longer)
rufáyya9 (thin)	árfa9 (thinner)
tikhíin (fat)	átkhan (fatter)
Hílw (nice/sweet)	áHla (nicer/sweeter)
lazíiz (delicious)	alázz (more delicious)
muhímm (important)	ahámm (more important)
gidíid (new)	ágdad (newer)

And the important irregular comparative:

kwáyyis (good)	áHsan (better)

The equivalent in Arabic to the English word 'than' (as in 'thinner than') is **min**, which literally means 'from':

bínti áTwal min íbni.	My daughter is taller than my son.
faránsa á'rab min il-maksíik.	France is nearer than Mexico.

You can add attached pronouns to the word **min** to produce the meaning 'than me/you/him', etc.):

ána áTwal mínn<u>ak</u>.	I'm taller than <u>you</u>.
híyya ákbar mínn<u>i</u>.	She's older than <u>me</u>.

To give the meaning of 'much', **bi-kitíir** ('by a lot') is added at the end of the comparison:

il-9arabíyya di ághla bi-kitíir.	This car is much more expensive.

To express the superlative ('the ...est/the most ...'), simply add the comparative in front of the thing being described, or use **il-**:

ahámm(a) Háaga	the most important thing
ákbar kabíina	the biggest cabin

6 Numbers

number	translation
wáaHid	one
itnáyn	two
taláata	three
arbá9a	four
khámsa	five
sítta	six
sáb9a	seven
tamánya	eight
tís9a	nine
9áshara	ten
Hidáashar	eleven
itnáashar	twelve
talatáashar	thirteen

arba9táashar	fourteen
khamastáashar	fifteen
sittáashar	sixteen
saba9táashar	seventeen
tamantáashar	eighteen
tisa9táashar	nineteen
9ishríin	twenty
talatíin	thirty
arba9íin	forty
khamsíin	fifty
sittíin	sixty
sab9íin	seventy
tamaníin	eighty
tis9íin	ninety
míyya	one thousand
mitáyn	two hundred
tultumíyya	three hundred
rub9umíyya	four hundred
khumsumíyya	five hundred
suttumíyya	six hundred
sub9umíyya	seven hundred
tumnumíyya	eight hundred
tis9umíyya	nine hundred
alf	one thousand
alfáyn	two thousand
milyóhn	one million

wi/w- ('and') is used to join units and tens, with the units coming first:

wáaHid wi-9ishríin	twenty-one (*lit.* 'one and twenty')
sáb9a wi-tamaníin	eighty-seven
míyya wi-9áshara	one hundred and ten
tis9umíyya khámsa wi-9ishríin	nine hundred and twenty-five

All numbers above ten are followed by a singular noun:

sittáashar lohn	sixteen colours
khámsa w-arba9íin bint	forty-five girls

A shorter form of the numbers 3–10 are used in front of a noun:

árba9 'umSáan	four shirts
tálat galaalíib	three galabeyyas
táman mudarrisíin	eight teachers

The numbers 3–10 are followed by a plural noun. From 11 upwards the number is followed by a *singular* noun:

khámas 'umSáan	five shirts
sába9 wiláad	seven children
Hidáashar 'amíiS	eleven shirts (*lit.* 'shirt')
khamsíin raghíif	fifty loaves (*lit.* 'loaf')

■ The dual

Two items are usually expressed by using a special dual ending: **-áyn**. If the singular word ends with the feminine **-a** this changes to **-t** when the dual ending is added (or **-it** after two consonants):

siríir	a bed
siriiráyn	two beds
tufáaHa	an apple
tuffaaHtáyn	two apples

7 Demonstratives

Egyptian Arabic makes no distinction between 'this' and 'that', or 'these' and 'those' (*demonstratives*). However, the demonstratives do change depending on the gender and number of what they refer to: **da** for a masculine word, **di** for a feminine word and **duul** for plurals:

da kháali.	This/That [is] my uncle.
di Súura.	This/That [is a] picture.

miin duul?	Who [are] these/those?

If you want to say the equivalent of 'this/that wedding' (rather than 'this/that is a wedding'), you need to make the noun definite by adding il and then add da/di/duul *after* the combination:

il-fáraH da	that wedding (*lit.* 'the wedding that')
iS-Súura di	this picture ('the picture this')
il-wiláad duul	those children ('the children those')

8 Construct phrases (iDáafa)

A construct phrase, or iDáafa, is made by putting two nouns or more directly together:

ábu widáad	father of Widaad/Widaad's father
sandawítsh Ta9míyya	(a) falafel sandwich ('sandwich [of] falafel')
Tába' bilíila	(a) bowl of sweet porridge

The feminine ending -a changes to -it when the noun is first in a construct phrase:

sálaTit sabáanikh	spinach salad
Súurit bínti	my daughter's picture

If the construct phrase is definite (i.e. *the* bowl of porridge), then the article il- is added *only* to the second word:

Tába' il-bilíila	the bowl of porridge
Tába' il-yohm	the dish of the day
sálaTit is-sabáanikh	the spinach salad

9 Nouns of place

Arabic has a special pattern for words that decribe the place where something happens, and these are called *nouns of place*. For example, from the root kh/b/z ('baking') you get mákhbaz (bakery, 'place of baking') and from the root **s/g/d** ('kneeling in prayer') you get **másgid** (mosque, 'place of kneeling').

The pattern is to add **má-** to the root and then **a**, or less commonly **i**, between the second and third root consonants (**máC^{1}C^{2}aC^3** or **máC^{1}C^{2}iC^3**). In addition, nouns of place sometimes include the feminine ending **-a**, for example **madrása** (school, 'place of studying') from the root **d/r/s** ('studying').

There are many nouns of place and recognizing the pattern will help you build your vocabulary.

  máktab (office, place of writing) root = **k/t/b**

  máSna9 (factory, place of manufacture) root = **S/n/9**

  madrása (school, place of studying) root letters = **d/r/s**

  máT9am (restaurant, place of eating) root = **T/9/m**

The plural pattern for most nouns of place is **maC^{1}áaC^{2}iC^3**, e.g.

  mákhbaz ➜ **makháabiz** (bakeries)

  madrása ➜ **madáaris** (schools)

10 Sentences/questions without verbs

There is no equivalent of the English 'is', 'am' or 'are' (the verb 'to be') in Arabic. So you can make simple sentences and questions without any verb:

  ána min buur sa9íid.   I [am] from Port Said.

  híyya samîira.   She [is] Samira.

  ínta kamáal?   [Are] you *(masc.)* Kamal?

  húwwa min aswáan.   He [is] from Aswan.

  ínti min maSr?   [Are] you *(fem.)* from Egypt?

The position of question words, such as **miin?** (who?), **fayn?** (where?) or **ímta?** (when?), is flexible and they are often put at the end of the question:

| miin da?/da miin? | Who's that? |
| fayn iS-Súura di?/
iS-Súura di fayn? | Where's this picture [taken]? |

■ Negative

mish (also pronounced **mush**) means 'not' and is used to make simple phrases and sentences negative:

| ána mish duktúur. | I'm not a doctor. |
| di mish úmmi. | That's not my mother. |

11 Want/need

The equivalent of the English 'want' is **9áawiz**, also pronounced **9áayiz**, changing to **9áwza/9áyza** in the feminine and **9awzîin/9ayzîin** in the plural.

(ána) 9áawiz	I *(masc.)* want
(ána) 9áwza	I *(fem.)* want
(íHna) 9awzîin	we want
(húwwa) 9áawiz	he wants, etc.

miHtáag ('need') works in a similar way to **9áawiz**:

(ána) miHtáag	I *(masc.)* need
(ána) miHtáaga	I *(fem.)* need
(íHna) miHtaagíin	we need

■ Negative

miHtáag and **9áawiz** are made negative with **mish**:

| mish miHtaagíin | we don't need |
| húwwa mish 9áawiz | he doesn't want |

12 Active participles

Active participles can be used to describe what is happening at the
moment (or in the near future).

Masculine	Feminine	Plural	Translation
náazil	názla	nazlíin	coming down/getting off
Táali9	Tál9a	Tal9íin	going up/heading to
láabis	lábsa	labsíin	wearing
9áarif	9árfa	9arfíin	knowing
náyim	náyma	naymíin	sleeping/asleep
SáaHi	SáHya	SaHyíin	awake
wáakil	wákla	waklíin	eating
sháarib	shárba	sharbíin	drinking

fiih khawáaga náazil.	There's a foreigner getting off.
ínta Táali9 il-míina búkra.	You're going to the port tomorrow.
il-itnáyn labsíin baraníiT.	The two [of them] are wearing hats.

You can also sometimes use active participles with **líssa** to mean
'just':

ána líssa wáakil.	I've just eaten.
íHna líssa sharbíin.	We've just had a drink.
ibrahíim líssa Táali9 il-míina.	Ibrahim has just gone [up] to the port.

■ Negative

As with other adjectives, active participles can be made negative
using **mish**:

húwwa mish láabis bádla.	He's not wearing a suit.
húmma mish nazlíin is-suu' innahárda.	They're not coming to the market today.

13 Present/future tense

The present/future tense is formed by adding prefixes and suffixes around a present stem.

■ Regular verbs

	Prefix/suffix	yíl9ab *(stem = l9ab)*
ána (I)	a-	ál9ab
ínta (you, *masc.*)	ti-	tíl9ab
ínti (you, *fem.*)	ti-/i	til9ábi
húwwa (he)	yi-	yíl9ab
híyya (she)	ti-	tíl9ab
íHna (we)	ni-	níl9ab
íntu (you, *pl.*)	ti-/u	til9ábu
húmma (they)	yi-/u	yil9ábu

	Prefix/suffix	yúkhrug *(stem = khrug)*
ána (I)	a-	ákhrug
ínta (you, *masc.*)	tu-	túkhrug
ínti (you, *fem.*)	tu-/i	tukhrúgi
húwwa (he)	yu-	yúkhrug
híyya (she)	tu-	túkhrug
íHna (we)	nu-	núkhrug
íntu (you, *pl.*)	tu-/u	tukhrúgu
húmma (they)	yu-/u	yukhrúgu

■ Irregular verbs

There are three main types of irregular verbs:

1 Verbs with the first root **hamza**.

   yáakul to eat; present stem = **áakul**

   yáakhud to take; present stem = **áakhud**

The present/future prefix is shortened to **y-, t-, n-**, etc., for example **yáakul** (he eats); **táakul** (she eats); **náakhud** (we take). There is no need to add a prefix at all for 'I': **áakul** (I eat); **áakhud** (I take).

2 Verbs with the middle root is **waaw** or **yaa** (*hollow verbs*).

   yirúuH to go; present stem = **ruuH**

   yizíid to increase; present stem = **ziid**

3 Verbs with the final root **waaw** or **yaa** (*defective verbs*).

   yíSHa to wake up; present stem = **SHa**

   yíb'a to become; present stem = **b'a**

   The basic present verb can be used as an invitation or suggestion:

táakul Ta9míyya?	Would you like to eat falafel? *(to a male)*
tirúuHi il-mátHaf?	Would you like to go to the museum? *(to a female)*
tu'9údu fil-bayt?	Would you like to stay in the house? *(to a group)*

   You can make the same verbs describe plans for the future by adding **Ha-** (or **H-** for the **ána** part of the verb):

íbni Ha-yináam ba9d il-gháda. lunch.	My son will sleep after
HarúuH in-náadi búkra.	I'll go to the club tomorrow.

■ Negative

The present is made negative by adding **ma ... -(i)sh** either side of the verb:

ma baHíbbish is-sámak.	I don't like fish.
ma nakhrúgsh yohm il-Had.	We don't go out [on] Sunday.

   The future is made negative by adding mish in front of the H(a)-:

mish Ha-yíwSal búkra.	He won't arrive tomorrow.

14 Past tense

■ Regular verbs

The past stem is formed by taking the three root letters and separating them with short vowels:

	Ending	yínzil *(to go down/get off)* *(past stem = nizil)*
ána (I)	-t	nizílt
ínta (you, *masc.*)	-t	nizílt
ínti (you, *fem.*)	-ti	nizílti
húwwa (he)	—	nízil
híyya (she)	-it	nízlit
íHna (we)	-na	nizílna
íntu (you, *pl.*)	-tu	nizíltu
húmma (they)	-u	nízlu

■ Irregular verbs

1 Verbs with the first root **hamza**.

    yáakul (to eat)   root = '/k/l   past stem = **kal**

    yáakhud (to take)   root = '/kh/d past stem = **khad**

2 Hollow verbs (with the middle root is **waaw** or **yaa**).

Hollow verbs have two past stems, a long **aa** in the middle for **húwwa**, **híyya** and **húmma**, and a short **u** or **i** for the other parts of the verb:

    yirúuH (to go)   root = r/w/H   past stem = **raaH/ruH**

    yibíi9 (to sell)   root = b/y/9   past stem = **baa9/bi9**

3 Defective verbs (with the final root **waaw** or **yaa**).

The past stem of a defective verb ends with a vowel, but it varies from verb to verb. The final vowel is also unstable and sometimes drops out or changes to **y**.

■ Negative

The past is made negative by using **ma** ... **-(i)sh**:

shírib/ma shiríbsh	he drank/he didn't drink
wiSílt/ma wiSíltish	I arrived/I didn't arrive
rígi9it/ma rigi9ítsh	she returned/she didn't return
shúfna/ma shufnáash	we saw/we didn't see

15 Modifying words

There are a number of useful words which can be used before a present verb to modify the meaning. Amongst the most common are:

■ **láazim** (have to/must)

íbni láazim yizáakir innahárda.	My son must study today.

■ **múmkin** (can/be allowed to)

múmkin nirúuH in-náadi?	Can we go to the club?

■ **il-mafrúuD** (should/supposed to)

il-mafrúuD yúkhrug dilwá'ti.	He's supposed to go out now.

■ **Darúuri** (need to)

il-wiláad Darúuri yináamu bádri.	The children need to sleep early.

Notice how the modifying words themselves don't change according to the subject, but the following verb does.

■ Negative

Modifying words are made negative with **mish**:

mish láazim á'9ud.	I don't have to sit down.
mish Darúuri túkhrug.	You don't need to go out.
mish múmkin niSTáad hína.	We can't fish here.

16 The verb 'to be': yikúun/kaan

Although the verb 'to be' (**yikúun/kaan**) is usually omitted in the present tense, it is essential in the past and the future.

húwwa ga9áan.	He's hungry.
kaan ga9áan.	He was hungry.
Ha-yikúun ga9áan.	He will be hungry.

yikúun/kaan is a hollow verb formed in a similar way to **yirúuH/raaH**:

	Present/future	Past
ána (I)	akúun	kunt
ínta (you, *masc.*)	tikúun	kunt
ínti (you, *fem.*)	tikúuni	kúnti
húwwa (he)	yikúun	kaan
híyya (she)	tikúun	káanit
íHna (we)	nikúun	kúnna
íntu (you, *pl.*)	tikúunu	kúntu
húmma (they)	yikúunu	káanu

■ After modifying words

As well as being used with **Ha-** for the future, **yikúun** is also used after modifying words such as **láazim** (have to), **múmkin** (can), and so on. Remember that you must use the appropriate form to agree with the subject.

il-bayt láazim yikúun háadi. The house must be peaceful.

iHtimáal yikúunu ga9aníin. They might be hungry.

■ As a second verb

yikúun is used as a second verb after expressions such as 'want' or 'like', again in the appropriate form to agree with the subject.

bínti 9áwza tikúun hína lámma l-wiláad yíSHu.	My daughter wants to be here when the children wake up.
ána baHíbb akúun mashghúul.	I like to be busy.

■ Before **fiih** and **9and**

kaan or **ma káansh** is used in front of standard phrases such as **fiih** ('there is/are') and **9and** ('to have') to make them refer to the past.

kaan fiih ghayTáan barsíim.	There were fields of clover.
ma kaansh fiih kull(i) da.	There wasn't all of this.
kaan 9ándi SáHba.	I had a (female) friend.
kaan fiih mu9áskar.	There was a camp.

Ha-yikúun ('will be') can be used in a similar way to refer to the future:

Ha-yikúun fiih Háfla hína búkra.	There'll be a party here tomorrow.
mish Ha-yikúun fiih akl.	There won't be any food.

17 Imperative

■ Regular and defective verbs

For regular verbs and defective verbs (ending in a vowel), the imperative is formed by taking the 'you' part of the verb and simply removing the initial **t-**.

tínzil you *(masc.)* go down ➔ **ínzil** go down! *(to a male)*

tinzíli you *(fem.)* go down ➔ **inzíli** go down! *(to a female)*

tinzílu you *(pl.)* go down ➔ **inzílu** go down! *(to a group)*

tíTla9 you *(masc.)* go up ➔ **íTla9** go up! *(to a male)*

tiTlá9i you *(fem.)* go up ➔ **íTlá9i** go up! *(to a female)*

tiTlá9u you *(pl.)* go up ➔ **íTlá9u** go up! *(to a group)*

túkhrug you *(masc.)* go out → **úkhrug** go out! *(to a male)*

tukhrúgi you *(fem.)* go out → **ukhrúgi** go out! *(to a female)*

tukhrúgu you *(pl.)* go out → **ukhrúgu** go out! *(to a group)*

tíSHa you *(masc.)* wake up → **íSHa** wake up! *(to a male)*

tíSHi you *(fem.)* wake up → **íSHi** wake up! *(to a female)*

tíSHu you *(pl.)* wake up → **íSHu** wake up! *(to a group)*

■ Other irregular verbs

For irregular verbs that have a long vowel in the middle *(hollow)* or that start with a long vowel, the initial **t-** and the following vowel are removed for the imperative:

tirúuH you *(masc.)* go → **ruuH** go! *(to a male)*

tirúuHi you *(fem.)* go → **rúuHi** go! *(to a female)*

tirúuHu you *(pl.)* go → **rúuHu** go! *(to a group)*

tibíi9 you *(masc.)* sell → **bii9** sell! *(to a male)*

tibíi9i you *(fem.)* sell → **bíi9i** sell! *(to a female)*

tibíi9u you *(pl.)* sell → **bíi9u** sell! *(to a group)*

táakhud you *(masc.)* take → **khud** take! *(to a male)*

tákhdi you *(fem.)* take → **khúdi** take! *(to a female)*

tákhdu you *(pl.)* take → **khúdu** take! *(to a group)*

■ Negative

A negative instruction is made in one of two ways:

1 Add **ma-** and **-sh** either side of the present verb:

ma tinzílsh!	don't go down! *(to a male)*
ma tukhrugísh!	don't go out! *(to a female)*
ma takhdúsh!	don't take! *(to a group)*

2 Add **baláash** in front of the present verb:

baláash tinzíl!	don't go down! *(to a male)*
baláash tukhrúgi!	don't go out! *(to a female)*
baláash tákhdu!	don't take! *(to a group)*

18 Forms of the verb

Verbs in different 'forms' with the same root consonants usually have related meanings. There are ten 'forms' altogether, including the basic verbs which are counted as the first form. Western Arabic scholars generally refer to the forms of the verb using Roman numerals, i.e. form I (basic verbs), form II, form III, form IV, etc. Form IX is very rare and form IV is uncommon in Egyptian Arabic, leaving seven significant variations.

	Present/Past	*Main features*
Form II	yikhállaS/khállaS (to finish; root **kh/l/S**)	doubling of middle root
Form III	yisáafir/sáafir (to travel; root **s/f/r**)	long **áa** after first root
Form IV	yún9ish/án9ash (to refresh; root n/9/sh)	á before first root in past
Form V	yitmárran/itmárran (to train; root **m/r/n**)	additional **t** before first root; doubling of middle root
Form VI	yit'áabil/it'áabil (to meet up; root **'/b/l**)	additional **t** before first root; long **áa** after first root
Form VII	yinbísiT/inbásaT (to enjoy; root **b/s/T**)	additional **n** before first root
Form VIII	yishtághal/ishtághal (to work; root **sh/gh/l**)	additional **t** between first and second root
Form X	yistáhlik/istáhlak (to consume; root **h/l/k**)	additional **st** before first root

Certain meanings are associated with each form, although these are not always obvious in individual verbs. Here is a some other meaning patterns that you may find useful:

Form	Meaning patterns
Form II	• carrying out an action on someone/ something else • doing something intensely or repeatedly
Form III	• trying to do something • doing something with someone else
Form V	• doing something to or for yourself; (reflexive of form II)
Form VI	• doing something together/collaborating in doing something
Form VII	• doing something to or for yourself; (reflexive of form I)
Form VIII	• similar to form VII
Form X	• asking to do something • considering something/someone to be

There are usually two to four verb forms that are possible with a particular root, but there may be up to five or six, or indeed none at all.

■ Active participles

Active participles can be formed from the forms of the verb by using the prefix **mu-** (or sometimes **mi-**) with the present tense pattern. These active participles have the meaning of doing something, and may also be used for the person who carries out the action, e.g.

yishághghal (to operate, form II) ➔ **mishághghal** operating

yisáafir (to travel, form III) ➔ **musáafir** travelling/traveller

yistáhlik (to consume, form X) ➔ **mustáhlik** consuming/consumer

19 Relative clauses

Arabic only uses the word **ílli** ('who/which') when referring to a definite noun (e.g. 'the girl'). When the meaning is indefinite (e.g. 'a girl') **ílli** is omitted:

ána shuft <u>il-bint ílli káanit</u> rákba HuSáan.
I saw <u>the girl who was</u> riding a horse.

ána shuft <u>bint káanit</u> rákba HuSáan.
I saw <u>a girl who was</u> riding a horse.

Arabic script supplement

This section gives the dialogues and other listening texts in the Arabic script.

If you are already familiar with the script from previous knowledge of Standard Arabic, or other Arabic-script languages such as Farsi or Urdu, you may prefer to read the dialogues in this form. But be aware that the colloquial language does not have hard-and-fast 'spelling' rules and you may see some words spelt differently in other contexts.

Alternatively, you may want to complete *Colloquial Arabic of Egypt* using the transliteration and then come back to this section at the end when you have completed the script sections included in each unit. You can compare the Arabic script to the transliterated version to help you become familiar with the Arabic letters and how they join.

Unit 1

Dialogue 1

— صباح الخير يا طنت.

— أهلا يا حسن. إزيك يابني؟

— الحمد لله. جابر صاحي؟

— أيوه، من بدري.

Dialogue 2

— ضيف رقم ١... اسمك إيه؟

— أنا اسمي منى. أنا من اسكندرية.

— أهلا منى. ضيف ٢... اسمك إيه؟

— أنا اسمي كمال. أنا من أسوان.

— ضيف ٣؟

— وأنا سميرة. أنا من بور سعيد.

Dialogue 3

— أهلا وسهلا يا مدام. اسم حضرتك؟

— ستانلي.

— ستانلي؟ حضرتك من اسكندرية؟!

— لا، لا. أنا من ليفربول. أنا انجليزية!

— اتفضلي. ترابيزة خمسة.

Exercise 7

— صباح الخير يا أستاذ.

— صباح النور.

— أنا وداد من النيل للسياحة. اسم حضرتك محمود أمين؟

— محمد أمين. أنا اسمي محمد أمين.

— أيوه محمد أمين – آسفة. أهلا وسهلا.

— أهلا بيكي.

— حضرتك من اسكندرية؟

— أيوه. وأنتي؟

— أنا من الجيزة.

— آه الجيزة...

Exercise 10

— أهلا، أنا اسمي ريتا ستانلي. أنا إنجليزية. أنا من ليفربول.

Unit 2

Dialogue 1

— يا حسن! تعال! أختك في الراديو!

— أختي؟

— بسرعة. قول لأبوك تعال!

— بابا! بابا! تعال اسمع بنتك في الراديو.

— بنتي؟ هات الراديو هنا يا حسن يابني.

— لا. احنا هنا! تعال أنت للراديو!

Exercise 6

— أنا اسمي سميرة وأنا من بور سعيد.
أخويا اسمه حسن وأمي اسمها ليلى.
بابا... أبويا... اسمه عثمان.

Dialogue 2

— مين دي يا جابر؟

— دي خطيبتي، وداد.

— وامتى الفرح إن شاء الله؟

— الفرح في الصيف.

— وده مين؟

— ده خالي أمين بتاع استراليا

— والصورة دي فين يا جابر؟

— شرم الشيخ.

Unit 3

Dialogue 1

— تشرب شاي يابني؟

— لا شكرا يا طنت. لسه شارب.

— تاكل طبق بليلة؟

— بليلة؟ أنا أموت في البليلة!

— طيب اقعد يابني!

Dialogue 2

— تشربي إيه حضرتك؟ عصير؟ كولا؟ كركديه؟

— ميه من فضلك. طبق اليوم إيه؟

— طبق اليوم كباب وكفتة. وعندنا ورق عنب، سبانخ، اومليت.
حضرتك تحبي مصري؟

— أيوه. هـات لي الكبـاب وسلطة.

— واحد كبـاب وسلطة!

Exercise 8

— تشربي إيه حضرتك؟ عصير؟ كولا؟ كركديه؟

— عصير ليمون من فضلك.

— وحضرتك تشرب إيه؟

— قزازة كولا.

— عصير وكولا...تاكلي إيه يا آنسة؟

— هـات لي بـامية ورز.

— وحضرتك؟

— سبانخ وسلطة من فضلك.

— واحد بامية ورز وواحد سبانخ وسلطة!

Dialogue 3

— اسم حضرتك إيه يا مدام؟

— اسمي زينب سرحان.

— وحضرتك بتشتغلي إيه؟

— أنا مدرسة — مدرسة كيميا.

— واسم حضرتك إيه يا أستاذ؟

— أنا الدكتور أحمد منير.

— وحضرتك بتشتغل هنا في مصر؟

— لا مش هنا. أنا دكتور في فرنسا.

— وحضرتك يا آنسة؟

— أنا اسمي سامية نور وأنا مضيفة في مصر للطيران.

Unit 4

Dialogue 1

— آلو؟ النيل للسياحة؟ محمد موجود؟

— لا، مش موجود يا فندم. معاك وداد.

— أهلا وداد. فيه كابينة بين الأقصر وأسوان؟

— أيوه، فيه كابينة لوكس... كبيرة.

— فيها كم سرير؟

— سريرين فوق بعض وتليفزيون جنب الباب.

— وفيها كم شباك؟

— شباك واحد. بين السرير والترابيزة.

Exercise 4

— أهلاً! أنا فين؟ أنا قدام الباب.

— أنا جنب الشباك.

— أنا تحت السرير.

— أنا وراء الترابيزة.

— أنا تحت البورتريه.

— أنا بين الراديو والتليفزيون.

— أنا على السرير.

— أنا قدام الترابيزة.

— أنا على الترابيزة.

Dialogue 2

— العربية جديدة؟ مبروك عليك!

— الله يبارك فيك.

— فيها تكييف؟

— لا، ما فيهاش. بس فيها سي دي.

— سي دي؟ فين؟

— أهو، تحت الراديو.

— الكرسي مريح. ده جلد يا جابر؟

— لا. ما فيش في الموديل ده جلد.

— أمال؟

— الكبيرة، الألفين سي سي فيها جلد وتكييف.

— طيب. يللا بينا.

Exercise 12

— أوضة النوم بتاعتي كبيرة. فيها شباك كبير وبلكونة. سريري
جنب الشباك وفيه بورتريه لماما فوق السرير. فيها ترابيزة
وكرسي مريح وفيه كمان ترابيزة صغيرة في البلكونة. بس
ما فيهاش تكييف.

Unit 5

Dialogue 1

— تعال معايا خان الخليلي.

— بالعربية الجديدة؟

— طبعا. عاوزين جلبية لوداد، وكنكة نحاس لأمي.

— وأنا كمان محتاج قميص أبيض للشغل.

— فكرة. وأنا برضه عاوز قمصان جديدة.

Dialogue 2

— اديني علبة جبنة رومي وربع كيلو زيتون.

— حاضر يا مدام. وحضرتك محتاجة عيش؟

— هات لي اثناشر رغيف بلدي، من فضلك.

— إيه كمان؟

— عاوزين طباق ورق وشوك بلاستك.

— ماشي.

— بكام التفاح؟

— التفاح بعشرة جنيه.

— عشرة؟ ليه؟ ده بثمانية في كل حتة.

Exercise 6

— صباح الخير. اديني نص كيلو جبنة بيضا لو سمحت.

— حاضر.

— وهات لي عشرة أرغفة شامي.

— إيه كمان؟

— عاوزين قزازة كولا كبيرة وثلاث علب عصير.

— ده كله يا بيه؟

— بكام الزيتون؟

— الربع كيلو بعشرين جنيه.

— ماشي اديني ربع كيلو من فضلك.

Dialogue 3

— مساء الخير. عاوز جلابية حريمي صيفي.

— مقاس إيه؟

— وسط. زيك انتي كده.

— الألوان عندنا أصفر لموني وأزرق فاتح وبنفسجي.

— حلوة البنفسجي. بكام دي لو سمحتي؟

— دي بمية وعشرة، والزرقا والصفرا بخمسة وتسعين.

Exercise 13

— صباح الخير. عاوز قميص شتوي.

— مقاس إيه؟

— كبير. الألوان عندكم إيه؟

— عندنا أبيض وأخضر غامق وبني.

— حلو الأخضر. بكام ده لو سمحتي؟

— ده بخمسة وثمانين.

Unit 6

Dialogue 1

— يا ابراهيم، أنت طالع المينا في بورسعيد بكرة عشان مستر
لورنس بتاع صن شاين كروز.

— شكله إيه مسترلورنس ده؟

— طويل وشعره أحمر. عينيه ملونة ولابس نظارة. استنى عند
سلم المركب.

— ماشي يا مدام وداد.

Exercise 4

— ١ الراجل ده قصير وشعره أسود. عنده شنب وودانه كبيرة
شوية.

— ٢ الست دي شعرها قصير ولابسة نظارة.

— ٣ الراجل ده طويل ورجليه طويلة كمان. هو أصلع ولكن بشنب.

— ٤ الست دي شعرها طويل وأسود. عينيها جميلة.

Exercise 5

— أيوه يا مدام. أنا طالع المطار دلوقتي، لكن شكلكم إيه؟

— أنا طويلة وشعري أسود وعينيا بني.

— وأبو حضرتك، شكله إيه؟

— هو عجوز، شعره أبيض وعنده شنب وابني طويل.
شعره أحمر وقصير.

— ماشي يامدام. استنوني عند السلم الكبير.

Dialogue 2

— يا مدام وداد، أنا عند سلم المركب. فيه خواجة نازل لابس
نظارة شمس وبدلة زرقة كحلي، ومعاه واحدة ست لابسة
فستان أخضر.

— أيوه يا ابراهيم، يعني هو مستر لورانس وللا مش هو؟

— أنا مش عارف يا مدام. شعره الأحمر مش باين عشان الاثنين
لابسين برانيط.

— طيب، عنده كام سنة يا براهيم؟

— حوالي زي أربعين خمسين كده.

— طيب يا ابراهيم... اسأله "Are you Mr Lawrence?"؟

Exercise 10

— يا ابراهيم، اسمع. أنت طالع المطار بكرة عشان سنيورا سنشين.
عندها حوالي أربعين سنة كده. شكلها طويلة ورفيعة. شعرها
إسود وقصير ولابسة نظارة . دايما لابسة جونلة طويلة وبلوزة
بيضا.

Unit 7

Dialogue 1

— احنا رايحين فرنسا في شهر العسل.

— يعني مش رايحين المكسيك؟

— لا، لغينا المكسيك لأنها بعيدة. أبعد من فرنسا بكثير.
أنا ماباحبش الطيران الطويل.

— ولا أنا. فرنسا قريبة ... أقرب من المكسيك. كده أحسن فعلا.

— وكمان الأكل في فرنسا لذيذ.

— عندك حق. الأكل اللذيذ مهم جدا.

— أهم حاجة في شهر العسل!

Dialogue 2

— بكام تذكرة الأقصر رايح جاي من فضلك؟

— بالطيارة ولا بالقطر حضرتك؟

— أرخص حاجة إيه؟

— الأوتوبيس! بس الرحلة طويلة ومش مريحة قوي.

— والطيارة؟

— الطيارة غالية، أغلى من القطر بكثير. القطر درجة أولى سعره

معقول. حضرتك عاوزة كام تذكرة؟

— ثلاثة... اثنين كبار وطفل واحد. فيه تخفيضات للأطفال؟

— أيوه الأطفال بنص السعر.

— طيب، خللينا في القطر أحسن.

Exercise 8

— بكام تذكرة أسوان رايح جاي من فضلك؟

— بالطيارة ولا بالقطر حضرتك؟

— أرخص حاجة إيه؟

— القطر بس الرحلة أطول.

— طيب، خللينا في الطيارة.

— حضرتك عاوز كام تذكرة؟

— خمسة... اثنين كبار وثلاث أطفال. فيه تخفيضات للأطفال؟

— لا ما فيش، للأسف.

Dialogue 3

— أنا باحب الكلاب. أبويا عنده ثلاث كلاب وولف.

— يا ساتر! أنا ما باحبش الكلاب. أحنا عندنا قطة سيامي.
القطط أحسن من الكلاب.

— القطط دي مالهاش فايدة.

— إزاي؟ دي مفيدة قوي. بتمسك الفيران ونظيفة زي الفل.

— فيران؟ الكلاب بتمسك حرامية، مش فيران!

Unit 8

Exercise 4

— الأوضة فيها تكييف، مافيهاش راديو لكن فيها تليفزيون بالألوان.
فيها كمان كرسي مريح بس الأوضة صغيرة والسرير مش كبير.
فيها ترابيزة جنب السرير وعليها كمبيوتر بس مش بالانترنت.

Exercise 7

— أنا عاوز كباب وسلطة خضرة.

— وتشرب إيه حضرتك؟

— هات لي عصير ليمون.

— وحضرتك؟

— عندكم بامية حلوة النهارده؟

— إن شاء الله. تحبي أجيب لحضرتك رز مع البامية؟

— أيوه، رز أبيض. وهات لي كباية كركديه.

— حاضر. والمدام؟ تحبي تاكلي إيه حضرتك؟

— فيه سبانخ يا متر؟

— لا، يا مدام مافيش سبانخ النهادة.

— طب هـات لي ورق عنب وسلطة وقزازة كولا.

Unit 9

Dialogue 1

— يا ابراهيم، اسمع... بكرة الخميس وأنت طالع المطار عشان
مستر نديم من فرع عمان.

— الساعة كام الطيارة؟

— الساعة خمسة الصبح.

— يا ساتر! بدري قوي!

— معلهش يا ابراهيم، يوم الجمعة أجازة. بس أنت مشغول من
السبت عشان الفوج الياباني.

— رايحين فين؟

— السبت رايحين الأهرام بدري حوالي الساعة ستة ونص ...
وبعد الظهر كله في المتحف المصري. الحد عندهم حجز في
مطعم فلفلة الساعة واحدة الا ربع ورايحين خان الخليلي بعد
الغدا.

— خان الخليلي؟ زحمة والمرور وحش قوي هناك!

Dialogue 2

— أنا مضيفة في مصر للطيران وساكنة في مصر الجديدة.
الساعة خمسة ونص باصحى وبآكل حاجة خفيفة وباخرج
من البيت الساعة ستة وربع. باوصل المطار الساعة سبعة
بالظبط.

الأثنين والأربع والسبت بنسافر عمان، والخميس والحد
بنسافر أسوان مرتين، مرة الصبح ومرة الظهر. الثلاث أجازة
وباروح النادي بعد الظهر حوالي الساعة خمسة بالعب باسكت
بول مع أصحابي ومع نادية بنت عمي.
الجمعة بأقعد في البيت آكل وأنام!

Exercise 11 (model answer)

— الساعة ثمانية حاخرج من البيت وحاوصل المكتب الساعة
ثمانية ونص. الساعة حداشر حاطلع المطار. عندي حجز
للغداء في مطعم النيل الساعة واحدة إلا ربع. حاروح مدرسة
مروان الساعة اثنين وثلث. حاخرج من المكتب حوالي الساعة
ستة ونص علشان العب باسكت بول مع أصحابي في النادي
الساعة سبعة وربع.

Dialogue 3

— منى، أنتي بتدرسي إيه؟
— أنا بادرس في علوم اسكندرية تخصص كيميا.
— وأنت يا كمال بتدرس إيه؟
— أنا في معهد الفنادق، وباتمرن في الشيراتون.
— عظيم. وأنتي يا سميرة؟
— أنا عايشة في بور سعيد وباحضر ماجستير لغات شرقية في
جامعة القناة.
— ما شاء الله يا سميرة. مستعدين للأسئلة يا شباب؟
— مستعدين!

Exercise 12

— أنا عايشة في بور سعيد وباحضر ماجستير لغات شرقية في
جامعة القناة. كل يوم باصحي الساعة سبعة وباشرب شاي
الساعة سبعة ونص. باخرج من البيت الساعة تمانية بأوصل
الجامعة في نص ساعة.
باقعد في مكتبة الجامعة ساعتين ثلاثة كدة وباكل سندويتش
حوالي الساعة اتناشر. بأدرّس لغات للطلاب بعد الظهر
وباروح البيت الساعة ثلاثة الا ربع. عموما باروح النادي
حوالي الساعة ستة ألعب تنس مع أصحابي.

Unit 10

Dialogue 1

— منى، أنتي هواياتك إيه؟
— أنا باحب ألعب اسكواش. أنا كابتن فريق الكلية. وكمان باحب
الموسيقى وروايات نجيب محفوظ.
— وأنت يا كمال؟ هواياتك إيه؟
— باحب ألعب كورة وأنا غاوي الانترنت. كل يوم لازم اقعد
ساعتين ثلاثة قدام الكومبيوتر. ما باخرجش من البيت قبل
ما أصبح على الكومبيوتر!
— ها! ها! وأنتي يا سميرة؟
— للأسف دلوقتي ماعنديش وقت لهوايتي – صيد السمك مع
بابا وحسن أخويا. كل يوم جمعة هما بيطلعوا الصيد وأنا
باقعد أذاكر.
— معلهش يا سميرة. بعد الماجستير ممكن تصطادي سمك البحر كله!

Dialogue 2

— شركة النيل للسياحة ناوية تفتح فرع جديد في شرم الشيخ.
الحجوزات في مكتبنا بتاع ميدان الأوبرا والحجوزات في
موقعنا على الانترنت كثير جدا وبتزيد حوالي عشرين في
المية كل سنة.
تجهيز الفرع الجديد مابياخذش وقت. مهندس الديكور بتاعنا
سريع وممكن يخلص شغله قبل ما يبتدي الموسم. أنا رايحة
شرم الشيخ وحاشوف مكان مناسب وأنا هناك.

Unit 11

Dialogue 1

— آلو؟ أيوه يا مدام، أنا ابراهيم. ده مستر لورنس عاوز ينزل
وسط البلد لوحده.
— ليه يا ابراهيم؟
— بيقول عاوز يروح ميدان التحرير عشان يزورالمتحف وبعدين
عاوز ينزل محطة رمسيس عشان يحجز في قطر الأقصر.
— المتحف والمحطة؟ أخاف ليتوه يا إبراهيم.
— ماتخافيش يا مدام. أنا حاوصفله السكة كويس.

Exercise 6

— عايز تروح السوق معايا يا جابر؟ أنا محتاج شوية حاجات.
— دلوقتي مش ممكن. المفروض أروح البنك وبعدين السفارة
الفرنساوي عشان الفيزا و وبعدين المحطة عشان أحجز لأمي.
— يا ساتر! حا تخلّص الساعة كام؟

— حوالي اتناشر واحدة كده.

— طب، خلَّص حاجتك وممكن ننزل وسط البلد بعد الظهر.

— ماشي. عاوز تروح السينما؟

— آه فكرة. نتقابل عند السينما الساعة اتنين. وأنا حاشتري سي دي من محل الموسيقى بعد الفيلم.

Dialogue 2

— حاوصفلك المتحف والمحطة منين.

الأول اطلع كوبري ستة اكتوبر وانزل بعد البرج. خلليك دوغري على الكورنيش وخد شمال عند الهيلتون حتلاقي المتحف على اليمين.

بالنسبة للمحطة خلليك في شارع رمسيس على طول لغاية الميدان نفسه. خللى بالك، مدخل المحطة بعد تاني إشارة تحت الكوبري جنب محل كبير بيبيع سندوتشات فول وطعمية اسمه أبو وردة.

Exercise 10

— البنك؟ الأول خلليك دوغري في الشارع ده وبعدين خد تالت شارع يمين والبنك على الشمال.

— المتحف؟ خدي أول شارع شمال واطلعي دوغري لغاية الإشارة. المتحف على اليمين.

— المحطة؟ اطلعي على طول لغاية الإشارة وخدي يمين. حاتلاقي المحطة على الشمال قبل الكوبري.

— عاوز السفارة الأمريكية؟ خليك دوغري في الشارع ده وبعدين خد تاني شارع شمال. السفارة على الشمال قبل السينما.

Unit 12

Dialogue 1

— ازيك يا عريس؟ انبسطت في فرنسا؟

— قوي قوي.

— وصلتوا امتى؟

— وصلنا يوم السبت.

— ووداد؟ لسة بتخاف من الطيارات؟

— أيوة، بس خدت مسكّن من الدكتور.

— فعلا؟ وعملتوا ايه هناك؟

— رحنا أماكن كتيرة – متاحف وبرج ايفيل، ونزلنا في مركب
على نهر السين – حلو النهر. شفنا كل حاجة من المركب –
الكنايس القديمة، والمباني الجميلة، تماثيل ذهب...

— وكلتوا كويس؟

— أنا كلت سمك لذيذ ومحار لكن وداد ما بتحبش السمك فكلت
لحمة وفراخ وحاجات زي كده. وطبعا جربنا الحلويات –
أحسن حلويات في الدنيا!

— يا سلام يا سيدي. وإيه كمان؟

— الناس هناك طبعا بيشربوا النبيذ الفرنساوي المشهور بس
إحنا شربنا مشاريب منعشة جدا معمولة من النعناع والرمان

— نعناع ورمان؟ ده ايه الجمال ده؟!

— أيوه، آخر جمال، بس خلاص، رجعنا دلوقتي.

Dialogue 2

— أنا أستاذ في كلية الطب، جامعة القاهرة. السنة اللي فاتت رحت إعارة في جامعة "ادنبره". سافرنا انا وعيلتي اسكتلندا في أغسطس ولقينا شقة في وسط "ادنبره"، قريبة من الجامعة. الأولاد راحوا المدرسة في سبتمبر وقعدنا هناك عشر شهور لغاية نهاية السنة الدراسية في يونيو. رجعنا مصر في يوليو. انبسطنا في "ادنبره" واحتمال نرجع تاني في المستقبل.

Exercise 10

— السنة اللي فاتت شفت الدنيا كلها! الأول سافرت لندن في يوليو وزرت عمتي هناك. بعدين لفيت أوروبا بالقطر: فرنسا في أغسطس وايطاليا في سبتمبر. انبسطت قوي في ايطاليا عشان باحب الباستا والآيس كريم! في اكتوبر خدت طيارة لنيو يورك وعملت جولة في أمريكا شهرين. ومن لوس آنجيلوس سافرت اليابان وده كان في الشتاء – في ديسمبر. من اليابان رحت الصين في يناير – بلد عظيمة – وأخيرا في مارس زرت الهند شهر بحاله ورجعت مصر آخر أبريل.

Unit 13

Dialogue 1

— ده شارع الهرم – دايما زحمة! شفت كل العربيات والمباني
والمطاعم والمحلات؟ زمان ما كانش فيه كل ده. كان فيه
غيطان برسيم ونخل وحمير. أنا فاكرة لما كنت صغيرة كان
عندي صاحبة كانت عايشة هنا جنب الترعة في بيت جميل
هادي. بس دلوقتي في مكان بيتها حاتلاقي خمس عمارات!
جدي قال لي إن في التلاتينات والأربعينات كان فيه معسكر
تبع الجيش الانجليزي، هناك في الصحراء عند أبو الهول. طبعا
الانجليز مشوا من زمان، من سنة ١٩٥٤، لكن لسة فيه
اسطبلات لغاية دلوقتي والناس تقدر تركب خيل هناك عندهم.

Dialogue 2

— احنا سافرنا الأقصر بالطيارة، وبعدين خدنا فلوكة من
الأقصر لأسوان. كانت رحلة جميلة في النيل. المراكبي طبخ
لنا سمك ورز. لما وصلنا أسوان رحنا أبو سمبل بالأوتوبيس.
السنة اللي فاتت رحنا الأقصر بتاكسي من الغردقة. خدنا
السكة اللي بتروح من سفاجا. المشوار خد له حوالي ثلاث
ساعات لكن احنا انبسطنا لأن السواق كان مشغّل شريط أغاني
أفلام زمان. أنا بأحب الأفلام القديمة أكثر من الأفلام الجديدة
لأن أفلام زمان متكلفة ومعمولة بذمة.

Exercise 13 (model)

— رحتوا فين في الأجازة السنة اللي فاتت؟

— رحنا البحر الأحمر.

— سافرتوا بالأوتوبيس؟

— لا، سافرنا شرم الشيخ بالطيارة.

— مع العيلة؟

— آه، كلهم.. مراتي والثلاث بنات.

— وعملتوا ايه هناك؟

— يعني.. اصطدنا كثير ونزلنا مرة بالمركب.

— قعدتوا في شرم الشيخ ولا رحتوا حتة تانية؟

— رحنا طابا بالأوتوبيس.

— رحلة طويلة! عملتوا ايه ثلاث ساعات؟

— فعلا المشوار خد له حوالي ثلاث ساعات لكن السواق كان مشغّل فيلم قديم.

— عظيم! يعني انبسطتوا في البحر الأحمر.

— قوي. احتمال نرجع في المستقبل.

Unit 14

Dialogue 1

— مطعم النيل، صباح الخير.

— أيوه، مطعم النيل؟

— أيوه. صباح الخير يا فندم.

— صباح النور. لو سمحت عاوزين نحجز ترابيزة لخمسة يوم الجمعة الجاية.

— تحت أمرك يا فندم. لحظة معايا من فضلك...

— الجمعة ١٦ حضرتك؟

— أيوه مظبوط. الجمعة الجاية على طول.

— ترابيزة لخمسة. باسم مين حضرتك؟

— باسمي أنا. جابر عبد الوهاب.

— جابر عبد الوهاب. حضرتك حتشرفنا الساعة كام إن شاء الله؟

— واحدة ونص، اثنين. بعد صلاة الجمعة كده.

— أهلا بحضرتك يا فندم.

— مين معايا؟

— أنا متر أبو السعود.

— أهلا بيك يا متر. باقولك إيه وحياتك أنا عاوز ترابيزة حلوة على النيل على طول.

— إن شاء الله يا بيه بس حضرتك عارف طبعا يوم الجمعة بيبقى زحمة شوية معلش.

— لا يابو السعود وحياتك. ما تكسفنيش. أنا حيكون معايا جماعة أجانب. لازم نقعدهم على النيل.

— إن شاء الله يا فندم.

— خلاص. اتفقنا يا بو السعود. سلامه عليكم.

— مع ألف سلامة يا جابر بيه.

Dialogue 2

— سميرة... حتأكلي صاحبتك إيه؟

What do you want to eat, Jane? -

Something typically Egyptian! -

— اطلبولها ملوخية بالأرانب.

— لا يا جابر، مش معقول. العيال الانجليز بيربوا الأرانب في البيوت زي القطط والكلاب والحاجات دي عندنا.

— حتقول علينا متوحشين لو قلنالها حنأكلك أرنب.

— نطلب لها ورق عنب مثلا؟

— آه. ورق عنب يبقى جميل.

Jane, have you tried stuffed vine leaves? -

Yes, dolmades! We had it in Greece. It was good. -

— او كي. خلاص. نطلبلها ورق عنب مع فراخ مثلا أو لحمة بانيه.

— مع كباب أحسن علشان الكباب مصري أصيل.

— أيوه صح. وانتي يا سميرة، حتاكلي إيه؟

— والله أنا محتارة بين البامية وبين البسلة.

— أنا شخصيا حاطلب بامية.

— طب خلاص. أطلب أنا البسلة، وأنا أدوقك بسلتي، وانتي تدوقيني باميتك!

— أنا محتار يا جماعة. آكل سمك مقلي ولا فراخ؟

— إحنا ممكن ننقي سمكة كبيرة ونقسمها.

— ماشي. وحنطلب جمبري طبعا.

— طبعا.

— هه؟ جاهزين يا جماعة نطلب؟

— جاهزين.

— يا متر... يا أبو السعود... احنا جاهزين.

Unit 15

Exercise 4

— عملت إيه في الأجازة يا جابر؟

— رحت بيت جدي في بلد صغيرة جنب التل الكبير.

— سافرت بالعربية الجديدة طبعا.

— لا والله سافرت بالقطر لأنه أسهل وأسرع والبيت جنب المحطة.

— وعملت إيه هناك؟ الريف مش هادي قوي؟

— لا أبدا، الناس هناك حياتهم بسيطة لكن جميلة جدا. بيصحوا بدري وبيأكلوا الفراخ والبط قبل الفطار.

— يعني أنت تعرف تأكل فراخ وبط؟

— طبعا أعرف، وأعرف كمان أأكل الحصان بتاع جدي اللي اسمه منصور. أنا اتعلمت ركوب الخيل على منصور، بس دلوقتي منصور عنده عشرين سنة، مش زي زمان.

— ما فيش حاجة زي زمان يا جابر.

— عندك حق، زمان بيت جدي كان دايما مليان ناس. عمي وعمتي وولادهم لكن دلوقتي البيت بقى فاضي تقريبا ومافيش غير جدي وجدتي.

— يا خسارة.

— لا مش قوي كده، كلنا بنحاول نروح هناك في الأعياد والمناسبات السعيدة.

Key to exercises

Unit 1

Exercise 1
1 – SabáaH il-khayr.
– SabáaH in-nuur.
2 – áhlan.
– áhlan bíiki.
3 – masáa' il-khayr.
– masáa' in-nuur.
4 – izzáyak?
– il-Hámdu lilláah.
5 – má9a s-saláama.
– alláah yisallímik.

Exercise 2
1 áhlan yaa HáSan 2 áhlan biik 3 masáa' il-khayr yaa Tant
4 masáa' in-nuur 5 izzáyak? 6 izzáayik? 7 il-Hámdu lilláah
8 SabáaH il-khayr yaa gáabir 9 má9a s-saláama yábni
10 alláah yisallímak

Exercise 3
taláata	3
itnáyn	2
khámsa	5
arbá9a	4
wáaHid	1

Exercise 4
1d; 2e; 3a; 4c; 5f; 6b

Exercise 5
1 ísmik eh? 2 ismáhaa eh? 3 ísmak eh? 4 ínti min lú'Sur?
5 ínta gáabir? 6 húwwa min iskindiríyya?

Exercise 6
This is a speaking exercise and the main aim is fluency. The script is provided for you in the unit, but try to complete the conversation on the recording without referring to it.

Exercise 7

1 false **2** true **3** true **4** true **5** false

Exercise 8

1 ínta máSri? **2** ínti maSríyya? **3** ána ingilíizi. **4** ána ingilizíyya.
5 húwwa amriikáani. **6** híyya amriikaaníyya. **7** HaDrítak amriikáani?
8 la', ána iskutlándi. **9** HaDrítik amriikaaníyya? **10** la', ána iskutlandíyya.

Exercise 9

1 ínti maSríyya? **2** híyya iskutlandíyya. **3** ána amriikaaníyya.
4 HaDrítik ingilizíyya? **5** ána ostoralíyya. **6** híyya ostoralíyya?

Exercise 10

*There is no correct answer for these open-ended speaking
exercises. The aim is to encourage you to talk about yourself and
your environment using the language taught in the unit. If you can,
try to find an Egyptian who can listen to you. You could also record
your own description and listen critically to your accent and
language – a useful self-assessment.*

Unit 2

Exercise 1

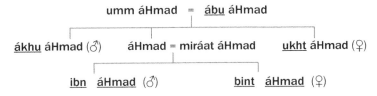

Exercise 2

1 húmma hína? **2** íntu fir-rádyo! **3** íHna min iskindiríyya.
4 íntu min buur saa9íid? **5** húmma fi aswáan. **6** íHna fi maSr.

Exercise 3

1 abúki (your *fem.* father) **2** ibn(í)na (our son) **3** úkhti (my sister)
4 ísmak (your *masc.* name) **5** umm(ú)ku (your *pl.* mother)
6 akhúhum (their brother) **7** bíntik (your *fem.* daughter)
8 wiláaduh (his children) **9** góhzhaa (her husband)
10 akhúya (my brother) **11** miráatak (your *masc.* wife)
12 ísmuh (his name) **13** abúna (our father)
14 wiláadhum (their children)

Exercise 4

1 húwwa ísmuh kamáal. **2** bíntik hína? **3** abúna min aswáan.
4 góhzhaa ísmuh 9osmáan. **5** ukht(ú)hum fi r-rádyo.
6 úmmak ism(á)haa láyla.

Exercise 5

1 – ísmak eh?
  – ána ísmi Hásan.

2 – ísmik eh?
  – ána ísmi samîira.

3 – bíntik ism(á)haa eh?
  – bínti ism(á)haa móna.

4 – abúku ísmuh eh?
  – abúna ísmuh kamáal.

5 – miráatuh ism(á)haa eh?
  – miráatuh ism(á)haa láyla.

5 – ibn(ú)ku ismuh eh?
  – ibn(í)na ismuh áHmad.

Exercise 6

(model answer – yours may vary slightly)

ána ísmi widáad w-ána min ig-gîiza.

akhúya ísmuh hiláal wi-úkhti ism(á)haa sáara.
úmmi ism(á)haa fawzíyya wi-bába … abúya … ísmuh ánwar.

Exercise 7

Open-ended speaking exercise. See Unit 1, Exercise 10.

Exercise 8

*For these kinds of prompted audio exercises, you will hear a model
response on the recording for you to check your answer.*

Exercise 9

1 *masculine* il-ibn **2** *masculine* ir-ráqam **3** *feminine* il-umm
4 *masculine* iS-Sayf **5** *masculine* iS-SabáaH **6** *feminine*
it-tarabáyza **7** *masculine* il-khaal **8** *masculine* il-masáa'
9 *feminine* il-khaala **10** *masculine* iD-Dayf

Exercise 10

1 miin da? **2** da kháali Hásan. **3** miin di? **4** di bint Hásan.

5 wi-miin duul? **6** duul wiláadhaa. **7** wiS-Súura di? **8** da akhúya fi sharm ish-shaykh.

Exercise 11

You will hear a model response on the recording.

Exercise 12

1 miin duul? **2** miin di? **3** fayn iS-Súura di?
4 il-rádyo bitáa9 miin? **5** il-fáraH ímta? **6** khaTíbtak fayn?

Exercise 13

You will hear a model response on the recording.

Exercise 14

1e; **2**f; **3**a; **4**d; **5**c; **6**b

Unit 3

Exercise 1

1 tíshrab áhwa? **2** tákul ba'láwa? **3** tákli ba'láwa?
4 tíshrabi kárkaday? **5** tíshrab Háaga sá9a? **6** tákul basbúusa?
7 tákli basbúusa? **8** tíshrabi áhwa?

Exercise 2

You will hear a model response on the recording.

Exercise 3

1 tákul basbúusa yaa gáabir? **2** la' shúkran, líssa wáakil. **3** áywa min fáDlik. **4** tíshrabi shay yaa widáad? **5** la' shúkran yaa Tant, líssa shárba. **6** tákul Tába' bilîila yaa Hásan? **7** ána amúut fil-bilîila. **8** Táyyib u'9úd yábni.

Exercise 4

1e; **2**c; **3**b; **4**f; **5**d; **6**a

Exercise 5

You will hear a model response on the recording.

Exercise 6

1 9andáhaa akh ísmuh tom. **2** 9andína bint ismáhaa náadya.
3 ínti 9ándik wiláad? **4** 9andúku kárkaday? **5** ána 9ándi ibn.
6 widáad 9andáhaa akh ísmuh gamáal. **7** gáabir 9ánduh khaal fi buur sa9îid. **8** áHmad wi-miráatuh 9andúhum Dayf.

Exercise 7

1 Tába' bilíila (bowl of porridge) **2** Tába' ruzz (bowl of rice)
3 izáazit/kubbáayit kóhla (bottle/glass of cola) **4** kubbáayit shay
(glass of tea) **5** Tába'/sandawítsh Ta9míyya (plate/sandwich of
falafel) **6** Tába' bámya (plate of okra) **7** Tába'/sandawítsh fuul
(plate/sandwich of beans) **8** kubbáayit 9aSíir laymúun (glass of
lemon juice)

Exercise 8

	Water	Lemon juice	Cola	Spinach	Okra	Kebab	Rice	Salad
Widaad	✔				✔		✔	
Gaber			✔	✔				✔

Exercise 9

You will hear a model response on the recording.

Exercise 10

1 ána muhandísa fi amríika. **2** híyya muDíifa fi maSr
liT-Tayaráan. **3** híyya mudarrísit kímya. **4** ínti mumassíla yaa
madáam? **5** ána Taalíba fi-iskindiríyya. **6** ínti Taalíba hína?

Exercise 11

1 ána mumássil. **2** ána mumassíla. **3** ínti duktúura? **4** ínta Táalib?
5 húwwa muHáasib fi-iskindiríyya. **6** híyya muHaamíya fi amríika.
7 ána muDíifa fi maSr liT-Tayaráan. **8** ínti mudarrísit kímya?

Exercise 12

1 la', ána mish iskutlándi (iskutlandíyya). **2** la', ána mish min
Glasgow. **3** la', di mish bínti. **4** la', da mish íbni. **5** la', ísmi mish
Stanley. **6** la', ána mish mumássil (mumassíla).

Exercise 13

1 húmma mudarrisíin. **2** húmma muhandisíin. **3** íHna
mumassilíin. **4** íntu mumassilíin? **5** húmma maSriyyíin.
6 húmma ostoraliyyíin. **7** íHna muHaasbíin. **8** íntu muhandisíin?

Exercise 14

Open-ended speaking exercise. See Unit 1, Exercise 10.

Exercise 15

1 ab **2** bint **3** akh **4** ukht **5** ibn

Unit 4

Exercise 1
You will hear a model response on the recording.

Exercise 2
c; d; e; f; a; b

Exercise 3
1 fiih mushkíla? **2** ik-kabíina fíihaa tarabáyza. **3** fiih takíif?
4 fiih 9arabíyya? **5** il-9arabíyya fíihaa kaam baab? **6** fiih bank
ganb il-'áhwa.

Exercise 4

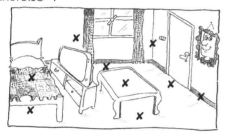

Exercise 5
1 il wálad fi k-kabíina. **2** is-siríir ganb il-baab. **3** ána 'uddáam
ish-shibbáak. **4** it-tilifizyóhn 9ála t-tarabáyza. **5** is-siríir bayn
it-tarabáyza wil-baab. **6** ir-rádyo wára it-titifizyóhn.

Exercise 6
1 il-bint ganbáhaa. **2** ána waráhum. **3** híyya 'uddáamhaa.
4 is-siríir táHtuh. **5** núura ganbúku. **6** fíihaa kaam siríir?
7 widáad mawgúuda fiih? **8** il-áhwa uddáamuh.

Exercise 7
You will hear a model response on the recording.

Exercise 8
1d; **2**h; **3**g; **4**f; **5**c; **6**a; **7**e; **8**b

Exercise 9
1 náyim **2** shárba **3** SáHya **4** wáakil **5** wákla **6** sharbíin
7 naymíin **8** náyma

Exercise 10
1 ma fiish Súura foh' is-siríir. **2** ma fiiháash takíif?
3 il-9arabíyya mish 'adíima. **4** ma fiish kúrsi ganb il-baab.
5 ik-kúrsi mish muríiH. **6** ma fiish CD taHt ir-rádyo.
7 il-wiláad mish mawguudíin. **8** ma fiiháash shibbáak?
9 il-bayt mish kibíir. **10** ma fiish bank 'uráyyib min hína?

Exercise 11
1 ish-shibbáak **2** kúrsi **3** tilifizyóhn/rádyo **4** il-baab/wit-tarabáyza
5 is-siríir

Exercise 12
1 false **2** true **3** false **4** true **5** false **6** false

Exercise 13
Open-ended speaking exercise. See Unit 1, Exercise 10.

Exercise 14
a**7** (two); b**4** (between); c**1** (next to); d**9** (brother); e**10** (milk);
f**3** (but); g**2** (tea); h**11** (house); i**8** (sister); j**5** (under); k**6** (uncle)

Unit 5

Exercise 1
1 (ána) 9áwza sálaTa. **2** (íntu) 9awzíin galaalíib? **3** (ínti) 9áwza
áhwa? **4** (húwwa) 9áawiz shay. **5** (íHna) 9awzíin 9arabíyya gidíida.
6 (híyya) 9áwza kánaka naHáas? **7** (húmma) 9awzíin kabíina lux.
8 (ínta) 9áawiz 'umSáan?

Exercise 2
1 widáad miHtáaga galabíyya. **2** gáabir miHtáag 'amíiS.
3 umm(i) gáabir miHtáaga kánaka. **4** gáabir wi-Hásan miHtaagíin
'umSáan. **5** ábu Hásan miHtáag shíisha.
6 umm(i) w-ábu gáabir miHtaagíin 9aysh.

Exercise 3
1 tálat 'umSáan **2** khámas galaalíib **3** 9áshar mudarrisíin **4** árba9
muhandisíin **5** ínti 9áwza árba9 galaalíib? **6** la', ána 9áwza taláata.
7 íntu miHtaagíin sába9 'umSáan? **8** la', íHna miHtaagíin khámsa.

Exercise 4
1 9ílba/9ílab (box, packet, tin) **2** bank/bunúuk (bank)

3 Tába'/Tubáa' (plate, dish) **4** 'amîiS/'umSaan (shirt)
5 galabíyya/galaalîib (galabeyya) **6** raghîif/raghífa (loaf)
7 tarabáyza/tarabayzáat (table) **8** muhándis/muhandisîin (engineer)
9 shóhka/shúwak (fork) **10** tilifóhn/tilifohnáat (telephone)

Exercise 5

1 iddîini Hidáashar 'amîiS, min fáDlak. **2** iddîini tálat galaalîib, min fáDlak. **3** iddîini itnáashar shóhka biláastik, min fáDlak. **4** iddîini sitt Tubáa', min fáDlak. **5** iddîini árba9 9îlab, min fáDlak. **6** iddîini 9áshar raghífa, min fáDlak. **7** iddîini Hidáashar Tába' wára', min fáDlak. **8** iddîini táman 'umSaan, min fáDlak.

Exercise 6

1 true **2** true **3** false **4** false **5** true **6** false

Exercise 7

You will hear a model response on the recording.

Exercise 8

1 waladáyn **2** baytáyn **3** bintáyn **4** shibbaakáyn **5** Taba'áyn
6 shohktáyn **7** laymuumtáyn **8** mushkiltáyn **9** Taalibáyn **10** bayDtáyn

Exercise 9

5 khámsa	**8** tamánya
11 Hidáashar	**16** sittáashar
22 itnáyn wi-9ishrîin	**46** sítta w-arba9îin
75 khámsa wi-sab9îin	**90** tis9îin
62 itnáyn wi-sittîin	**31** wáaHid wi-talatîin
106 míyya wi-sítta	**158** míyya tamánya wi-khamsîin

Exercise 10

You will hear a model response on the recording.

Exercise 11

1 – bikáam ik-kánaka?
   – bi-sab9íin.

2 – bikáam kîilu it-tufáaH?
   – bi-itnáashar.

3 – bikáam ish-shúwak?
   – bi-arbá9a wi-khamsîin.

4 – bikáam il-galabíyya?
   – bi-míyya wi-khamastáashar.

5 – bikáam rub9 kíilu zaytúun?
   – bi-talatíin.

6 – bikáam it-tarabáyza?
   – bi-mitáyn wi-khamsíin.

7 – bikáam nuSS(i) kíilu gíbna?
   – bi-wáaHid wi-9ishríin.

8 – bikáam ish-shíisha?
   – bi-míyya wi-tis9íin.

Exercise 12
– 9áawiz 'amíiS Sáyfi.
– HáaDir. 9indína ázra' gháami' wi-áHmar.
– il-ázra' Hílw.
– w-eh kamáan?
– miHtáag kamáan galabíyya kibíira. 9andúku galaalíib Sáfra?
– la', bass 9andína galaalíib báyDa wi-galaalíib banafsígi.
– bikáam il-báyDa law samáHti?

Exercise 13
– SabáaH il-khayr. 9áawiz 'amíiS shítwi.
– ma'áas eh?
– kibíir. il-alwáan 9indúku eh?
– 9andína ábyaD w-ákhDar gháami' wi-búnni.
– Hílw il-ákhDar. bi-káam da law samáHti?
– da bi-míyya khámsa wi-tamaníin gináyh.

Exercise 14
You will hear a model response on the recording.

Exercise 15
a6; b5; c1; d2; e3; f4

Unit 6

Exercise 1
1 sháklik eh? **2** íbnak shákluh eh? **3** shaklúhum eh? **4** Hásan
shákluh eh? **5** umm(i) gáabir shakláhaa eh? **6** bíntik shakláhaa
eh? **7** shaklúku eh? **8** il-wiláad shaklúhum eh?

Exercise 2

1 húwwa Tawíil. **2** híyya rufayyá9a. **3** úmmi 9agúuza. **4** ibraahíim 'uSáyyar wi-tikhíin. **5** Hásan Tawíil bi-shánab. **6** bínti Tawíil wi-rufayyá9a. **7** abúya áSla9 bi-shánab. **8** húwwa shaabb bi-da'n?

Exercise 3

1 shá9ruh **2** manakhíiri **3** bo'ak **4** 9aynáyki **5** Sawáabi9haa **6** iidáyna **7** widáanik **8** shánabuh **9** rigláyya **10** 9aynáyhum

Exercise 4

1b; **2**c; **3**d; **4**a

Exercise 5

You will hear a model response on the recording.

Exercise 6

You will hear a model response on the recording.

Exercise 7

1 híyya lábsa fustáan. **2** húmma labsíin baraníiT. **3** ínti lábsa guníIla. **4** ána láabis bádla. **5** ána lábsa bilúuza. **6** húwwa láabis naDDáara. **7** íntu labsíin baláaTi. **8** íHna labsíin shurabáat.

Exercise 8

1 híyya lábsa burnáyTa. **2** húmma Tal9íin il-míina búkra. **3** ínti 9árfa widáad? **4** íHna líssa waklíin. **5** híyya názla síllim il-márkib. **6** húmma líssa sharbíin. **7** ána lábsa banTalóhn. **8** íntu SaHyíin? **9** húmma naymíin. **10** íHna mish 9arfíin.

Exercise 9

1 bíntak 9andáhaa kaam sána? 9andáhaa talatáashar sána.
2 ibnúku 9ánduh kaam sána? 9ánduh tálat siníin.
3 íntu 9andúku kaam sána? ána 9ándi itnáyn wi-9ishríin sána wi-híyya 9andáhaa wáaHid wi-9ishríin sána.
4 ínti 9ándik kaam sána? 9ándi arba9íin sána.
5 góhzik 9ánduh kaam sána? 9ánduh Hawáali khámsa wi-arba9íin sána.
6 wiláadi 9andúhum kaam sána? áHmad 9ánduh tísa9 siníin wi-láyla 9andáhaa arba9atáashar sána.
7 ábu gáabir 9ánduh kaam sána? 9ánduh itnáyn wi-tamaníin sána.
8 ukht Hásan 9andáhaa kaam sána? 9andáhaa saba9táashar sana.

Exercise 10

Your drawing or notes should show a 40-year-old tall, thin woman with short black hair, glasses and wearing a long skirt and a white blouse.

Exercise 11

I'm tall and <u>thin</u> and I'm <u>twenty-five</u> years old. My hair is <u>black</u> and short and my <u>eyes</u> are brown. I'm <u>wearing</u> a dark blue <u>suit</u> and <u>green</u> shirt and... ah, and I have a <u>moustache</u>.

Exercise 12

1 Danny **2** David **3** Donald **4** Dorothy **5** Daisy **6** Derek

Unit 7

Exercise 1

1 la'ánnak **2** la'ánnuh **3** la'annína **4** la'ánnik **5** la'annúhum
6 la'annáhaa **7** la'annúku

Exercise 2

1 íHna rayHíin faránsa la'annáhaa 'urayyíba.
2 il-akl áHsan fi faránsa la'ánnuh lazíiz gíddan.
3 íHna mish rayHíin amríika la'ánni ma baHíbbish iT-Tayaráan iT-Tawíil.
4 lagháyna k-kabíina la'annáhaa Sughayyára.
5 húwwa mish 9áwwiz bilíila la'ánnuh líssa wáakil.
6 ínta mish miHtáag tilifóhn la'ánnak wálad Sugháyyar.
7 il-wiláad mish 9awzíin kóhla la'annúhum líssa sharbíin.
8 íntu hína la'annúku 9awzíin máyya?

Exercise 3

1 tikhíin, tikhíina, átkhan **2** kibíir, kibíira, ákbar **3** bi9íid, bi9íida, áb9ad **4** Tawíil, Tawíila, áTwal **5** lazíiz, lazíiza, alázz **6** gháali, ghálya, ághla **7** 'uSáyyar, 'uSayyára, á'Sar **8** gidíid, gidíida, ágdad **9** kwáyyis, kwáyyisa, áHsan **10** Hilw, Hílwa, áHla

Exercise 4

1 gáabir á'Sar min Hásan. **2** il-maksíik áb9ad min faránsa. **3** il-9arabíyya di áSghar bi-kitíir. **4** 9awzíin il-ákbar min fáDlak. **5** fayn á'rab maTáar? **6** wiláadna áTwal mínna. **7** akhúhaa áShgar mínhaa. **8** bass ána ákbar mínnuh. **9** it-tiin áHla bi-kitíir innahárda. **10** kída áHsan.

Exercise 5

You will hear a model response on the recording.

Exercise 6

1 bikáam tazkárit ig-gíiza bil-otobíis? **2** bikáam tazkárit aswáan biT-Tayyáara? **3** bikáam tazkárit is-sways bil-márkib? **4** bikáam tazkárit

faránsa biT-Tayyáara? **5** bikáam tazkárit iz-zamáalik bil-otobíis?
6 bikáam tazkárit lú'Sur bil-'aTr? **7** bikáam tazkárit il-maksíik
biT-Tayyáara? **8** bikáam tazkárit sharm ish-shaykh bil-márkib?

Exercise 7
You will hear a model response on the recording.

Exercise 8

Information	
Destination:	Aswan
Means of transport:	Plane
Number of tickets:	5
Number of adults:	3
Number of children:	2
Discounts for children?:	No

Exercise 9
You will hear a model response on the recording.

Exercise 10
You will hear a model response on the recording.

Exercise 11
1 yes (dog and spinach) **2** no (cat and dog) **3** no (donkey and
apples) **4** yes (cow and olives) **5** yes (okra and cat) **6** yes (duck
and rabbit) **7** no (cow and spinach) **8** no (cat and milk)

Exercise 12
1 ána ma baHíbbish il-bámya. **2** ána ma baHíbbish iz-zaytúun.
3 ána mish muwáafi'. **4** fí9lan ma 9andáksh(i) Ha' yaa ibrahíim.
5 la', ma 9andakíish Ha' yaa widáad. **6** ána ma baHíbbish il-fuul
bil-laymúun. **7** wála ána.

Exercise 13
Open-ended speaking exercise. See Unit 1, Exercise 10.

Exercise 14
a**2**; b**6**; c**5**; d**3**; e**1**; f**4**

Unit 8

Exercise 1

1 widáad min maSr. híyya maSríyya. **2** Pierre min faránsa. húwwa
faransáawi. **3** Maria min il-maksíík. híyya maksiikíyya. **4** Holly min
ostorálya. híyya ostoralíyya. **5** Ronny min amríika. húwwa amriikáani.
6 Jack min ingiltáara. húwwa ingilíizi.

Exercise 2

ána kháalid wi-di 9íIti. ana 9ándi ukht Sughayárra ismáhaa sáara.
híyya 9andáhaa khámas siníin. wi-9ándi akh ísmuh 9omar wi-húwwa
9ánduh táman siníin. abúyaa ísmuh walíid wi-9ánduh shánab kibíir.
úmmi ismáhaa móna wi-híyya áHsan umm!

Exercise 3

1 il-9arabíyya ma fiiháash takíif. **2** húwwa mish 9áwwiz bilíila.
3 ána mish miHtáag gázma lish-shughl. **4** húwwa mish min faránsa.
5 ána ma baHíbbish iT-Tayaráan iT-Tawíil. **6** ma fiish faar taHt ik-kúrsi.
7 híyya mish lábsa fustáan ábyaD. **8** íHna mish nazlíin wusT il-bálad
bil-otobíis.

Exercise 4

1 takíif ✔ **2** tarabáyza ✔ **3** tilifizyóhn ✔ **4** siríir kibíir ✘
5 rádyo ✘ **6** kúrsi muríiH ✔ **7** kombyúutir bil-internet ✘

Exercise 5

1 fiiháa takíif. **2** fiiháa tarabáyza. **3** fiiháa tilifizyóhn. **4** ma fiiháash
siríir kibíir. **5** ma fiiháash rádyo. **6** fiiháa kúrsi muríiH. **7** ma fiiháash
kombyúutir bil-internet.

Exercise 6

(model answer – yours may vary slightly)

búkra ínta ráayiH il-maTáar 9asháan 'Mister Ross' min shírkit
Beachtime. húwwa Tawíil wi-9ánduh shánab. láabis naDDáara
wi-bádla zár'a.

Exercise 7

	Meal	Drink
Man	kebab and green salad	lemon juice
Woman 1	okra and rice	hibiscus tea
Woman 2	stuffed vine leaves and salad	cola

Exercise 8

13 talatáashar **6** sítta **5** khámsa **27** sáb9a wi-9ishríin
72 itnáyn wi-sab9íin **18** tamantáashar **14** arba9táashar
39 tís9a wi-talatíin **44** arbá9a w-arba9íin **100** míyya
140 míyya w-arba9íin **250** miyyitáyn wi-khamsíin

Exercise 9

1 'amíiS/'umSáan (shirt) **2** tilifizyóhn/tilifizyohnáat (television)
3 Tába'/Tubáa' (plate) **4** lohn/alwáan (colour) **5** shóhka/shúwak
(fork) **6** bádla/bídal (suit) **7** rigl/rigláyn (leg) **8** naDDáara/
naDDaráat (pair of glasses) **9** takhfíiD/takhfiiDáat (discount)
10 raghíif/raghífa (loaf)

Exercise 10

ána ísmi nádya hiláal w-ána min iz-zamáalik fi maSr. 9ándi ukht
wi-akh. úkhti, sámya, Tawíila 'áwi, áTwal mínni bi-kitíir. bass ána ákbar
mínhaa fi s-sinn. akhúya, Táari', 9ánduh khamastáashar sána.
húwwa árfa9 wi-á'Sar min sámya. abúna muHáami fi máktab kibíir
fiz-zamáalik – wi-ummína mumassíla t-tilifizyóhn.

Unit 9

Exercise 1

You will hear a model response on the recording.

Exercise 2

1 innahárda it-taláat. búkra il-árba9. **2** búkra ig-gúm9a. innahárda
il-khamíis. **3** búkra is-sabt. bá9da búkra il-Hadd. **4** áHmad gayy
yohm ig-gúm9a. innahárda il-khamíis. áHmad gayy búkra.
5 innahárda il-khamíis. bá9da búkra is-sabt. **6** bá9da búkra il-árba9.
búkra it-taláat. **7** innahárda il-árba9. búkra il-khamíis. **8** búkra
il-itnáyn. innahárda il-Hadd. **9** iT-Tayáara gáyya yohm il-Hadd.
innahárda ig-gúm9a. iT-Tayáara gáyya bá9da búkra. **10** bá9da búkra
il-Hadd. innahárda ig-gúm9a.

Exercise 3

1 is-sáa9a tamánya. **2** is-sáa9a arbá9a. **3** is-sáa9a khámsa wi-
nuSS. **4** is-sáa9a itnáashar ílla rub9. **5** is-sáa9a itnáyn wi-tilt.
6 is-sáa9a sába9 wi-rub9. **7** is-sáa9a tís9a wi-9áshara.
8 is-sáa9a wáHda ílla khámsa.

314 Key to exercises

Exercise 4
You will hear a model response on the recording.

Exercise 5
1 madrása/madáaris (school) 2 maghsála/magháasil (laundry)
3 máT9am/maTáa9im (restaurant) 4 mátHaf/matáaHif (museum)
5 másgid/masáagid (mosque) 6 máktab/makáatib (office)
7 máTbakh/maTáabikh (kitchen) 8 mákhbaz/makháabiz (bakery)

Exercise 6
1 (yohm) it-taláat rayHíin il-mátHaf il-máSri is-sáa9a 9áshara.
2 (yohm) il-árba9 rayHíin máT9am Nefertiti is-sáa9a wáHda wi-nuSS.
3 (yohm) il-khamíis rayHíin iskandiríyya is-sáa9a sáb9a wi-rub9.
4 (yohm) ig-gúm9a rayHíin másgid maHámmad 9áli is-sáa9a arbá9a
wi-nuSS.
5 (yohm) is-sabt rayHíin khaan il-khalíili is-sáa9a khámsa.
6 (yohm) il-Hadd rayHíin il-maTáar is-sáa9a tís9a ílla rub9.

Exercise 7
1 til9ábi basketball? 2 tirúuH in-náadi? 3 nígi innaháarda?
4 yú'9ud fil-bayt? 5 tishrábu shaay? 6 anáam ba9d il-gháda?
7 yáklu faláafel? 8 tígu in-náadi? 9 níshrab máyya? 10 ákhrug
ba9d il-fiTáar?

Exercise 8
1 bi-yíSHa is-sáa9a khámsa wi-nuSS. 2 bi-til9ábi basketball?
3 báwSal il-maTáar is-sáa9a sáb9a biZ-ZabT. 4 bi-nirúuH in-náadi
má9a aS-Háabna. 5 bi-yukhrúgu bádri. 6 bi-táakul Háaga khafíifa.
7 bi-tirúuH in-náadi yohm is-sabt. 8 bi-tígu hína ba9d il-gháda?

Exercise 9
sámya muDíifa fi maSr liT-Tayaráan. is-sáa9a khámsa wi-nuSS(i) bi-
tíSHa wi-bi-táakul Háaga khafíifa wi-bi-túkhrug min il-báyt is-sáa9a
sítta wi-rub9. bi-tíwSal il-maTáar is-sáa9a sáb9a biZ-ZabT.

il-itnáyn wil-árba9 wis-sabt bi-yisáafru 9amáan, wil-khamíis wil-Hadd
bi-yisáafru aswáan marratáyn – márra S-SubH wi-márra D-Duhr.

it-taláat agáaza wi-bi-tirúuh in-náadi ba9d iD-Duhr. Hawáali is-sáa9a
khámsa bi-tíl9ab basketball má9a aS-Háabhaa wi-má9a náadya bint
9ámm(a)haa.

ig-gúm9a bi-tí'9ud fil-bayt táakul wi-tináam!

Exercise 10

1 búkra HáSHa bádri. **2** yohm ig-gúm9a Ha-nisáafir 9amáan.
3 yohm is-sabt sámya Ha-tirúuH in-náadi. **4** Ha-tígu má9a
aS-Háabkum? **5** il-wiláad Ha-yináamu ba9d il-9ásha. **6** Háakul
Háaga khafíifa is-sáa9a khámsa. **7** Ha-tákli fil-bayt? **8** góhzi
Ha-yúkhrug min il-máktab is-sáa9a sáb9a wi-nuSS.

Exercise 11

You will hear a model response on the recording.

Exercise 12

Activity	Time
Wake up	7.00AM
Drink tea	7.30AM
Leave house	8.00AM
Arrive at university	7.30AM
Sandwich break	12 noon
Go home	2.45PM
Go to club with friends	6.00PM

Exercise 13

Open-ended speaking exercise. See Unit 1, Exercise 10.

Exercise 14

You will hear a model response on the recording.

Unit 10

Exercise 1

You will hear a model response on the recording.

Exercise 2

1 ma baHíbbish ál9ab kúra. **2** baHíbb ál9ab basketball. **3** ma
baHíbbish Sayd is-sámak. **4** baHíbb il-muusíiqa. **5** ma baHíbbish
ál9ab ténnis. **6** ma baHíbbish il-'iráaya. **7** baHíbb rukúub il-khayl.
8 ma baHíbbish ál9ab golf.

Exercise 3

Open-ended speaking exercise. See Unit 1, Exercise 10.

Exercise 4

1 láazim arúuH dilwá'ti. **2** múmkin niSTáad sámak innahárda?
3 Darúuri yíSHu is-sáa9a sítta wi-nuSS. **4** il-mafrúuD tishrábi Háaga.
5 móna láazim tizáakir saa9táyn taláata. **6** múmkin il-wiláad
yil9ábu kúra innahárda? **7** múmkin til9ábu golf fin-náadi.
8 abúya darúuri yináam bádri. **9** múmkin a'9úd fil-bayt?
10 il-mafrúuD tizáakir kull(i) yohm.

Exercise 5

You will hear a model response on the recording.

Exercise 6

1 ma bi-niHíbbish rukúub il-khayl. **2** móna mish gháwya Sayd is-sámak.
3 ma 9andakíish wa't l-hiwáaytik? **4** ma fiish shibbáak ganb
is-siríir. **5** mish láazim nirúuH il-mádrasa. **6** mish múmkin ál9ab
má9ak? **7** ma bi-yiHíbbish riwayáat nagíib maHfúuZ.
8 it-taláat ma barúuHsh in-náadi. **9** búkra kamáal mish Ha-yíl9ab
iskwáash. **10** mish Darúuri átla9 il-maTáar.

Exercise 7

You will hear a model response on the recording.

Exercise 8

(model answers – yours may vary slightly)

1 mish láazim tíshrab kóla. **2** il-mafrúuD tíshrab máyya.
3 il-mafrúuD tíl9ab kúra. **4** il-mafrúuD táakul sálaTa. **5** mish láazim
ti'9úd 'uddáam ik-kombyúutir. **6** il-mafrúuD tíl9ab iskwáash.
7 mish láazim ti'9úd 'uddáam it-tilifizyóhn.

Exercise 9

1 Ha-nishúuf makáan munáasib w-íHna hináak. **2** láazim ashúuf
khálti w-ána fi maSr. **3** múmkin yikhállas shúghluh wi-húwwa fil-
máktab. **4** kamáal bi-yáakul wi-húwwa 'áa9id 'uddáam ik-kombyúutir.
5 múmkin tishrábi ik-kóla wi-ínti wá'fa. **6** madáam díina náwya
tishúuf máktab munáasib wi-híyya fi sharm ish-shaykh.

Exercise 10

<u>shírkit</u> in-niil lis-siyáaHa náwya tíftaH <u>far9</u> gidíid fi sharm ish-shaykh.
il-Huguuzáat fi maktábna bitáa9 <u>miidáan</u> il-úubraa, wil-Huguuzáat
fi <u>mawqí9na</u> 9ála l-internet, <u>kitíir</u> gíddan wi-bi-tizíid <u>Hawáali</u> 9ishríin
fil-míyya kull(i) <u>sána</u>. tag-híiz il-far9 ig-gidíid ma bi-yaakhúdsh(i) wa't.
<u>muhándis</u> id-diikór bitáa9na saríi9 wi-múmkin yikhállaS <u>shúghluh</u>

'ábl(i) ma yibtídi <u>il-múusim</u>. ána ráyHa sharm ish-shaykh wi-<u>Hashúuf</u> makáan munáasib w-ána <u>hináak</u>.

Exercise 11

1 máktab/makáatib (office) **2** far9/furúu9 (branch) **3** másgid/ masáagid (mosque) **4** agáaza/agazáat (holiday) **5** náadi/nawáadi (club) **6** SáaHib/aS-Háab (friend) **7** kombyúutir/ kombyuutiráat (computer) **8** su'áal/as'íla (question) **9** hiwáaya /hiwaayáat (hobby/pastime) **10** máT9am/maTáa9im (restaurant) **11** lúgha/ lugháat (language) **12** bádla/bídal (suit) **13** 'amíiS/ 'umSáan (shirt) **14** kalb/kiláab (dog) **15** makáan/amáakin (place/location) **16** mudárris/mudarrisíin (teacher)

Exercise 12

1 il-furúu9 di gidíida. (These branches are new.) **2** il-9arabiyyáat di Sughayyára. (These cars are small.) **3** il-amáakin di mish munásba. (These locations are not suitable.) **4** il-Huguuzáat mawgúuda 9ála k-kombyúutir. (The bookings are present on the computer.) **5** il-maTáa9im bi9íida 9an miidáan il-úubraa. (The restaurants are far from Opera Square.) **6** il-Tayaráat bi-tíwSal yohm il-gúm9a. (The planes arrive on Friday[s].) **7** il-makáatib ig-gidíida Ha-táakhud wa't. (The new offices will take time.) **8** il-'umSáan Sughayyára. íHna 9awzíin ákbar mínhaa. (The shirts are small. We want bigger ones.) **9** il-bunúuk hináak wil-matáaHif 'uddáamhaa. (The banks are over there and the museums are in front of them.) **10** il-ma9áahid Ha-tíftaH búkra. (The institutes will open tomorrow.) **11** il-ówaD fíihaa tilifizyohnáat wi-saráayir muríiHa. (In the rooms there are televisions and comfortable beds.) **12** ik-kiláab bi-tiHíbb il-láHma wil-'óTaT bi-tiHíbb il-lában. (Dogs like meat and cats like milk.)

Unit 11

Exercise 1

You will hear a model response on the recording.

Exercise 2

**1** law samáHt, il-bank patch — il-bank mináyn? **2** law samáHt, il-maHáTTa mináyn? **3** law samáHt, il-mustáshfa mináyn? **4** law samáHt, il-mátHaf mináyn? **5** law samáHt, is-síinima mináyn? **6** law samáHt, il-maTáar mináyn?

To ask a woman, you should change 'law samáHt' to 'law samáHti'.

Exercise 3

(model answers – yours may vary slightly)

1 ána 9áawiz/9áwza arúuH il-bank fi sháari9 in-niil.
2 ána 9áawiz/9áwza arúuH fúndu' Nefertiti fi miidáan it-taHríir.
3 ána 9áawiz/9áwza áakul fi máT9am in-niil fi sháari9 musáddaq.
4 ána 9áawiz/9áwza arúuH il-maHáTTa fi miidáan ramsíis.
5 ána 9áawiz/9áwza azúur il-mátHaf il-máSri fi wusT il-bálad.
6 ána 9áawiz/9áwza arúuH sifáarit amríika fi 'Garden City'.
7 ána 9áawiz/9áwza azúur khálti fil-mustáshfa.
8 ána 9áawiz/9áwza áakul fi máT9am filfíla fi sháari9 Tala'at Harb.

Exercise 4

1 yizúur **2** nirúuH **3** tíSHa **4** tíb'i **5** táklu **6** yizíid **7** yizúuru
8 yáakhud **9** tináami **10** áakhud **11** yíSHu **12** tirúuHu **13** nináam
14 tizúuru **15** tizíid

Exercise 5

(model answers – yours may vary slightly)

1 húwwa 9áawiz yirúuH il-bank fi sháari9 in-niil.
2 húmma 9awzíin yirúuHu fúndu' Nefertiti fi miidáan it-taHríir.
3 híyya 9áwza táakul fi máT9am in-níil fi sháari9 musáddaq.
4 íntu 9awzíin tirúuHu il-maHáTTa fi miidáan ramsíis.
5 widáad 9áwza tizúur il-mátHaf il-máSri fi wusT il-bálad.
6 gáabir 9áawiz yirúuH sifáarit amríika fi 'Garden City'.
7 íHna 9awzíin nizúur khalítna fil-mustáshfa.
8 il-wiláad 9awzíin yáklu fi máT9am filfíla fi sháari9 Tala'at Harb.

Exercise 6

	Hassan	Gaber
Hospital		
Bank		✔
French Embassy		✔
Station		✔
Cinema	✔	✔
Market	✔	
Music Shop	✔	

Exercise 7

1 rúuHu! **2** izîli! **3** náamu! **4** kul! **5** ughrúgu! **6** iTlá9i! **7** íSHi! **8** khúdu!
9 bii9! **10** kúli! **11** ishrábu! **12** zuur! **13** iHgízi! **14** iTlá9u! **15** bîi9i!

Exercise 8

1 iTlá9u is-síllim. (Go up the stairs.) **2** inzíli bá9d táani isháara.
(Go down after the second lights.) **3** ukhrúgu min il-bayt is-sáa9a
sáb9a. (Go out of the house at 7 o'clock.) **4** khúdi áwwil sháari9
shimáal. (Take the first street left.) **5** ruuH il-mádrasa asháan
ibrahîim. (Go to the school for Ibrahim.) **6** ishrábi Háaga sáa9a.
(Drink something cold.) **7** náamu bádri. (Sleep early.) **8** kúli Háaga
'ábl il-mádrasa. (Eat something before school.) **9** bîi9u il-9arabíyya.
(Sell the car.) **10** zuur il-máTHaf. (Visit the museum.)

Exercise 9

1 ma tiTla9úsh is-síllim. / baláash tiTlá9u is-síllim.
2 ma tinzilísh bá9d táani isháara. / baláash tinzíli bá9d táani isháara.
3 ma tukhrugúsh min il-bayt is-sáa9a sáb9a. / baláash tukhrúgu min
il-bayt is-sáa9a sáb9a. **4** ma takhdîish áwwil sháari9 shimáal. /
baláash tákhdi áwwil sháari9 shimáal. **5** ma tirúuHsh il-mádrasa
asháan ibrahîim / baláash tirúuH il-mádrasa asháan ibrahîim.
6 ma tishrabísh Háaga sáa9a. / baláash tishrábi Háaga sáa9a.
7 ma tinaamúsh bádri. / baláash tináamu bádri. **8** ma taklísh Háaga
'ábl il-mádrasa. / baláash tákli Háaga 'ábl il-mádrasa. **9** ma
tibii9úsh il-9arabíyya. / baláash tibîi9u il-9arabíyya. **10** ma tizúursh
il-máTHaf. /baláash tizúur il-máTHaf.

Exercise 10

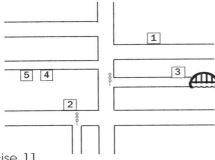

Exercise 11

You will hear a model response on the recording.

Exercise 12

You will hear a model response on the recording.

Exercise 13

1 shimáal (left) **2** yimíin (right) **3** dúghri (straight on) **4** síinima (cinema) **5** yizúur (to visit/he visits) **6** sháari9 (street)

Unit 12

Exercise 1

1 wiSîlt **2** ríg9it **3** nízlu **4** shiríbt **5** wiSîltu **6** rigí9na **7** nizîlti **8** ríg9u **9** shírib **10** nizîlt

Exercise 2

1 kalt **2** ráaHit **3** SíHyu **4** záadit **5** shúftu **6** khádna **7** bí9ti **8** záaru **9** SiHít **10** ruHt **11** shaaf **12** SiHítu **13** zaad **14** zurt **15** bí9na

Exercise 3

imbáariH widáad wi-gáabir _nízlu_ wusT il-bálad. il-áwwil gáabir _raaH_ maHáll il-muusíiqa wi-láakin widáad _ráaHit_ il-mustáshfa wi-záarit_ kháalhaa. wi-ba9dáyn húmma l-itnáyn _sháafu_ film gidíid wi-_kálu_ sámak fi máT9am 9ála k-korníish.

Exercise 4

You will hear a model response on the recording.

Exercise 5

You will hear a model response on the recording.

Exercise 6

1d; **2**f; **3**a; **4**c; **5**b; **6**e

Exercise 7

1 ma raaHítsh il-bank imbáariH. **2** záarit náadya fil-mustáshfa. **3** ma khallaSítsh ir-riwáaya. **4** nízlit wusT il-bálad. **5** ma li9bítsh iskwáash má9a záyna. **6** ma khadítsh il-fustáan lit-tárzi. **7** ráaHit il-maHáTTa.

Exercise 8

Open-ended speaking exercise. See Unit 1, Exercise 10.

Exercise 9

You will hear a model response on the recording.

Exercise 10

1 England *July* 2 France *August* 3 Italy *September*
4 USA *October* 5 Japan *December* 6 China *January*
7 India *March* 8 Egypt *April*

Exercise 11

1 manSúur 9ánduh táman siníin. 9iid miláaduh arbá9a abríil.
2 bashíir 9ánduh talatíin sána. 9iid miláaduh khámsa wi-9ishríin
oghúsTus. 3 fáTma 9andáhaa 9áshar siníin. 9iid miláadhaa tís9a
oktúubir. 4 áHmad 9ánduh taláata wi-árba9íin sána. 9iid miláaduh
saba9táashar disámbir. 5 núura 9andáhaa saba9táashar sána. 9iid
miláadhaa itnáashar yanáayir. 6 sáara 9andáhaa khámsa wi-9ishríin
sána. 9iid miláadhaa áwwil/wáahid fibráayir. 7 muHámmad 9ánduh
khamastáashar sána. 9iid miláaduh sáb9a máayo. 8 wisáam
9ánduh itnáashar sána. 9iid miláaduh wáaHid wi-talatíin yúulio.

Exercise 12

Open-ended speaking exercise. See Unit 1, Exercise 10.

Exercise 13

1h; 2i; 3e; 4k; 5d; 6a; 7c; 8f; 9j; 10l; 11b; 12g

Unit 13

Exercise 1

1 sánat alf wi-tis9umíyya wi-sittíin 2 sánat alfáyn w-arbá9a
3 sánat alf wi-tis9umíyya wi-tis9íin 4 sánat alf wi-khumsumíyya wi-
sab9íin 5 sánat alfáyn wi-9ishríin 6 sánat alf wi-tumnumíyya
khámsa wi-tamaníin 7 sánat alfáyn wi-tisa9táashar 8 sánat alf wi-
tis9umíyya itnáyn wi-sab9íin 9 sánat alfáyn wi-tís9a 10 sánat alfáyn
arbá9a wi-talatíin

Exercise 2

1 kúnna ga9aníin. 2 ma kaanúush fil-bayt. 3 Hakúun fil-bank.
4 gíddi kaan másri. 5 mish Ha-nikúun hináak. 6 Ha-tikúunu
fil-qáahira búkra? 7 iS-SaHrá kaan háadi. 8 bínti Ha-tikúun
mashghúula. 9 il-ghayTáan káanit kibíira. 10 ínta ma kúntish
fil-madrása?

Exercise 3

1 láazim nikúun fil-madrása. 2 íbni 9áwwiz yikúun hína.
3 iHtimáal yikúunu min aswáan. 4 múmkin yikúun mumássil.
5 baHíbb akúun il-áwwil. 6 mish 9awzíin nikúun ga9aníin.

Exercise 4

1 kaan 9ándi SáaHib 9áayish hína. **2** kaan fiih mátHaf fi wusT il-bálad.
3 káanu muhandisíin? **4** ma kaansh fiih bank ganb is-síinima.
5 kaan 9andína 9aSíir tufáaH. **6** kúnna mashghuulíin.
7 kaan 9ándak SáaHib hináak? **8** ma kaansh 9ándi 9arabíyya.

Exercise 5

1 Ha-yikúun 9ándi SáaHib 9áayish hína. **2** Ha-yikúun fiih mátHaf fi
wusT il-bálad. **3** Ha-yikúunu muhandisíin? **4** mish Ha-yikúun fiih bank
ganb is-síinima. **5** Ha-yikúun 9andína 9aSíir tufáaH. **6** Ha-nikúun
mashghuulíin. **7** Ha-yikúun 9ándak SáaHib hináak? **8** mish
Ha-yikúun 9ándi 9arabíyya.

Exercise 6

(model answer – yours may vary)

min mí'it sána kaan fiih nakhl kitíir, bass dilwá'ti fiih 9imáaraat.

kaan fiih ghayTáan wi-HiSína, bass dilwá'ti fiih shawáari9 wi-
9arabiyyáat kitíira.

ma kaansh fiih síinima hína wálla maHalláat. kaan fiih bass
shuwáyyit buyúut.

il-bálad káanit gamíila wi-hádya bass dilwá'ti záHma.

Exercise 7

Open-ended exercise. See Unit 1, Exercise 10.

Exercise 8

1 kúnna bi-niStáad fit-tír9a. **2** úkhti káanit lábsa fustáan áHmar.
3 káanu gáyyiin il-Háfla? **4** kúnti náyma? **5** kúnt bál9ab ténnis kull
yohm. **6** ma kúntish bi-tírkab il-khayl? **7** íbni kaan Ha-yíl9ab kúra
bass kaan ta9báan. **8** kúuna Ha-nizáakir bass kúuna mashguulíin.

Exercise 9

You will hear a model response on the recording.

Exercise 10

1 (íHna) khalláSna il-9aysh. **2** ukhtáhaa inbásaTit? **3** abúya bi-
yishtághal bil-layl fi máT9am Sugháyyar. **4** il-wiláad it'áablu 9and
is-síinima ba9d il-madrása. **5** (ána) batmárran kull yohm fin-náadi.
6 (húmma) sáafru iskindiríyya imbáariH leh? **7** Darúuri nishtághal
yohm il-Hadd. **8** (íntu) istahláktu kull is-sámak is-sána di?

Exercise 11

1 muHáasib ➔ yiHáasib H/s/b (form III), *to calculate*
2 mumássil ➔ yimással m/s/l (form II), *to act/to represent*
3 mitkállif ➔ yitkállaf k/l/f (form V), *to cost*
4 mistá9gil ➔ yistá9gil 9/g/l (form X), *to be in a hurry*
5 mudárris ➔ yidárras d/r/s (form II), *to teach*
6 mustá9mil ➔ yistá9mil 9/m/l (form X), *to use*
7 musákkin ➔ yisákkan s/k/n (form II), *to calm*
8 mitgáwwiz ➔ yitgáwwiz g/w/z (form V), *to get married*
9 mukhtálif ➔ yikhtálaf kh/l/f (form VIII), *to differ*

Exercise 12

5; 6; 4; 7; 2; 3; 1

Exercise 13

You will hear a model response on the recording.

Exercise 14

Open-ended exercise. See Unit 1, Exercise 10.

Exercise 15

The registration number is **875138**.

Exercise 16

a khámsa **b** talatáashar **c** 9ishríin **d** sítta wi-tamaníin **e** míyya
f mitáyn wi-khamsíin **g** alf wi-tultumíyya, arbá9a w-arba9íin
h alf wi-tis9umíyya, sáb9a wi-tis9íin **i** alfáyn **j** alfáyn w-itnáashar
k alfáyn wi-9ishríin **l** alfáyn, tamánya wi-khamsíin

Unit 14

Exercise 1

1 9awzíin níHgiz tarabáyza li-khámsa yohm it-taláat ig-gáyy.
2 9awzíin níHgiz tarabáyza li-arbá9a yohm is-sabt ig-gáyy.
3 9awzíin níHgiz tarabáyza li-sítta yohm il-árba9 ig-gáyy.
4 9awzíin níHgiz tarabáyza li-itnáyn yohm ig-gúm9a ig-gáyya.
5 9awzíin níHgiz tarabáyza li-tamánya yohm il-Had ig-gáyy.
6 9awzíin níHgiz tarabáyza li-khamastáashar yohm il-khamíis ig-gáyy.

Exercise 2

1 ma9lésh **2** láHZa ma9áaya **3** taHt ámrak **4** miin ma9áaya?
5 SabáaH il-khayr yaa fándim **6** ittafá'na

Exercise 3
You will hear a model response on the recording.

Exercise 4
1 Ha-nîigi is-sáa9a tamánya. **2** úmmi gat imbáariH. **3** widáad Ha-tîigi tishúufna yohm ig-gúm9a ig-gáyya. **4** ta9áala hína yaa Hásan! **5** bági hína kull yohm khamîis. **6** 9áawiz tîigi in-náadi? **7** gum imbáariH bass ma kúntish hína. **8** láazim tîigu dilwá'ti. **9** gáabir ma bi-yigîish hína kull yohm gúm9a. **10** ta9áalu hína yaa wiláad! **11** ma gaytîish leh? **12** il-muhándis ma gehsh is-sáa9a sítta.

Exercise 5

	kebab	chicken	fish	prawns	peas	okra	vine leaves
Jane	✔						✔
Samira			✔				
Widaad					✔		
Gaber		✔	✔				
Hassan		✔	✔				

Exercise 6
1 HáTlub il-firáakh má9a ruzz. **2** HáTlub il-bámya má9a 9aysh. **3** HáTlub gambári máshwi. **4** HáTlub ik-kabáab má9a sálaTa. **5** HáTlub il-firáakh má9a bisílla. **6** HáTlub is-sámak il-má'li wi-gambári. **7** HáTlub muluukhíyya bil-aráanib. **8** HáTlub wára 9ínab wil-banáyh.

Exercise 7
1 I try/I attempt **2** she dressed **3** I explain to him **4** you *(fem.)* got married **5** we fed **6** you *(masc.)* choose **7** he benefitted **8** they seated me **9** we will give you a taste **10** he gets annoyed

Exercise 8
1 'a99adúni **2** bi-yitDáayi' **3** afahhímuh **4** itgawwízti **5** baHáawil **6** Ha-nidawwá'ik **7** tikhtáar **8** istafáad **9** labbísit **10** akkílna

Exercise 9
Open-ended speaking exercise. See Unit 1, Exercise 10.

Exercise 10
1 stuffed vine leaves 50
2 okra 70
3 prawns 120

4 fish with rice 95
5 molokheyya 45
6 fried chicken 65
7 cola 14
8 lemon juice 23

Unit 15

Exercise 1

Present	Past	English
yirúuH	raaH	to go
yí9mil	9ámal	to make/to do
yisáafir	sáafir	to travel
yáakul	kal	to eat
yishúuf	shaaf	to see
yíSHa	SíHi	to wake up
yíigi	geh	to come
yikúun	kaan	to be
yi'ákkil	ákkil	to feed
yinbísiT	inbásaT	to enjoy
yitmárran	itmárran	to train/to practise
yiHáawil	Háawil	to attempt/to try
yistáHlik	istáHlik	to consume
yíwSal	wíSil	to arrive

Exercise 2

1 yohm il-itnáyn is-sáa9a tamánya **2** yohm il-khamíis is-sáa9a itnáyn
3 yohm ig-gúm9a is-sáa9a arbá9a **4** yohm is-sabt is-sáa9a tamánya
wi-nuSS **5** yohm il-Hadd is-sáa9a arbá9a wi-nuSS **6** yohm it-taláat
is-sáa9a áshara wi-rub9 **7** yohm ilt-árba9 is-sáa9a wáHda ílla rub9
8 yohm ig-gúm9a ig-gáyya is-sáa9a sítta wi-tilt

Exercise 3

1 yohm il-Hadd saafírt bayt gíddi bil-9arabíyya. **2** 9umúuman
bi-ni'ákkil il-HuSáan is-sáa9a sítta. **3** inbasáTtu l-agáaza yaa wiláad?
4 il-bálad kaan háadi wi-jamíil. **5** báSHa kull yohm is-sáa9a sáb9a wi-
nuSS. **6** 9ammíti Ha-tiHáawil tíigi yohm it-taláat. **7** Hásan itmárran
tálat sa9áat fin-náadi yohm il-khamíis. **8** iT-Tayyáara Ha-tiwSál yohm
is-sabt is-sáa9a itnáyn wi-tilt. **9** húmma ma shaafúush il-máT9am
ganb il-maHáTTa. **10** Ha-ti9míli eh yohm ig-gúm9a ig-gáyya?

Exercise 4

1 ✗ 2 ✓ 3 ✓ 4 ✓ 5 ✗ 6 ✗ 7 ✗ 8 ✓

Exercise 5

1 e 2 k 3 k 4 f 5 a 6 j 7 d 8 b 9 c 10 g 11 i 12 h

Exercise 6

1 áHmad ma bi-yiHíbbish il-'iráaya. 2 ma ruHtíish il-bank leh?
3 mish láazim núkhrug is-sáa9a taláata. 4 húmma mish naymíin
dilwá'ti. 5 mish Ha-yikúun fiih alk fil-Háfla. 6 il-wiláad ma inbasTúush
imbáariH? 7 ána ma basaafírsh aswáan fish-shíta. 8 ma fiish
masharíib fit-taláaga. 9 samíira ma rig9ítsh min il-madrása. 10 ma
takhdúsh/baláash tákhdu áwwil sháari9 9ála l-yimíin.

Exercise 7

1 mátHaf/matáaHif (museum) 2 agáaza/agazáat (holiday)
3 kullíiya/kulliiyáat (college) 4 muhándis/muhandisíin (engineer)
5 shahr/shuhúur (month) 6 9imáara/9imaráat (apartment building)
7 bayt/buyúut (house) 8 maHáTTa/maHaTTáat (station) 9 film/
afláam (film) 10 HuSáan/HiSína (horse) 11 burg/abráag (tower)
12 ghayT/ghayTáan (field) 13 náadi/nawáadi (club) 14 bank/
bunúuk (bank) 15 ríHla/riHláat (journey) 16 mádkhal/madáakhil
(entrance) 17 madrása/madáaris (school) 18 shá''a/shú'a'
(apartment) 19 fawg/afwáag (group) 20 agnábi/agáanib (foreigner)

Exercise 8

You will hear a model response on the recording.

Exercise 9 *(Model directions. Yours may vary.)*

1 khud áwwil sháari9 9ála l-shimáal. il-bank 9ála l-shimáal ba9d
il-isháara. 2 9ála Tuul min hína wi-khúdi táalit sháari9 9ála l-yimíin.
il-maHáTTa 9ála l-shimáal. 3 dúghri min hína wi-ba9dáyn khúdu táalit
sháari9 9ála l-shimáal. is-síinima 9ála l-yimíin ganbj il-mátHaf.
4 khud áwwil sháari9 9ála l-yimíin. il-mustáshfa 9ála l-yimíin.
5 khúdi táani sháari9 9ála l-yimíin 9ánd il-isháara. khallíiki dúghri wil-
burg hináak. 6 9ála Tuul min hína wi-khúdu táalit sháari9 9ála
l-yimíin. il-maTáar 9ála l-shimáal ba9d il-maHáTTa. 7 khud táani
sháari9 9ála l-shimáal. khallíiki dúghri wil-kúbri hináak. 8 khúdu áwwil
sháari9 9ála l-shimáal. maHáTTit il-otobíis 9ála l-yimíin 'udáam il-bank.

Exercise 10

Open-ended speaking exercise. See Unit 1, Exercise 10.

English–Arabic glossary

This section is an English–Arabic glossary of the key words appearing in *Colloquial Arabic of Egypt*. The unit number in which the word first appears is given in the right-hand column.

The Arabic script is shown alongside the transliteration, but be aware that the colloquial language does not have hard-and-fast spelling rules and you may see some words spelt differently in other contexts.

Note the following:

1 *Plurals* are given after the singular (in transliteration).

2 *Verbs* are shown in the present followed by the past and given in the **huwwa** form (*third person masculine*). See Structure summary for more details on how to form verbs.

A

a little/somewhat	شوية shuwáyya	14
a long time ago	زمان/من زمان zamáan/min zamáan	13
about/approximately	حوالي Hawáali	9
above each other	فوق بعض foh' ba9D	4
above/over	فوق foh'	4
accountant	محاسب muHáasib (pl. muHaasbíin)	3
actor	ممثل mumássil (pl. mumassilíin)	3
actually/really	فعلا fí9lan	7
adults	كبار kubáar	7
afraid, to be	يخاف/خاف yikháaf/khaaf	11
after	بعد ba9d	9
after (+ verb)	بعد ما ba9d(i) maa	10
afternoon	بعد الظهر ba9d id-Duhr	9
ago	من min (+ period of time)	13
agree, to	يتفق/اتفق yittífi'/ittáfa'	14
air conditioning	تكييف takíif (pl. takiifáat)	4
airport	مطار maTáar (pl. maTaráat)	6
also	كمان kamáan	5
always	دايما dáyman	13
American	أمريكاني amriikáani (pl. amriikáan)	1
and	و wi/w-	1
anything else?	إيه كمان؟ eh kamáan?	5
apartment building	عمارة 9imáara (pl. 9imaráat)	13
apple	تفاحة tuffáaHa (pl. tuffáaH)	5
April	أبريل abríil	12
approximately/about	حوالي Hawáali	6
army	جيش gaysh (pl. giyúush)	13
arrive, to	يوصل/وصل yíwSal/wíSil	9
as regards/in relation to	بالنسبة لـ... bin-nísba li...	11
ask him	اسأله is'áluh	6
at your service	حاضر HáaDir	5
at your service	تحت أمرك taHt ámrak (fem. ámrik)	14

August	أغسطس	oghúsTus	12
auntie	طنت	Tant	1
Australia	أستراليا	ostorálya	2
Australian	أسترالي	ostoráali (pl.ostoraliyyíin)	1
authentic/original	أصيل	aSíil	14
available	موجود	mawgúud	4
awake	صاحي	SáaHi	1

B

balcony	بلكونة	balakóhna (pl. balakohnáat)	4
bald	أصلع	áSla9	6
ball/football/soccer	كورة	kúra (pl. kúwar)	10
bank	بنك	bank (pl. bunúuk)	11
bathroom	حمام	Hammáam (pl. Hammamáat)	4
be careful/watch out	خللي بالك	khálli báalak (fem. khálli báalik)	11
beautiful	جميل	gamíil	12
because	لأن	la'ánn	7
bed	سرير	siríir (pl. saráayir)	4
bedroom	أوضة النوم	ohDt in-nóhm	4
beer	بيرة	bíira	3
before	قبل	'abl	9
before (+ verb)	قبل ما	'ábl(i) maa	10
behind	ورا	wára	4
belonging to/relating to	تبع	taba9	13
between	بين	bayn	4
big	كبير	kibíir	4
birthday	عيد ميلاد	9iid miláad	12
black	أسود	íswid (fem. sóhda)	5
blouse	بلوزة	bilúuza (pl. biluzáat)	6
blue	أزرق	ázra' (fem. zár'a)	5
boat	مركب	márkib (pl. maráakib)	6

boatman	مراكبي	marákbi (pl. marakbíyya)	13
book/reserve, to	يحجز/حجز	yíHgiz/Hágaz	10
booking/reservation	حجز	Hagz (pl. Huguuzáat)	9
boots (pair of)	بوت	buut (pl. buutáat)	6
bottle	قزازة	izáaza (pl. azáayiz)	3
boy/child	ولاد	wálad (pl. wiláad)	1
branch	فرع	far9 (pl. furúu9)	9
bread	عيش	9aysh	3
breakfast	فطار	fiTáar	9
bridge	كوبري	kúbri (pl. kabáari)	11
bring!	هات!	haat! (fem. háati)	2
bring me ...	هات لي ...	háatli ... (fem. haatíili)	3
broadcaster	مذيع	muzíi9 (pl. muzii9íin)	1
brother	أخو	akh(u) (pl. ikhwáat)	2
brown	بني	búnni	5
building	مبنى	mábna (pl. mabáani)	12
bus/coach	اوتوبيس	otobíis (pl. otobiisáat)	7
busy	مشغول	mashgúul	9
but	بس	bass(i)	4
by herself	لوحدها	li-waHdáhaa	11
by himself	لوحده	li-wáHduh	11
by myself	لوحدي	li-wáHdi	11

C

cabin	كابينة	kabíina (pl. kabáayin)	4
cake	كيك	kayk	10
camp; encampment	معسكر	mu9áskar	13
can/possible	ممكن	múmkin	10
can/to be able	يقدر/قدر	yí'dar/'ídir	13
canal (small irrigation)	ترعة	tír9a (pl. tíra9)	13
captain (of a sports team)	كابتن	káabtin (pl. kabáatin)	10
car	عربية	9arabíyya (pl. 9arabiyyáat)	4
cat	قطة	'óTTa (pl. 'óTaT)	7

catch, to	يمسك/مسك	yímsik/mísik	7
cheapest/cheaper	أرخص	árkhaS	7
cheese	جبنة	gíbna	5
chemistry	كيميا	kímya	3
chicken	فراخ	firáakh	12
child	طفل	Tifl (pl. aTfáal)	7
children	ولاد/أولاد	awláad/wiláad	2/12
choose, to	ينقي/نقى	yiná"i/ná"a	14
church	كنيسة	kiníisa (pl. kanáayis)	12
cinema	سينما	síinima (pl. siinimáat)	11
city centre/downtown	وسط البلد	wusT il-bálad	11
clean	نظيف	niDíif	7
clear	واضح	wáadiH	10
clover	برسيم	barsíim	13
club	نادي	náadi (pl. nawáadi)	9
coat	بالطو	bálToh (pl. baláaTi)	6
coffee/café	قهوة	áhwa	3
cola	كولا	kóhla	3
college	كلية	kullíiya (pl. kulliiyáat)	10
colour	لون	lohn (pl. alwáan)	5
coloured	ملون	miláwwin	6
come!	تعال!	ta9áala! (fem. ta9áali)	2
come this way; here you are	اتفضل	itfáDDal (fem. itfaDDáli)	1
come, to	ييجي/جه	yíigi/geh	14
comfortable	مريح	muríiH	4
coming/next	الجاي	ig-gáyy	14
company/business	شركة	shírka (pl. shirkáat)	10
computer	كمبيوتر	kombyúutir (pl. kombyuutiráat)	10
congratulations	مبروك	mabrúuk	4
connected with	بتاع	bitáa9	2
cook, to	يطبخ/طبخ	yúTbukh/Tabakh	13
copper	نحاس	naHáas	5

corniche	كورنيش	korníish	11
correct/right	مضبوط	maZbúuT	14
cousin, daughter of (paternal) uncle	بنت عم	bint 9ámm	9
cow	بقرة	bá'ara (pl. bá'ar)	7
crowded	زحمة	záHma	9
customer/client	زبون	zibúun (pl. zabáayin)	10

D

dark (colour)	غامق	gháami'	5
dark blue	أزرق كحلي	ázr'a kóHli	6
daughter	بنت	bint (pl. banáat)	2
December	ديسمبر	disámbir	12
delicious	لذيذ	lazíiz	7
describe, to	يوصف/وصف	yíwSif/wáSaf	11
desert	صحراء	SaHrá	13
dining room	أوضة السفرة	ohDt is-súfra	4
dinner	عشاء	9ásha	9
disappoint/embarrass, to	يكسف/كسف	yíksif/kásaf	14
discount	تخفيض	takhfíiD (pl. takhfiiDáat)	7
dish of the day	طبق اليوم	Tába' il-yohm	3
distance/errand/task	مشوار	mishwáar (pl. mashawíir)	13
dock/port	ميناء	míina (pl. mawáani)	6
doctor	دكتور	duktúur (pl. dakáktra)	3
dog	كلب	kalb (pl. kiláab)	7
door	باب	baab (pl. bibáan)	4
don't …!	بلاش …!	baláash …!	11
donkey	حمار	Humáar (pl. Himíir)	7
dress	فستان	fustáan (pl. fasatíin)	6
drink	مشروب	mashrúub (pl. masharíib)	12
drink, to	يشرب/شرب	yíshrab/shírib	12
driver	سواق	sawwáa' (pl. sawwa'íin)	13
duck	بطة	báTTa (pl. baTT)	7

E

ear	ودن	widn (*pl.* widáan)	6
early	بدري	bádri	9
Eastern	شرقي	shárqi (*fem.* sharqíyya)	9
easy	سهل	sahl	10
eat, to	ياكل/كل	yáakul/kál	9
Egypt Air	مصر للطيران	maSr liT-Tayaráan	3
Egyptian	مصري	máSri (*pl.* máSriyyíin)	1
eight	ثمانية	tamánya (táman)	5
eighteen	ثمنتاشر	tamantáashar	5
eighty	ثمانين	tamaníin	5
eleven	حداشر	Hidáashar	5
embassy	سفارة	sifáara (*pl.* sifaráat)	11
end/finish	نهاية	niháaya	12
engineer	مهندس	muhándis (*pl.* muhandisíin)	3
England	انجلترا	ingiltára	7
English (nationality)	انجليزي	ingilíizi (*pl.* ingilíiz)	1
enjoy, to	ينبسط/انبسط	yinbísiT/inbásaT	12
entrance	مدخل	mádkhal (*pl.* madáakhil)	11
every/all	كل	kull	10
every day	كل يوم	kull yohm	10
everyone/'you lot'	يا جماعة	yaa gamáa9a	14
everywhere	في كل حتة	fi kull Hitta	5
exactly	بالضبط	biZ-ZabT	9
exit	مخرج	mákhrag (*pl.* mahkáarig)	11
expensive	غالي	gháali (*fem.* ghálya)	7
eye	عين	9ayn (*pl.* 9aynáyn)	6

F

falafel	طعمية	Ta9míyya	3
famous	مشهور	mash-húur	12
far	بعيد	bi9íid	6

fast	سريع	saríi9	10
fat	تخين	tikhíin	6
father	أب (أبو)	ab(u)	2
fava beans	فول	fuul	3
February	فبراير	fibráayir	12
feed, to	يأكل/أكل	yi'ákkil/ákkil	14
felucca	فلوكة	filúuka (pl. faláayik)	13
fiancé(e)	خطيب/خطيبة	khaTíib (fem. khaTíiba)	2
field	غيط	ghayT (pl. ghayTáan)	13
fifteen	خمستاشر	khamastáashar	5
fifty	خمسين	khamsíin	5
film/movie	فيلم	film (pl. afláam)	13
find, to	يلاقي/لاقى	yiláa'i/lá'a	11
fine ('thanks be to God')	الحمد لله	il-Hámdu lilláah	1
finger	صباع	Sobáa9 (pl. Sawáabi9)	6
finish, to	يخلص/خلص	yikhállaS/khállaS	10
first	أول	áwwil	11
first class	درجة أولى	dáraga úula	7
first/firstly	الأول	il-áwwil	11
fish	سمك	samak	10
fish/hunt, to	يصطاد/اصطاد	yiSTáad/iSTáad	10
fishing	صيد السمك	Sayd is-sámak	10
five	خمسة	khámsa (khámas)	1
flat/apartment	شقة	shá''a (pl. shú'a')	12
flight attendant	مضيف	muDíif/muDíifa	3
flip-flops	شبشب	shíbshib (pl. shabáashib)	6
flying	طيران	Tayaráan	7
food	أكل	akl	7
for	لـ	li-	5
for example	مثلا	másalan	14
for/because of	عشان	9asháan	6
foreigner	أجنبي	agnábi (pl. agáanib)	14
foreigner (slang)	خواجة	khawáaga	6
forks	شوكة	shóhka (pl. shúwak)	5

forty	أربعين	arba9íin	5
four	أربعة	arbá9a (árba9)	1
fourteen	أربعتاشر	arba9atáashar	5
France	فرنسا	faránsa	3
Friday	الجمعة	ig-gúm9a	9
fried	مقلي	má'li	14
friend	صاحب	SáaHib (pl. aS-Háab)	9
future	مستقبل	mustá'bal	12

G

galabeyya: *Egyptian robe*	جلابية	galabíyya (pl. galaalíib)	5
getting down/getting off	نازل	náazil	6
give (someone) a taste	دوق/يدوق	yidáwwa'/dáwwa	14
give me	اديني	iddíini	5
glass	كباية	kubbáaya (pl. kubbayáat)	3
glasses (pair of)	نظارة	naDDáara (pl. naDDaaráat)	6
go (away)/walk, to	يمشي/مشي	yímshi/míshi	13
go down/get down, to	ينزل/نزل	yínzil/nízil	10
go, to	راح/يروح	yirúuH/raaH	9
God help us!	يا ساتر!	yaa sáatir!	7
going (to)	رايح	ráayiH (pl. rayHíin)	7
gold	ذهب	dahab	12
good afternoon/evening	مساء الخير	masáa' il-khayr	1
good morning	صباح الخير	SabáaH il-khayr	1
goodbye	مع السلامة	má9a s-saláama	1
grandfather	جد	gidd	13
grandmother	جدة	gídda	13
great!	عظيم!	9aZíim!	9
green	أخضر	ákhDar (fem. KháDra)	5
grilled	مشوي	máshwi	14
group	جماعة	gamáa9a	14
group (of tourists)	فوج	fawg (pl. afwáag)	9
guest	ضيف	Dayf (pl. Diyúuf)	1

H

English	Arabic	Transliteration	No.
hair	شعر	shá9r	6
half	نص	nuSS	5
half past …	الساعة … ونص	is-sáa9a … wi-nuSS	9
hall	صالة	Sáala (pl. Saaláat)	4
hand	ايد	iid (pl. iidáyn)	6
happy	مبسوط	mabsúut (pl. mabsuutíin)	6
hat	برنيطة	burnáyTa (pl. baraníiT)	6
have to/must	لازم	láazim	10
have to/essential	ضروري	Darúuri	10
have/has	عند	9ánd + possessive ending	3
he	هو	húwwa	1
heading up to/going to	طالع	Táali9	6
Heliopolis	مصر الجديدة	maSr ig-gidíida	1
hello	اهلا	áhlan	1
hello? (as on the telephone)	آلو؟	aló?	4
here	هنا	hína	2
herself	نفسها	nafsáhaa	11
hibiscus tea	كركديه	karkaday	3
himself	نفسه	náfsuh	11
hobby	هواية	hiwáaya (pl. hiwayáat)	10
holiday	أجازة	agáaza (pl. agazáat)	9
honeymoon	شهر العسل	shahr il-9ásal	7
honour, to	يشرف/شرف	yishárraf/shárraf	14
horse	حصان	HuSáan (pl. HiSína)	7
horses	خيل	khayl	13
hospital	مستشفى	mustáshfa (pl. mustashfayáat)	11
hotel	فندق	fúndu' (pl. fanáadi')	9
house	بيت	bayt (pl. buyúut)	9
how (come)?	إزاي؟	izzáay?	7
how are you?	إزيك	izzáayak (fem. izzáayik)	1
How do I get to …?	منين؟	… mináyn?	11
how many?	كام؟	káam?	6

how much?	بكام؟	**bikáam?**	5
How old is he?	عنده كام سنة؟	**9ánduh kaam sána?**	6
hundred	مية	**míyya**	5
hungry	جعان	**ga9áan** (*pl.* **ga9aníin**)	13
husband	جوز	**gohz**	2

I

I	أنا	**ána**	1
I adore ...	أنا أموت في...	**ána amúut fi ...**	3
I agree (*masc./fem.*)	أنا موافق	**ána muwáafi'/muwáf'a**	7
I don't know	أنا مش عارف	**ána mish 9áarif**	6
I don't like	أنا ما باحبش	**ána ma baHíbbish**	7
I like	أنا باحب	**ána baHíbb**	7
I mean/so/well	يعني	**yá9ni**	6
I'm from ...	أنا من...	**ána min ...**	1
I've just eaten.	لسه واكل	**líssa wáakil** (*fem.* **wákla**)	3
I've just had a drink.	لسه شارب	**líssa sháarib** (*fem.* **shárba**)	3
idea	فكرة	**fíkra** (*pl.* **afkáar**)	5
If Gods wills/God willing	إن شاء الله	**in sháa' alláah**	2
important	مهم	**muhímm**	7
in	في	**fi**	4
in front of	قدام	**'uddáam**	4
in the place of	في مكان	**fi makáan**	13
increase, to	يزيد/زاد	**yizíid/zaad**	10
institute	معهد	**má9had** (*pl.* **ma9áahid**)	9
integrity/honesty	ذمة	**zímma**	13
intending to	ناوي	**náawi** (*pl.* **nawyíin**)	10
Islamic headscarf	حجاب	**Higáab**	6

J

| January | يناير | **yanáayir** | 12 |
| journey | رحلة | **ríHla** (*pl.* **riHláat**) | 7 |

juice	عصير 9aSíir	3
July	يوليو yúulio	12
June	يونيو yúunio	12

K

kebab	كباب kabáab	3
keen on	غاوي gháawi (fem. gháwya)	10
keep (pets)/breed/ bring up, to	يربي/ربى yirábbi/rábba	14
kid	عيل 9áyyil (pl. 9ayyáal)	14
kilo	كيلو kíilu	5
kitchen	مطبخ máTbakh (pl. maTáabikh)	9

L

ladies'/women's	حريمي Haríimi	5
language	لغة lúgha (pl. lugháat)	9
last year	السنة اللي فاتت is-sána ílli fáatit	12
laundry	مغسلة maghsála (pl. magháasil)	9
lavish	متكلف mitkállif	13
lawyer	محامي muHáami (pl. muHaamiyíin)	3
leather	جلد gild	4
leave/exit, to	يخرج/خرج yúkhrug/khárag	9
left (hand side)	شمال shimáal	11
leg/foot	رجل rigl (pl. rigláyn)	6
lemon-yellow (adj.)	لموني laymúuni	5
let's stick to/let's stay with	خللينا في khallíina fi	7
library/bookshop	مكتبة maktába (pl. maktabáat)	9
light (weight)	خفيف khafíif	9
light (coloured)	فاتح fáatiH	5
lights (traffic)	إشارة isháara (pl. isharáat)	11
like this	كده kída	5
like; similar to	زي zayy	5

lime/lemon	لمون laymúun	3
listen, to	يسمع/سمع yísma9/sími9	13
live in	ساكن في sáakin fi (pl. sakníin fi)	9
living room	أوضة القعاد ohDt il-o9áad	4
loaf	رغيف raghíif (pl. raghífa)	5
lunch	غدا gháda	9
luxury/first class	لوكس lux	4

M

Madam	مدام madáam	1
made from	معمول من ma9múul min	12
maître	متر metr	1
make/do/create, to	يعمل/عمل yí9mil/9ámal	10
March	مارس máaris	12
market	سوق suu' (pl. aswaa')	11
masters (degree)	ماجستير majistáyr	9
May	مايو máayo	12
may/might	احتمال iHtimáal	12
me neither/nor I	ولا أنا wála ána	7
me too	أنا كمان ána kamáan	7
meat	لحمة láHma	12
medicine (study)	الطب iT-Tibb	12
medium (sized)	وسط wásaT	5
Mexico	المكسيك il-maksíik	7
milk	لبن lában	3
minced meat	كفتة kófta	3
mint	نعناع ni9náa9	12
Miss, young woman	آنسة áanisa (pl. aanisáat)	3
model (of car, etc.)	موديل modáyl	4
Monday	الأثنين il-itnáyn	9
month	شهر shahr (pl. shuhúur)	12
more expensive	أغلى ághla	7
morning (in the)	الصبح iS-SubH	9
mosque	مسجد másgid (pl. masáagid)	9

mother	أم	umm	2
mouse	فار	faar (*pl.* firáan)	7
mouth	بق	bo'	6
museum	متحف	mátHaf (*pl.* matáaHif)	9
music	موسيقى	muusíiqa	10
my name's ...	أنا اسمي	ána ísmi ...	1
myself	نفسي	náfsi	11

N

name	اسم	ism (*pl.* asáami)	1
near	قريب	'uráyyib	6
need	محتاج	miHtáag (*pl.* miHtaagíin)	5
never mind	معلش	ma9lésh	9
new	جديد	gidíid	4
next to/near	جنب	ganb	4
nice/sweet	حلو	Hílw	5
nine	تسعة	tís9a (tísa9)	5
nineteen	تسعتاشر	tisa9táashar	5
ninety	تسعين	tis9íin	5
no	لا	la'	1
nose	مناخير	manakhíir	6
not	مش	mish	3
not here	مش هنا	mish hína	3
novel	رواية	riwáaya (*pl.* riwayáat)	10
November	نوفمبر	nofámbir	12
now	دلوقتي	dilwá'ti	10
number	رقم	ráqam	1

O

| o'clock | الساعة | is-sáa9a ... | 9 |
| October | اكتوبر | oktúubir | 12 |

of course	طبعا	Táb9an	5
office	مكتب	máktab (pl. makáatib)	9
OK, well	طيب	Táyyib	3
OK, fine	ماشي	máashi	5
okra, ladies' fingers	بامية	bámya	3
old	قديم	'adíim	4
old (person)	عجوز	9agúuz	6
olives	زيتون	zaytúun	5
omelette	اومليت	omlíit	3
on	على	9ála	4
on the left	على الشمال	9ála sh-shimáal	11
on the right	على اليمين	9ála l-yimíin	11
once	مرة	márra	9
one	واحد	wáaHid	1
one moment	لحظة معايا	láHZa ma9áaya	14
operate, to	يشغل/شغل	yishághghal/shághghal	13
order/ask for, to	يطلب/طلب	yúTlub/Tálab	14
over/finished	خلاص	khaláas	12
oysters	محار	maHáar	12

P

packet/box/tin	علبة	9ílba (pl. 9ílab)	5
pair of shoes	جزمة	gázma (pl. gízam)	6
pair of socks	شراب	shuráab (pl. shurabáat)	6
palm trees	نخل	nákhla (pl. nakhl)	13
pan fried/escalope	بانيه	banáyh	14
paper	ورق	wára'	5
patisserie/desserts	حلويات	Halawiyáat	12
peace on you	السلام عليكم	is-saláamuh 9aláykum	14
peaceful/quiet	هادي	háadi	13
peas	بسلة	bisílla	14
people	ناس	naas	12
per cent	في المية	fil-míyya	10
personally	شخصيا	shakhSáyyan	14

photo/picture	صورة	Súura (pl. Súwar)	2
place	مكان	makáan (pl. amáakin)	12
plane	طيارة	Tayyáara (pl. Tayyaráat)	7
plastic	بلاستك	biláastik	5
plate	طبق	Tába' (pl. Tubáa')	3
play, to	يلعب/لعب	yíl9ab/lí9ib	9
please	لو سمحت	law samáHt (fem. law samáHti)	5
please	من فضلك	min fáDlak (fem. fáDlik)	3
please (lit. 'on your life')	وحياتك	wiHyáatak (fem. -ik)	14
pomegranate	رمان	rummáan	12
pound (money)	جنيه	gináyh	5
prawns	جمبري	gambári	14
prayers	صلاة	Saláat	14
prepare, to	يحضر/حضر	yiHáDDar/HáDDar	9
price	سعر	sí9r (pl. as9áar)	7
problem	مشكلة	mushkíla (pl. masháakil)	4
professor	أستاذ	ustáaz (pl. asátza)	12
purple	بنفسجي	banafsígi	5
Pyramids (at Giza)	الأهرام	il-ahráam	9

Q

quarter	ربع	rub9	5
quarter past ...	الساعة... وربع	is-sáa9a ... wi-rub9	9
quarter to ...	الساعة... إلا ربع	is-sáa9a ... ílla rub9	9
question	سؤال	su'áal (pl. as'íla)	9
quickly	بسرعة	bi-súr9a	2

R

rabbit	أرنب	árnab (pl. aráanib)	7
radio	راديو	rádyo (pl. radyoháat)	2
ready	جاهز	gáaHiz (pl. gaaHzíin)	14

English	Arabic	Transliteration	No.
ready	مستعد	musta9íd	9
really ('by God')	والله	walláahi	14
really?	فعلا؟	fí9lan?	12
reasonable	معقول	ma9'úul	7
red	أحمر	áHmar (*fem.* Hámra)	5
referee	حكم	Hákam	13
refreshing	منعش	mun9ísh	12
remain, to	يبقى/بقى	yíb'a/bá'a	10
remember(ing)	فاكر	fáakir (*pl.* fakríin)	13
reservation	حجز	Hagz (*pl.* Huguuzáat)	9
restaurant	مطعم	máT9am (*pl.* maTáa9im)	9
return (ticket)	رايح جاي	ráayiH gáay	7
return, to	يرجع/رجع	yírga9/rígi9	12
rice	رز	ruzz	3
ride, to	يركب/ركب	yírkab/ríkib	13
right (hand side)	يمين	yimíin	11
room	أوضة	óhDa (*pl.* ówaD)	4
route/way	سكة	síkka (*pl.* síkak)	11

S

English	Arabic	Transliteration	No.
salad	سلطة	sálaTa (*pl.* salaTáat)	3
sandwich	سندوتش	sandawítsh (*pl.* sandawitsháat)	3
Saturday	السبت	is-sabt	9
savage	متوحش	mutawáHHish	14
say good morning to	يصبح/صبح	yiSábbaH/SábbaH	10
say, to	يقول/قال	yi'úul/'aal	11
school	مدرسة	madrása (*pl.* madáaris)	9
sciences	علوم	9ulúum	9
Scotland	اسكتلندا	iskutlánda	12
Scottish	اسكتلندي	iskutlándi (*pl.* iskutlandiyíin)	1
sea	بحر	baHr	10
season	موسم	múusim (*pl.* mawáawim)	10

seat, to	يقعد/قعد	yi'á99ad/á99ad	14
seat/chair	كرسي	kúrsi (pl. karáasi)	4
second/again	تاني	táani	11
sedative	مسكن	musákkin	12
		(pl. musakkináat)	
see, to	يشوف/شاف	yishúuf/shaaf	12
seeing/believing	شايف	sháayif (pl. shayfíin)	10
sell, to	يبيع/باع	yibíi9/baa9	11
September	سبتمبر	sibtámbir	12
seven	سبعة	sáb9a (sába9)	5
seventeen	سبعتاشر	saba9táashar	5
seventy	سبعين	sab9íin	5
share/split, to	يقسم/قسم	yí'sim/'ásam	14
she	هي	híyya	1
sheep	خروف	kharúuf (pl. khirfáan)	7
shirt	قميص	'amíiS (pl. 'umSáan)	5
shop/store	محل	maHáll (pl. maHalláat)	11
short	قصير	'uSáyyar	6
should	المفروض	il-mafrúuD	10
showing/obvious	باين	báayin	6
Siamese cat	قطة سيامي	'óTTa (pl. 'óTaT) siyáami	7
sir	بيه	beh	14
Sir/Madam	يا فندم	yaa fándim	4
Sir/Mr	أستاز	ustáaz	1
sister	أخت	ukht (pl. ukhwáat)	2
sit down!	اقعد!	u'9úd!	3
sitting/staying	قاعد	'áa9id (pl. 'a9díin)	10
sitting room (for guests)	صالون	Salóhn	4
six	ستة	sítta (sitt)	5
sixteen	ستاشر	sittáashar	5
sixty	ستين	sittíin	5
size	مقاس	ma'áas	5
skirt	جونلة	gunílla (pl. gunilláat)	6
sleep, to	ينام/نام	yináam/naam	9

small	صغير	Sugháyyar	4
small coffee pot	كنكة	kánaka (*pl.* kának)	5
son	ابن	ibn (*pl.* wiláad)	2
song	أغنية	ughníyya (*pl.* agháani)	13
speciality	تخصص	takháSSuS (*pl.* takhaSSuSáat)	9
Sphinx	أبو الهول	ábul-hohl	13
spinach	سبانخ	sabáanikh	3
square (town)	ميدان	miidáan (*pl.* mayaadíin)	10
squash	اسكواش	iskwáash	10
stable	اسطبل	isTábl (*pl.* isTabláat)	13
start/begin, to	يبتدئ/ابتدأ	yibtídi/ibtáda	10
station	محطة	maHáTTa (*pl.* maHaTTáat)	11
statue	تمثال	timsáal (*pl.* tamaasíil)	12
stay/remain, to	يقعد/قعد	yú'9ud/'á9ad	9
steps/stairs	سلم	síllim (*pl.* saláalim)	6
straight on	على طول	9ála Tuul	11
straight on	دوغري	dúghri	11
street	شارع	sháari9 (*pl.* shawáari9)	11
student	طالب	Táalib (*pl.* Tálaba)	3
study (a subject), to	يدرس/درس	yídris/dáras	9
study/revise, to	يذاكر/ذاكر	yizáakir/záakir	10
suit (man's)	بدلة	bádla (*pl.* bídal)	6
suitable	مناسب	munáasib	10
summer	الصيف	iS-Sayf	2
summer *adj.*	صيفي	Sáyfi	5
Sunday	الأحد	il-Hadd	9
sunglasses	نظارة شمس	naDDáarit shams	6
sweet porridge	بليلة	bilíila	3

T

| table | ترابيزة | tarabáyza (*pl.* tarabayzáat) | 1 |

tailor	ترزي	tárzi (*pl.* tarzíyya)	5
take, to	يأخذ/خذ	yáakhud/khad	10
tall/long	طويل	Tawíil (*pl.* Tuwáal)	6
tea	شاي	shay	3
teacher	مدرس	mudárris (*pl.* mudarrisíin)	3
team	فريق	faríi' (*pl.* fíra')	10
telephone	تليفون	tilifóhn (*pl.* tilifohnáat)	3
television	تليفزيون	tilivizyóhn (*pl.* tilivizyohnáat)	4
tell ...	قول لـ...	'uul li ... (*fem.* 'uuli li ...)	2
ten	عشرة	9áshara (9áshar)	5
terrible/awful	وحش	wíHish	9
thank you	شكرا	shukrán	3
that	إن	in	13
theatre	مسرح	másraH (*pl.* masáariH)	11
then	بعدين	ba9dáyn	11
there	هناك	hináak	12
there is/are	فيه	fiih	4
there is/are; it's got	فيها	fiihaa	4
there is not/are not	مافيش/ما فيهاش	ma fiish/ma fiiháash	4
they	هما	húmma	2
they have no use	مالهاش فايدة	maalháash fáyda	7
thief/burglar	حرامي	Haráami (*pl.* Haraamíyya)	7
thin	رفيع	rufáyya9	6
thing	حاجة	Háaga (*pl.* Haagáat)	7
third	ثالث	táalit	11
thirteen	ثلاثتاشر	talatáashar	5
thirty	ثلاثين	talatíin	5
this/that	ده	da (*fem.* di)	2
three	ثلاثة	taláata (tálat)	1
Thursday	الخميس	il-khamíis	9
ticket	تذكرة	tazkára (*pl.* tazáakir)	7
time	تعبان	wa't (*pl.* aw'áat)	10

tired	وقت	ta9báan! (pl. ta9baníin)	13
today	النهارده	innahárda	9
tomorrow	بكرة	búkra	6
too/also	برضه	bárDu	5
tower	برج	burg (pl. abráag)	11
traffic	مرور	murúur	9
train	قطار	'aTr (pl. 'uTuráat)	7
train, to	يتمرن/اتمرن	yitmárran/itmárran	9
travel, to	يسافر/سافر	yisáafir/sáafir	9
trousers	بنطلون	banTalóhn (pl. banTalohnáat)	6
try, to	يجرب/جرب	yigárrab/gárrab	12
Tuesday	الثلاثاء	it-taláat	9
twelve	اتناشر	itnáashar	5
twenty	عشرين	9ishríin	5
twenty past ...	الساعة... وثلث	is-sáa9a ... wi-tilt	9
twenty to ...	الساعة... إلا ثلث	is-sáa9a ... ílla tilt	9
twice	مرتين	marritáyn	9
two	اثنين	itnáyn	1

U

uncle/aunt, maternal	خال/خالة	kháal/kháala	2
uncle/aunt, paternal	عم/عمة	9amm/9ámma	2
under	تحت	taHt	4
unfortunately	للأسف	lil-ásaf	10
university	جامعة	gám9a (pl. gam9áat)	9
until/up to	لغاية	li-gháayit	11
useful	مفيد	mufíid	7

V

very	قوي؛ جدا	'áwi; gíddan	7
vine leaves (stuffed)	ورق عنب	wára' 9ínab	3
visit, to	يزور/زار	yizúur/zaar	11

W

wait!	استنى	istánna (*fem.* istánni)	6
waiter	جرسون	garsón	3
wake up, to	يصحى/صحي	yíSHa/SíHi	9
want	عاوز/عايز	9áawiz/9áayiz (*pl.* 9awzîin)	5
water	ميه	máyya	3
water pipe	شيشة	shíisha	5
wavering/undecided	محتار	miHtáar	14
we	إحنا	íHna	2
wearing	لابس	láabis	6
website	مواقع	mawqí9 (*pl.* mawáaqi9)	10
wedding	فرح	fáraH (*pl.* afráaH)	2
Wednesday	الأربع	il-árba9	9
welcome	أهلا وسهلا	áhlan wa sáhlan	1
well/good	كويس	kwáyyis	12
what do you do?	بتشتغل إيه؟	bi-tishtághal eh? (*fem.* bi-tishtághali eh?)	3
what does he/she look like?	شكله إيه؟	shákluh/shakáhaa eh?	6
what God wishes	ما شاء الله	mashaa'alláah	9
what then?	أمال؟	ummáal?	4
what would you like to drink?	تشرب إيه؟	tishráb eh? (*fem.* tishrábi eh?)	3
what would you like to eat?	تاكل إيه؟	tákul eh? (*fem.* tákli eh?)	3
what's the time?	الساعة كام؟	is-sáa9a kaam?	9
what's your name?	اسمك إيه؟	ísmak eh? (*fem.* ísmik eh?)	1
when	لما	lámma	13
when?	امتى؟	ímta?	2
where?	فين؟	fayn?	2
white	أبيض	ábyaD (*fem.* báyDa)	5
who?	مين؟	miin?	2
who/which	اللي	ílli	13
who's speaking?	مين معايا؟	miin ma9áaya?	14
why?	ليه؟	leh?	5

wife	مرات	miráat	2
window	شباك	shibbáak (*pl.* shababíik)	4
wine	نبيذ	nibíit	3
winter	الشتاء	ish-shíta	5
winter (*adj.*)	شتوي	shítwi	5
with	مع	má9a	5
with a beard	بذقن	bi-da'n	6
with a moustache	بشنب	bi-shánab	6
woman/lady	سيدة	sayyída (*pl.* sayyidáat)	3
work	شغل	shughl	5
work, to	يشتغل/اشتغل	yishtághal/ishtághal	10
world	الدنيا	id-dúnya	12
would you like ...?	تحب...؟	tiHíbb ...? (*fem.* tiHíbbi)	3

Y

year	سنة	sána (*pl.* siníin)	12
yellow	أصفر	áSfar (*fem.* Sáfra)	5
yes	أيوه	áywa	1
yesterday	امبارح	imbáariH	12
you (*fem. sing.*)	أنتي	ínti	1
you (*masc. sing.*)	أنت	ínta	1
you (*pl.*)	أنتو	íntu	2
you guys ('you youths')	يا شباب	yaa shabáab	9
you/your (polite/formal)	حضرتك	HaDrítak (*fem.* HaDrítik)	1
you're not right	ما عندكش حق	ma 9andákshi Ha' (*fem.* ma 9andakíish Ha')	7
you're right	عندك حق	9ándak Ha' (*fem.* 9ándik Ha')	7
youth	شاب	shaab	6

Arabic–English glossary

This section is an Arabic–English glossary of the key words appearing in *Colloquial Arabic of Egypt*. The unit number in which the word first appears is given in the right-hand column.

The Arabic words are listed in alphabetical order of the transliteration, as if they were English words – with the words beginning with ' (**qaaf**) and **9** (**9ayn**) listed after **z**. The lower case letters and their emphatic upper case equivalents (e.g. **t** and **T**) are alphabetized together. This will make it easier for you to find the entries. (However, it is *not* the order of the Arabic alphabet – see page 8.)

The Arabic script is shown alongside the transliteration, but be aware that the colloquial language does not have hard-and-fast spelling rules and you may see some words spelt differently in other contexts.

Note the following:

1 *Plurals* are given after the singular (in transliteration).

2 *Verbs* are shown in the present followed by the past and given in the **húwwa** form (*third person*). See Structure summary for more details on how verbs form.

A

áanisa (*pl.* **aanisáat**)	آنسة	Miss, young woman	3
ab(u)	أب (أبو)	father	2
abríil	أبريل	April	12
ábul-hohl	أبو الهول	Sphinx	13
ábyaD (*fem.* **báyDa**)	أبيض	white	5
agáaza (*pl.* **agazáat**)	أجازة	holiday	9
ághla	أغلى	more expensive	7
agnábi (*pl.* **agáanib**)	أجنبي	foreigner	14
áhlan	اهلا	hello	1
áhlan wa sáhlan	أهلا وسهلا	welcome	1
áHmar (*fem.* **Hámra**)	أحمر	red	5
áhwa	قهوة	coffee/café	3
akh(u) (*pl.* **ikhwáat**)	أخو	brother	2
ákhDar (*fem.* **KháDra**)	أخضر	green	5
akl	أكل	food	7
aló?	ألو؟	hello? (on the telephone)	4
amriikáani (*pl.* **amriikáan**)	أمريكاني	American	1
ána	أنا	I	1
ána baHíbb	أنا باحب	I like	7
ána amúut fi ...	أنا باموت في...	I adore ...	3
ána ísmi ...	أنا اسمي	my name's ...	1
ána kamáan	أنا كمان	me too	7
ána ma baHíbbish	أنا ما باحبش	I don't like	7
ána min ...	أنا من...	I'm from ...	1
ána mish 9áarif	أنا مش عارف	I don't know	6
ána muwáafi'	أنا موافق	I agree	7
arbá9a (**árba9**)	أربعة	four	1
arba9atáashar	أربعتاشر	fourteen	5
arba9íin	أربعين	forty	5
árkhaS	أرخص	cheapest/cheaper	7
árnab (*pl.* **aráanib**)	أرنب	rabbit	7

áSfar (fem. Sáfra)	أصفر	yellow	5
aSíil	أصيل	authentic/original	14
áSla9	أصلع	bald	6
awláad	أولاد	children	12
áwwil	أول	first	11
áywa	أيوه	yes	1
ázr'a kóHli	أزرق كحلي	dark blue	6
ázra' (fem. zár'a)	أزرق	blue	5

B

baab (pl. bibáan)	باب	door	4
báabaa	بابا	dad	10
bá'ara (pl. bá'ar)	بقرة	cow	7
ba9d	بعد	after	9
ba9d iD-Duhr	بعد الظهر	afternoon	9
ba9d(i) maa	بعد ما	after (+ verb)	10
ba9dáyn	بعدين	then	11
báayin	باين	showing/obvious	6
bádla (pl. bídal)	بدلة	suit	6
bádri	بدري	early	9
baHr (pl. biHúur)	بحر	sea	10
baláash ...!	بلاش	don't...!	11
balakóhna (pl. balakohnáat)	بلكونة	balcony	4
bálToh (pl. baláaTi)	بالطو	coat	6
bámya	بامية	okra, ladies' fingers	3
banafsígi	بنفسجي	purple	5
banáyh	بانيه	pan fried/escalope	14
bank (pl. bunúuk)	بنك	bank	11
banTalóhn (pl. banTalohnáat)	بنطلون	trousers	6
bárDu	برضه	too/also	5
barsíim	برسيم	clover	13
bass(i)	بس	but	4

báTTa (*pl.* **baTT**)	بطة	duck	7
bayn	بين	between	4
bayt (*pl.* **buyúut**)	بيت	house	4
beh	بيه	sir	14
bi-da'n	بذقن	with a beard	6
bi-shánab	بشنب	with a moustache	6
bi-súr9a	بسرعة	quickly	2
bi-tishtághal eh? (*fem.* **bi-tishtághali eh?**)	بتشتغل إيه؟	what do you do?	3
bi9íid	بعيد	far	6
bíira	بيرة	beer	3
bikáam?	بكام؟	how much?	5
bilíila	بليلة	sweet porridge	3
bilúuza (*pl.* **biluzáat**)	بلوزة	blouse	6
bin-nísba li	بالنسبة لـ	as regards/in relation to	11
bint (*pl.* **banáat**)	بنت	daughter	2
bint 9ámm	بنت عم	cousin, daughter of (paternal) uncle	9
bisílla	بسلة	peas	14
bitáa9	بتاع	connected with	2
biZ-ZabT	بالضبط	exactly	9
biláastik	بلاستك	plastic	5
bo'	بق	mouth	6
búkra	بكرة	tomorrow	6
búnni	بني	brown	5
burg (*pl.* **abráag**)	برج	tower	11
burnáyTa (*pl.* **baraníiT**)	برنيطة	hat	6
buut (*pl.* **buutáat**)	بوت	boots (pair of)	6

D

da (*fem.* **di**)	ده	this/that	2
dahab	ذهب	gold	12
dáraga úula	درجة أولى	first class	7

Darúuri	ضروري	have to/essential	10
Dayf (*pl.* Diyúuf)	ضيف	guest	1
dáyman	دايما	always	13
dilwá'ti	دلوقتي	now	10
disámbir	ديسمبر	December	12
dúghri	دوغري	straight on	11
duktúur (*pl.* dakáktra)	دكتور	doctor	3

F

fáakir (*pl.* fakríin)	فاكر	remember(ing)	13
faar (*pl.* firáan)	فار	mouse	7
fáatiH	فاتح	light (coloured)	5
far9 (*pl.* furúu9)	فرع	branch	9
fáraH (*pl.* afráaH)	فرح	wedding	2
faránsa	فرنسا	France	3
faríi' (*pl.* fíra')	فريق	team	10
fawg (*pl.* afwáag)	فوج	group (of tourists)	9
fayn?	فين؟	where?	2
fi	في	in	4
fi kull Hitta	في كل حتة	everywhere	5
fi makáan	في مكان	in the place of	13
fí9lan	فعلا	actually/really	7
fí9lan?	فعلا؟	really?	12
fibráayir	فبراير	February	12
fiih	فيه	there is/are	4
fiihaa	فيها	there is/are; it's got	4
fíkra (*pl.* afkáar)	فكرة	idea	5
fil-míyya	في المية	per cent	10
film (*pl.* afláam)	فيلم	film/movie	13
filúuka (*pl.* faláayik)	فلوكة	felucca	13
firáakh	فراخ	chicken	12
fiTáar	فطار	breakfast	9
foh'	فوق	above/over	4

foh' ba9D	فوق بعض	above each other	4
fúndu' (*pl.* fanáadi')	فندق	hotel	9
fustáan (*pl.* fasatíin)	فستان	dress	6
fuul	فول	fava beans	3

G

gáaHiz (*pl.* gaaHzíin)	جاهز	ready	14
ga9áan (*pl.* ga9aníin)	جعان	hungry	13
galabíyya (*pl.* galaalíib)	جلابية	galabeyya: *Egyptian robe*	5
gám9a (*pl.* gam9áat)	جامعة	university	9
gamáa9a	جماعة	group	14
gambári	جمبري	prawns	14
gamíil	جميل	beautiful	12
ganb	جنب	next to/near	4
garsón	جرسون	waiter	3
gaysh (*pl.* giyúush)	جيش	army	13
gáyy	جاي	coming/next	14
gázma (*pl.* gízam)	جزمة	pair of shoes	6
gháali (*fem.* ghálya)	غالية	expensive	7
gháami'	غامق	dark (colour)	5
gháawi (*fem.* gháwya)	غاوي	keen on	10
gháda	غدا	lunch	9
ghayT (*pl.* ghayTáan)	غيط	field	13
gibna	جبنة	cheese	5
gidd	جد	grandfather	13
gídda	جدة	grandmother	13
gíddan	جدا	very	7
gidíid	جديد	new	4
gild	جلد	leather	4
gináyh	جنيه	pound (money)	5
gohz	جوز	husband	2
gunílla (*pl.* gunilláat)	جونلة	skirt	6

H

háadi	هادي	peaceful/quiet	13
HáaDir	حاضر	at your service	5
Háaga (*pl.* Haagáat)	خاجة	thing	7
haat! (*fem.* háati)	هات!	bring!	2
háatli ... (*fem.* haatíili) ...	هات لي	bring me ...	3
HaDrítak (*fem.* HaDrítik)	حضرتك	you/your (polite/formal)	1
Hagz (*pl.* Huguuzáat)	حجز	reservation	9
Hákam	حكم	referee	13
Halawiyáat	حلويات	patisserie/desserts	12
Hammáam (*pl.* Hammamáat)	حمام	bathroom	4
Haríimi	حريمي	ladies'/women's	5
Hawáali	حوالي	approximately/about	6
Hidáashar	حداشر	eleven	5
Higáab	حجاب	Islamic headscarf	6
Hílw	حلو	nice/sweet	5
hína	هنا	here	2
hináak	هناك	there	12
hiwáaya (*pl.* hiwayáat)	هواية	hobby	10
híyya	هي	she	1
Humáar (*pl.* Himíir)	حمار	donkey	7
húmma	هما	they	2
HuSáan (*pl.* HiSína)	حصان	horse	7
húwwa	هو	he	1

I

ibn (*pl.* wiláad)	ابن	son	2
id-dúnya	الدنيا	world	12
iddíini	اديني	give me	5
ig-gúm9a	الجمعة	Friday	9
íHna	إحنا	we	2

iHtimáal	احتمال	may/might	12
iid (*pl.* iidáyn)	ايد	hand	6
il-ahráam	الأهرام	pyramids (at Giza)	9
il-árba9	الأربع	Wednesday	9
il-áwwil	أول	first/firstly	11
il-Hadd	الأحد	Sunday	9
il-Hámdu lilláah	الحمد لله	fine ('thanks be to God')	1
il-itnáyn	الأثنين	Monday	9
il-khamíis	الخميس	Thursday	9
il-mafrúuD	المفروض	should	10
il-maksíik	المكسيك	Mexico	7
ílli	اللي	who/which	13
imbáariH	امبارح	yesterday	12
ímta?	امتى؟	when?	2
in	إن	that	13
in sháa' alláah	إن شاء الله	If Gods wills/God willing	2
ingilíizi (*pl.* ingilíiz)		English (nationality)	1
ingiltára	انجليزي	England	7
innahárda	النهارده	today	9
ínta	أنت	you (*masc. sing.*)	1
ínti	أنتي	you (*fem. sing.*)	1
íntu	أنتو	you (*pl.*)	2
is'áluh	اسأله	ask him	6
is-sáa9a ...	الساعة	o'clock	9
is-sáa9a ... ílla rub9	الساعة... إلا ربع	quarter to ...	9
is-sáa9a ... ílla tilt	الساعة... إلا ثلث	twenty to ...	9
is-sáa9a ... wi-nuSS	الساعة ... ونص	half past ...	9
is-sáa9a ... wi-rub9	الساعة... وربع	quarter past ...	9
is-sáa9a ... wi-tilt	الساعة... وثلث	twenty past ...	9
is-sáa9a kaam?	الساعة كام؟	what's the time?	9
is-sabt	السبت	Saturday	9

is-sána ílli fáatit	السنة اللي فاتت	last year	12
iS-Sayf	الصيف	summer	2
iS-SubH	الصبح	morning (in the)	9
ish-shíta	الشتاء	winter	5
isháara (*pl.* isharáat)	إشارة	lights (traffic)	11
iskutlánda	إسكتلندا	Scotland	12
iskutlándi (*pl.* iskutlandiyíin)	إسكتلندي	Scottish	1
iskwáash	اسكواش	squash	10
ism (*pl.* asáami)	اسم	name	1
ísma9! (*fem.* ismá9i)	اسمع!	listen!	2
ísmak eh? (*fem.* ísmik eh?)	اسمك إيه؟	what's your name?	1
isTábl (*pl.* isTabláat)	اسطبل	stable	13
istánna (*fem.* istánni)	استنى	wait!	6
íswid (*fem.* sóhda)	أسود	black	5
it-taláat	الثلاثاء	Tuesday	9
iT-Tibb	الطب	medicine (study)	12
itfáDDal (*fem.* itfaDDáli)	اتفضل	come this way; here you are	1
itnáashar	اتناشر	twelve	5
itnáyn	اثنين	two	1
izzáay?	إزاي؟	how (come)?	7
izáaza (*pl.* azáayiz)	قزازة	bottle	3
izzáayak (*fem.* izzáayik)	إزيك	how are you?	1

K

káabtin (*pl.* kabáatin)	كابتن	captain (of a sports team)	10
kabáab	كباب	kebab	3
kabíina (*pl.* kabáayin)	كابينة	cabin	4
kalb (*pl.* kiláab)	كلب	dog	7
kamáan	كمان	also	5
kánaka (*pl.* kának)	كنكة	small coffee pot	5
kárkaday	كركديه	hibiscus tea	3

kayk	كيك	cake	10
kháal/kháala	خال/خالة	uncle/aunt, maternal	2
khafíif	خفيف	light (weight)	9
khaláas	خلاص	over/finished	12
khálli báalak (*fem.* khálli báalik)	خللي بالك	be careful/watch out	11
khallíina fi	خللينا في	let's stick to/let's stay with	7
khamastáashar	خمستاشر	fifteen	5
khámsa (khámas)	خمسة	five	1
khamsíin	خمسين	fifty	5
kharúuf (*pl.* khirfáan)	خروف	sheep	7
khaTíib (*fem.* khaTíiba)	خطيب	fiancé(e)	2
khawáaga	خواجة	foreigner (*slang*)	6
khayl	خيل	horses	13
kibíir	كبير	big	4
kída	كده	like this	5
kíilu	كيلو	kilo	5
kímya	كيميا	chemistry	3
kiníisa (*pl.* kanáayis)	كنيسة	church	12
kófta	كفتة	minced meat	3
kóhla	كولا	cola	3
kombyúutir (*pl.* kombyuutiráat)	كمبيوتر	computer	10
korníish	كورنيش	corniche	11
kubáar	كبار	adults	7
kubbáaya (*pl.* kubbayáat)	كباية	glass	3
kúbri (*pl.* kabáari)	كوبري	bridge	11
kull	كل	every/all	10
kull yohm	كل يوم	every day	10
kullíiya (*pl.* kulliyáat)	كلية	college/faculty	10
kúra (*pl.* kúwar)	كورة	ball/football/soccer	10
kúrsi (*pl.* karáasi)	كرسي	seat/chair	4
kwáyyis	كويس	well/good	12

L

la'	لا	no	1
láabis	لابس	wearing	6
láazim	لازم	have to/must	10
lában	لبن	milk	3
láHma	لحمة	meat	12
láHZa ma9áaya	لحظة معايا	one moment	14
lámma	لما	when	13
laymúun	لمون	lime/lemon	3
laymúuni	لموني	lemon-yellow (adj.)	5
law samáHt (fem. law samáHti)	لو سمحت	please	5
lazíiz	لذيذ	delicious	7
la'ánn	لأن	because	7
leh?	ليه؟	why?	5
li-gháayit	لغاية	until/up to	11
li-waHdáhaa	لوحدها	by herself	11
li-wáHdi	لوحدي	by myself	11
li-wáHduh	لوحده	by himself	11
li-...	لـ...	for	5
lil-ásaf	للأسف	unfortunately	10
líssa sháarib (fem. shárba)	لسه شارب	I've just had a drink	3
líssa wáakil (fem. wákla)	لسه واكل	I've just eaten	3
lohn (pl. alwáan)	لون	colour	5
lúgha (pl. lugháat)	لغة	language	9
lux	لوكس	luxury/first class	4

M

ma 9andákshi Ha' (fem. ma 9andakíish Ha')	ما عندكش حق	you're not right	7
ma fiish/ ma fiiháash	مافيش/ ما فيهاش	there is not/are not	4

ma'áas	مقاس	size	5
má'li	مقلي	fried	14
má9a s-saláama	مع السلامة	goodbye	1
má9á	مع	with	5
má9had (pl. ma9áahid)	معهد	institute	9
ma9lésh	معلش	never mind	9
ma9múul min	معمول من	made from	12
ma9'úul	معقول	reasonable	7
maalháash fáyda	مالهاش فايدة	they have no use	7
máaris	مارس	March	12
máashi	ماشي	OK, fine	5
máayo	مايو	May	12
mábna (pl. mabáani)	مبنى	building	12
mabrúuk	مبروك	congratulations	4
mabsúuT (pl. mabsuuTíin)	مبسوط	happy	4
madáam	مدام	Madam	1
mádkhal (pl. madáakhil)	مدخل	entrance	11
madrása (pl. madáaris)	مدرسة	school	9
maghsála (pl. magháasil)	مغسلة	laundry	9
maHáar	محار	oysters	12
maHáll (pl. maHalláat)	محل	shop/store	11
maHáTTa (pl. maHaTTáat)	محطة	station	11
majistáyr	ماجستير	masters (degree)	9
makáan (pl. amáakin)	مكان	place	12
mákhrag (pl. mahkáarig)	مخرج	exit	11
máktab (pl. makáatib)	مكتب	office	9
maktába (pl. maktabáat)	مكتبة	library/bookshop	9
manakhíir	مناخير	nose	6
marákbi (pl. marakbíyya)	مراكبي	boatman	13
márkib (pl. maráakib)	مركب	boat	6
márra	مرة	once	9
marritáyn	مرتين	twice	9

masáa' il-khayr	مساء الخير	good afternoon/evening	1
másalan	مثلا	for example	14
másgid (pl. masáagid)	مسجد	mosque	9
mashhúur	مشهور	famous	12
mashaa'alláah	ما شاء الله	what God wishes	9
mashgúul	مشغول	busy	9
mashrúub (pl. masharíib)	مشروب	drink	12
máshwi	مشوي	grilled	14
maSr ig-gidíida	مصر الجديدة	Heliopolis	1
maSr liT-Tayaráan	مصر للطيران	Egypt Air	3
másraH (pl. masáariH)	مسرح	theatre	11
máSri (pl. máSriyyíin)	مصري	Egyptian	1
máT9am (pl. maTáa9im)	مطعم	restaurant	9
maTáar (pl. maTaráat)	مطار	airport	6
máTbakh (pl. maTáabikh)	مطبخ	kitchen	9
mátHaf (pl. matáaHif)	متحف	museum	9
mawgúud	موجود	available	4
mawqí9 (pl. mawáaqi9)	موقع	website	10
máyya	ميه	water	3
maZbúuT	مضبوط	correct/right	14
metr	متر	maître	1
miHtáag (pl. miHtaagíin)	محتاج	need	5
miHtáar	محتار	wavering/undecided	14
miidáan (pl. mayaadíin)	ميدان	square (town)	10
miin ma9áaya?	مين معايا؟	who's speaking?	14
miin?	مين؟	who?	2
míina (pl. mawáani)	ميناء	dock/port	6
miláwwin	ملون	coloured	6
min (+ period of time)	من	ago	13
min fáDlak (fem. min fáDlik)	من فضلك	please	3

... mináyn?	منين؟	How do I get to ...?	11
miráat	مرات	wife	2
mish	مش	not	3
mish hína	مش هنا	not here	3
mishwáar (pl. mashawíir)	مشوار	distance/errand/task	13
mitkállif	متكلف	lavish	13
míyya	مية	hundred	5
modáyl	موديل	model (of car, etc.)	4
mu9áskar	معسكر	camp; encampment	13
mudárris (pl. mudarrisíin)	مدرس	teacher	3
muDíif/muDíifa	مضيف	flight attendant	3
mufíid	مفيد	useful	7
muHáami (pl. muHaamiyíin)	محامي	lawyer	3
muHáasib (pl. muHaasbíin)	محاسب	accountant	3
muhándis (pl. muhandisíin)	مهندس	engineer	3
muhímm	مهم	important	7
mumássil (pl. mumassilíin)	ممثل	actor	3
múmkin	ممكن	can/possible	10
mun9ísh	منعش	refreshing	12
munáasib	مناسب	suitable	13
muríiH	مريح	comfortable	4
murúur	مرور	traffic	9
musákkin (pl. musakkináat)	مسكن	sedative	12
mushkíla	مشكلة	problem	4
mustá'bal	مستقبل	future	12
musta9íd	مستعد	ready	9
mustáshfa (pl. mustashfayáat)	مستشفى	hospital	11

mutawáHHish	متوحش	savage	14
muusíiqa	موسيقى	music	10
múusim (*pl.* mawáasim)	موسم	season	10
muzíi9 (*pl.* muzii9íin)	مذيع	broadcaster	1

N

náadi (*pl.* nawáadi)	نادي	club	9
naas	ناس	people	12
náawi (*pl.* nawyíin)	ناوي	intending to	10
náazil	نازل	getting down/getting off	6
naDDáara	نظارة	glasses (pair of)	6
naDDáarit shams	نظارة شمس	sunglasses	6
naHáas	نحاس	copper	5
náfsi	نفسي	myself	11
náfsuh/nafsáhaa	نفسه/نفسها	himself/herself	11
nákhla (*pl.* nakhl)	نخل	palm trees	13
ni9náa9	نعناع	mint	12
nibíit	نبيذ	wine	3
niDíif	نظيف	clean	7
niháaya	نهاية	end/finish	12
nofámbir	نوفمبر	November	12
nuSS	نص	half	5

O

oghúsTus	أغسطس	August	12
óhDa (*pl.* ówaD)	أوضة	room	4
ohDt is-súfra	أوضة السفرة	dining room	4
ohDt in-nóhm	أوضة النوم	bedroom	4
ohDt il-o9áad	أوضة القعاد	living room	4
oktúubir	اكتوبر	October	12
omlíit	اومليت	omelette	3
ostoráali (*pl.* ostoraliyyíin)	أسترالي	Australian	1

ostorálya	أستراليا	Australia	2
otobíis (*pl.* otobiisáat)	اوتوبيس	bus/coach	7

R

ráayiH (*pl.* rayHíin)	رايح	going (to)	7
ráayiH gáay	رايح جاي	return (ticket)	7
rádyo (*pl.* radyoháat)	راديو	radio	2
raghíif (*pl.* raghífa)	رغيف	loaf	5
ráqam	رقم	number	1
rigl (*pl.* rigláyn)	رجل	leg/foot	6
ríHla (*pl.* riHláat)	رحلة	journey	7
riwáaya (*pl.* riwayáat)	رواية	novel	10
rub9	ربع	quarter	5
rufáyya9	رفيع	thin	6
rummáan	رمان	pomegranate	12
ruzz	رز	rice	3

S

SáaHi	صاحي	awake	1
SáaHib (*pl.* aS-Háab)	صاحب	friend	9
Sáala (*pl.* Saaláat)	صالة	hall	4
sáb9a (sába9)	سبعة	seven	5
sab9íin	سبعين	seventy	5
saba9táashar	سبعتاشر	seventeen	5
SabáaH il-khayr	صباح الخير	good morning	1
sabáanikh	سبانخ	spinach	3
sahl	سهل	easy	10
SaHrá	صحراء	desert	13
is-saláamuh 9aláykum	السلام عليكم	peace on you	14
Saláat	صلاة	prayers	14
sálaTa (*pl.* salaTáat)	سلطة	salad	3
Salóhn	صالون	sitting room (for guests)	4
sámak	سمك	fish	10

sána (pl. siníin)	سنة	year	12
sandawítsh (pl. sandawitsháat)	سندوتش	sandwich	3
saríi9	سريع	fast	10
sawwáa' (pl. sawwa'íin)	سواق	driver	13
Sayd is-sámak	صيد السمك	fishing	10
Sáyfi	صيفي	summer adj.	5
sayyída (pl. sayyidáat)	سيدة	lady/woman	3
shá''a (pl. shú'a')	شقة	flat/apartment	12
shá9r	شعر	hair	6
shaab	شاب	youth	6
sháari9 (pl. shawáari9)	شارع	street	11
sháayif (pl. shayfíin)	شايف	seeing/believing	10
shahr (pl. shuhúur)	شهر	month	12
shahr il-9ásal	شهر العسل	honeymoon	7
shakhSáyyan	شخصيا	personally	14
shárqi (fem. sharqiyya)	شكله إيه؟	Eastern	9
shay	شرقي	tea	3
shibbáak (pl. shababíik)	شاي	window	4
shíbshib (pl. shabáashib)	شباك	flip-flops	6
shíisha	شبشب	water pipe	5
shimáal	شيشة	left (hand side)	11
shírka (pl. shirkáat)	شمال	company/business	10
shítwi	شركة	winter (adj.)	5
shóhka (pl. shúwak)	شتوي	forks	5
shughl	شوك	work	5
shukrán	شغل	thank you	3
shuráab (pl. shurabáat)	شكرا	pair of socks	6
shuwáyya	شراب	a little/somewhat	14
sí9r (pl. as9áar)	شوية	price	7
sibtámbir	سعر	September	12
sifáara (pl. sifaráat)	سبتمبر	embassy	11
síinima (pl. siinimáat)	سفارة / سينما	cinema	11

síkka (*pl.* **síkak**)		route/way	11
síllim (*pl.* **saláalim**)	سكة	steps/stairs	6
siríir (*pl.* **saráayir**)	سلم	bed	4
sítta (**sitt**)	سرير	six	5
sittáashar	ستة	sixteen	5
sittíin	ستاشر	sixty	5
Sobáa9 (*pl.* **Sawáabi9**)	ستين	finger	6
su'áal (*pl.* **as'íla**)	صباع	question	9
Sugháyyar	سؤال	small	4
suu' (*pl.* **aswaa'**)	صغير	market	11
Súura	سوق	photo/picture	2
	صورة		

T

ta9áala! (*fem.* **ta9áali**)		come!	2
ta9báan! (*pl.* **ta9baníin**)	تعال!	tired	13
Ta9míyya	تعبان	falafel	3
Táali9	طعمية	heading up to/going to	6
Táalib (*pl.* **Tálaba**)	طالع	student	3
táalit	طالب	third	11
táani	ثالث	second/again	11
Táb9an	تاني	of course	5
Tába' (*pl.* **Tubáa'**)	طبعا	plate	3
Tába' il-yohm	طبق	dish of the day	3
taba9	طبق اليوم	belonging to/relating to	13
taHt	تبع	under	4
taHt ámrak (*fem.* **taHt ámrik**)	تحت / تحت أمرك	at your service	14
takháSSuS (*pl.* **takhaSSuSáat**)	تخصص	speciality	9
takhfíiD (*pl.* **takhfiiDáat**)	تخفيض	discount	7
takíif (*pl.* **takiifáat**)		air conditioning	4
tákul eh? (*fem.* **tákli eh?**)	تكييف / تاكل إيه؟	what would you like to eat?	3

taláata (tálat)	ثلاثة	three	1
talatáashar	ثلاثتاشر	thirteen	5
talatíin	ثلاثين	thirty	5
tamaníin	ثمانين	eighty	5
tamantáashar	ثمنتاشر	eighteen	5
tamánya (táman)	ثمانية	eight	5
Tant	طنت	auntie	1
tarabáyza (pl. tarabayzáat)	ترابيزة	table	1
tárzi (pl. tarzíyya)	ترزي	tailor	5
Tawíil (pl. Tuwáal)	طويل	tall/long	6
Tayaráan	طيران	flying	7
Tayyáara (pl. Tayyaráat)	طيارة	plane	7
Táyyib	طيب	OK, well	3
tazkára (pl. tazáakir)	تذكرة	ticket	7
Tifl (pl. aTfáal)	طفل	child	7
tiHíbb ...? (fem. tiHíbbi ...?)	تحب...؟	would you like ...?	3
tikhíin	تخين	fat	6
tilifóhn	تليفون	telephone	3
tilivizyóhn (pl. tilifizyohnáat)	تليفزيون	television	4
timsáal (pl. tamaasíil)	تمثال	statue	12
tír9a (pl. tíra9)	ترعة	canal (small irrigation)	13
tís9a (tísa9)	تسعة	nine	5
tisa9táashar	تسعتاشر	nineteen	5
tis9íin	تسعين	ninety	5
tishráb eh? (fem. tishrábi eh?)	تشرب إيه؟	what would you like to drink?	3
tufáaH	تفاح	apples	5

U

u'9úd!	اقعد!	sit down!	3
ughníyya (pl. agháani)	أغنية	song	13

ukht (*pl.* ukhwáat)	أخت	sister	2
umm	أم	mother	2
ummáal?	أمال؟	what then?	4
ustáaz	أستاذ	Sir/Mr	1
ustáaz (*pl.* asátza)	أستاذ	professor	12

W

wa't (*pl.* aw'áat)	وقت	time	10
wáaDiH	واضح	clear	10
wáaHid	واحد	one	1
wála ána	ولا أنا	me neither/nor I	7
wálad (*pl.* wiláad)	ولد	boy/child (*pl.* = children)	1
walláahi	والله	really ('by God')	14
wára	ورا	behind	4
wára'	ورق	paper	5
wára' 9ínab	ورق عنب	vine leaves (stuffed)	3
wásaT	وسط	medium (sized)	5
wi/w-	و	and	1
widn (*pl.* widáan)	ودن	ear	6
wíHish	وحش	terrible/awful	9
wiHyáatak (*fem.* waHyáatik)	وحياتك	please (*lit.* 'on your life')	14
wusT il-bálad	وسط البلد	city centre/downtown	11

Y

yá9ni	يعني	I mean/so/well	6
yaa fándim	يا فندم	Sir/Madam	4
yaa gamáa9a	يا جماعة	everyone/'you lot'	14
yaa sáatir!	يا ساتر!	God help us!	7
yaa shabáab	يا شباب	you guys ('you youths')	9
yáakhud/khad	يأخذ/خذ	take, to	10
yáakul/kál	يأكل/كل	eat, to	9
yanáayir	يناير	January	12

yi'á99ad/á99ad	يقعد/قعد	seat, to	14
yi'ákkil/ákkil	يأكل/أكل	feed, to	14
yí'dar/'ídir	يقدر/قدر	can/to be able	13
yí'sim/'ásam	يقسم/قسم	share/split, to	14
yi'úul/'aal	يقول/قال	say, to	11
yi'úul/'aal 9ála	يقول/قال على	call, to (someone)	14
yí9mil/9ámal	يعمل/عمل	make/do/create, to	10
yíb'a/bá'a	يبقى/بقى	remain, to	10
yibíi9/baa9	يبيع/باع	sell, to	11
yibtídi/ibtáda	يبتدئ/ابتدأ	start, to	10
yidáwwa'/dáwwa	يدوق/دوق	give (someone) a taste	14
yídris/dáras	يدرس/درس	study (a subject), to	9
yigárrab/gárrab	يجرب/جرب	try, to	12
yiHáDDar/HáDDar	يحضر/حضر	prepare, to	9
yíHgiz/Hágaz	يحجز/حجز	book/reserve, to	10
yíigi/geh	ييجي/جه	come, to	14
yikháaf/khaaf	يخاف/خاف	afraid, to be	11
yikhállaS/khállaS	يخلص/خلص	finish, to	10
yíksif/kásaf	يكسف/كسف	disappoint/embarrass, to	14
yíl9ab/lí9ib	يلعب/لعب	play, to	9
yiláa'i/lá'a	يلاقي/لاقى	find, to	11
yimíin	يمين	right (hand side)	11
yímshi/míshi	يمشي/مشي	go (away)/walk, to	13
yímsik/mísik	يمسك/مسك	catch, to	7
yiná''i/ná''a	ينقي/نقى	choose, to	14
yináam/naam	ينام/نام	sleep, to	9
yinbísiT/inbásaT	ينبسط/انبسط	enjoy, to	12
yínzil/nízil	ينزل/نزل	go down/get down, to	10
yirábbi/rábba	يربي/ربى	keep (pets)/breed/bring up, to	14
yírga9/rígi9	يرجع/رجع	return, to	12
yírkab/ríkib	يركب/ركب	ride, to	13
yirúuH/raaH	يروح/راح	go, to	9
yisáafir/sáafir	يسافر/سافر	travel (to), to	9

yiSábbaH/SábbaH	يصبح/صبح	say good morning to	10
yíSHa/SíHi	يصحى/صحي	wake up, to	9
yishághghal/shághghal	يشغل/شغل	operate, to	13
yishárraf/shárraf	يشرف/شرف	honour, to	14
yíshrab/shírib	يشرب/شرب	drink, to	12
yishtághal/ishtághal	يشتغل/اشتغل	work, to	10
yishúuf/shaaf	يشوف/شاف	see, to	12
yiSmá9/Simí9	يسمع/سمع	hear, to/listen, to	13
yiSTáad/iSTáad	يصطاد/اصطاد	fish/hunt, to	10
yitmárran/itmárran	يتمرن/اتمرن	train, to	9
yittífi'/ittáfa'	يتفق/اتفق	agree, to	14
yíwSal/wíSil	يوصل/وصل	arrive, to	9
yíwSif/wáSaf	يوصف/وصف	describe, to	11
yizáakir/záakir	يذاكر/ذاكر	study/revise, to	10
yizíid/zaad	يزيد/زاد	increase, to	10
yizúur/zaar	يزور/زار	visit, to	11
yú'9ud/'á9ad	يقعد/قعد	stay/remain, to	9
yúkhrug/khárag	يخرج/خرج	leave/exit, to	9
yúTbukh/Tábakh	يطبخ/طبخ	cook, to	13
yúTlub/Tálab	يطلب/طلب	order/ask for, to	14
yúulio	يوليو	July	12
yúunio	يونيو	June	12

Z

záHma	زحمة	crowded	9
zamáan/min zamáan	زمان/من زمان	a long time ago	13
zaytúun	زيتون	olives	5
zayy	زي	like; similar to	5
zibúun (pl. zabáayin)	زبون	customer/client	10
zímma	ذمة	integrity/honesty	13

ʾ (qaaf)

'áa9id (pl. 'a9díin)	قاعد	sitting/staying	10
'abl	قبل	before	9
'ábl(i) maa	قبل ما	before (+ verb)	10
'adíim	قديم	old	4
'amíiS (pl. 'umSáan)	قميص	shirt	5
'aTr (pl. 'uTuráat)	قطار	train	7
'áwi	قوي	very	7
'óTTa (pl. 'óTaT)	قطة	cat	7
'óTTa (pl. 'óTaT) siyáami	قطة سيامي	Siamese cat	7
'uddáam	قدام	in front of	4
'uráyyib	قريب	near	6
'uSáyyar	قصير	short	6
'uul li ... (fem. 'uuli li ...)	قول لـ...	tell ...	2

9 (9ayn)

9áawiz (pl. 9awzíin)	عاوز	want	5
9áayish fi (pl. 9ayshíin fi)	عايش في	live in	9
9agúuz	عجوز	old (person)	6
9ála	على	on	4
9ála l-yimíin	على اليمين	on the right	11
9ála sh-shimáal	على الشمال	on the left	11
9ála Tuul	على طول	straight on	11
9amm/9ámma	عم/عمة	uncle/aunt, paternal	2
9an	عن	from	10
9ánd + possessive ending	عند	have/has	3
9ándak Ha' (fem. 9ándik Ha')	عندك حق	you're right	7
9ánduh kaam sána?	عنده كام سنة؟	How old is he?	6

9arabíyya (*pl.* **9arabiyyáat**)	عربية	car	4
9ásha	عشاء	dinner	9
9asháan	عشان	for/because of	6
9áshara (**9áshar**)	عشرة	ten	5
9aSíir	عصير	juice	3
9ayn (*pl.* **9aynáyn**)	عين	eye	6
9aysh	عيش	bread	3
9áyyil (*pl.* **9ayyáal**)	عيل	kid	14
9aZíim!	عظيم!	great!	9
9iid miláad	عيد ميلاد	birthday	12
9ílba (*pl.* **9ílab**)	علبة	packet/box/tin	5
9imáara (*pl.* **9imaráat**)	عمارة	apartment building/ block of flats	13
9ishríin	عشرين	twenty	5
9ulúum	علوم	sciences	9